D0593021

A STUDY OF LAND REFORMS
IN UTTAR PRADESH

A Study of
LAND REFORMS
IN UTTAR PRADESH

by BALJIT SINGH
and SHRIDHAR MISRA

HD
879
.U8
S54

EAST-WEST CENTER PRESS, HONOLULU

© Research Programmes Committee
Planning Commission
Government of India
1964

Published in India, 1964, by Oxford Book &
Stationery Co., Calcutta

American edition (for sale outside India,
Pakistan, Ceylon, and Burma), 1965, by
the East-West Center Press, Honolulu

Library of Congress Catalog Card No. 65-17358

ACKNOWLEDGEMENT

THIS STUDY was sponsored by the Research Programmes Committee of the Planning Commission and was financed by a grant for it. We are grateful to the Member-Secretary and the Research Programmes Committee for this kind assistance. The U.P. State Government extended to us all facilities required for the collection of official data from the Revenue Department, Board of Revenue and from the district and tehsil headquarters of the sample area. The revenue records of the sample villages were also made available to us. We wish to record here our appreciation of the co-operation extended to us for this study by the various agencies of the U.P. Government.

The study commenced in June, 1960 and the investigation team went to the field in August. It remained there for nearly six months. Statistical analysis and tabulation took about another eight months and the drafting of the report was completed in January, 1962.

During the course of investigation more than 20 persons worked on the Research Staff of the Project. They all discharged their duties ungrudgingly in spite of severe odds against their work in the field. At times they had to put in more work than normal and such occasions were many, particularly during the later stages. We wish to record our appreciation of the excellent manner in which the Research Staff discharged its duties.

Shri S. P. Dikshit and Shri L. S. Agarwal who have been associated with this study throughout its course have been mainly responsible for the supervision of field investigation and tabulation of the data. They discharged their duties with zeal and enthusiasm. Miss I. Z. Husain assisted the Director at the stage of finalising the draft of the Report. Her assistance was valuable.

We had also the benefit of consultation with several members of the Department, particularly with Dr. P. L. Rawat who was first a Field Controller in this Project and later on joined the Department. He was also responsible for preparing the preliminary drafts of several chapters. His assistance is gratefully acknowledged.

We also called from time to time on Professor A. R. Roy, Head of the Department of Statistics in the University, for technical advice on statistical matters. It was a very valuable assistance that we received from him. We also wish to acknowledge our debt to the University of Lucknow which gave us all the facilities for this study and transferred the services of one of us on a whole-time basis for acting as a Joint Director of the Project. Finally, we wish to thank our Secretarial Staff for the nice and efficient manner in which they handled their job.

BALJIT SINGH
Director

SHRIDHAR MISRA
Joint Director

Lucknow
January, 1962

CONTENTS

SECTION I

APPENDICES

        Location   177
        Area of Villages   177
        Cultivated Area   178
        Irrigation   179
        Double Cropping   182
        Population   183
        Occupational Pattern   184

APPENDIX II. CONCEPTS, DEFINITIONS AND
     EXPLANATIONS   ..   ..   185—193

        Variables   185
        Regions   185
        Household and their Members   ..   188
        Occupation and Industry   188
        Castes   190

LIST OF TABLES

LIST OF TABLES IN APPENDICES I TO V

LIST OF DIAGRAMS

LIST OF STATISTICAL TABLES

SECTION I

CHAPTER 1

ORIGIN, SCOPE AND METHOD

1.1. INTRODUCTION

The recent phase of land reforms started in this State with the enactment of the Uttar Pradesh Zamindari Abolition and Land Reforms Act 1950, known as the Principal Act, and has culminated in the passing of the Uttar Pradesh Imposition of Ceiling on Land Holdings Act 1960. The Principal Act was revised thrice, i.e. in 1952, 1954 and 1956. The U.P. Land (Amendment) Act 1958 received the assent in November, 1959. These legislative measures apply generally to the whole of Uttar Pradesh and make provisions for the following:

(a) Removal of intermediaries and vesting of estates in the State

(b) Payment of compensation to the intermediaries

(c) Payment of rehabilitation grant to small landowners dispossessed of their rights

(d) Establishment of Land Management Committees or *Gaon Sabhas* and *Gaon Samajs*

(e) Creation of new tenures with fixity of rights and possession to the tillers of soil

(f) General prohibition of sub-letting and safeguarding of the interests of existing sub-tenants

(g) Prevention of subdivision of holdings

(h) Formation of cooperative farm of uneconomic holdings

(i) Ceiling on future acquisition of holdings

(j) Ceiling on existing holdings

(k) No reservation of rights of resumption

(l) Assessment of land revenue on the aggregate holding area in a village

(m) Revision of land revenue not earlier than forty years from the commencement of the Principal Act

(n) Collection of land revenue by *Gaon Panchayats*

(o) Vesting of common land in the village community.

Before the abolition of *zamindari* the main types of tenures that prevailed were *sir*, *khudkasht*, Fixed Rate Tenancy, Exproprietary Tenancy, Occupancy Tenancy and Hereditary Tenancy. With the abolition of *zamindari* only three types of tenures were recognised, viz. *bhumidhari*, *sirdari* and *asami*. Besides these there was the *adhivasi* tenure of the transitional character which was abolished in 1954. A provision has also been made for compulsory consolidation of holding under the U.P. Consolidation of Holdings Act of 1954, and for voluntary redistribution of land under the U.P. *Bhoodan Yojna* Act of 1952.

1.2. ORIGIN

The Research Programmes Committee of the Planning Commission has sponsored a phased programme of studies of land reforms to examine the impact of recent land legislation particularly that of the abolition of intermediaries. Its Committee of Direction suggested that such studies should examine the land system as it existed prior to reforms, the major basic purposes of land reforms, the major provisions of legislative measures, the scope and agencies of implementation of the legislative measures on the one hand and the immediate and anticipatory effects of such land reforms on landowners, tenants and agricultural workers on the other.

Land reorganisation in the State has proceeded along three distinctive but inter-related lines, i.e. (*a*) abolition of *zamindari* and establishment of new land tenures, (*b*) consolidation of holdings and voluntary land redistribution and (*c*) Cooperative farming. We wanted to study all these aspects but that would have required more time and larger effort than devoted to the present study. We have, therefore, confined this study, as suggested by Technical Sub-Committee on Land Reforms and Cooperation, to the first aspect only, i.e. the structural changes in ownership of holdings, area under different types of tenures, the implementation of land legislation and their impact on different classes in the countryside. The Research Programmes Committee sanctioned an initial grant of Rs. 66,500/- for such a survey covering the entire State under our scheme entitled "Survey of the Economic and Social Effects of Land Reforms in U.P." This was communicated to us in May, 1960 and work on the scheme started in June, 1960.

1.3. SCOPE AND METHOD

Zamindari was abolished in the State with effect from July, 1952 from the bulk of the rural area[1] i.e. from 6.02 crore acres out of a total area of 7.26 crore acres. The total area of holdings in the portion of the State to which Zamindari Abolition and Land Reforms Act applies was 4.60 crore acres in 1959-60, the latest year for which published figures are available and forms 98.04% of the total area of holdings in the State excluding Hill Pattis of Kumaun Division and Tehri-Garhwal. It was only in that year that the Act was extended to Rampur District. Even now *zamindari* has not been abolished in about 2% of the total area. The total amount of compensation payable to the intermediaries for the whole State is estimated at about Rs. 68.79 crores out of which Rs. 59.73 crores or 86.8% of the total had been paid up by May 31, 1958. In addition, a Rehabilitation Grant of about Rs. 70 crores is payable to the expropriated small zamindars. The total area of holdings in the portion of the State where *zamindari* has been abolished is to the extent of 33.28% under *bhumidhars* and 65.92% under *sirdars*. The remaining area consitituting less than 1% of the area is held by *asamis* and occupiers of land without title. *Adhivasis*, as reported earlier, have been merged with these main tenures. Land Management Committees have been constituted all over the State and are charged with the general supervision, management and control of all lands vested in the *Gaon Samaj*. They had earmarked 3.17 million acres of land for common use of the community on planned basis and had completed demarcation of wasteland and forests in 38 districts by 1956-57. They had allotted to *sirdars* 109 thousand acres of land in that year for cultivation. Besides, they have also been protecting common land of the *Gaon Samaj* from private encroachment.

The scope of the present study may be defined as region by region macro-study of the main features of land legislation in the State, the lags and frictions in its implementation and its impact on various classes and on the rural economy as a whole.

For this purpose we have tried to compare the picture before *zamindari* abolition with that after it in sample villages scattered all over the

---

[1] The U.P. Zamindari Abolition and Land Reforms Act, 1950 was applied on July 1, 1952 to the entire State except to (*i*) Pargana of Kaswar Raja in the Banaras district, (*ii*) South of Kaimur Range in Mirzapur district, (*iii*) Former Banaras State, (*iv*) Rampur State, (*v*) Tehri-Garhwal State, (*vi*) Pargana Jaunsar Bawar of Dehra-dun district, (*vii*) Government Estates, (*viii*) Enclaves absorbed in U.P., (*ix*) Urban Areas and (*x*) Districts of Kumaun Division except Kashipur Tehsil of Nainital. But since then the Act has been applied to areas under (*i*), (*ii*), (*iii*) and (*viii*) above in 1953, (*iv*) in 1954 and (*vii*) in 1955. Separate Acts have been passed for areas under (*vi*) and (*ix*). The Act is still not applicable to Nainital, Tehri-Garhwal and Almora of the Kumaun Division of the newly created districts of Uttar Kashi, Pithoragarh and Chamoli in the Uttarakhand Division.

State except the Hill districts of the Kumaun region. The design of our study is based on the principle of "before and after". We have taken for comparison three yeais before the *zamindari* abolition, viz. 1948-49, 1949-50 and 1950-51 and the years 1957-58, 1958-59 and 1959-60. The latter years do not represent the period immediately following the enforcement of the Zamindari Abolition and Land Reforms Act in 1952 and leaves a gap of five years in between. To a certain extent this may obscure the situation as it emerged immediately after *zamindari* abolition. But this was necessary since the purpose of our study is not to study these transitional problems but to focus attention on the effects and bring to light the lags of land reform measures.

1.4. Statistical Design of the Enquiry and Coverage

The investigation covers the entire State excepting the administrative division of Kumaun and the newly formed division of Uttarakhand. In both these latter divisions the land system differs from the rest of the State and the Principal Act abolishing *zamindari* is not applicable. It also excludes certain small areas elsewhere in the State where *zamindari* has not yet been abolished. This leaves 9 administrative divisions with 572 parganas.

Further, since it was intended to study the effects of *zamindari* abolition without involving the impact of consolidation of holdings, 157 parganas, where consolidation work had either been in operation or completed by March, 1960, were excluded. This left a total of 415 parganas. Three parganas were then selected at random from each of the 9 divisions with probability proportional to the area of each pargana. This gave a sample of 27 parganas distributed over 25 districts.

At the second stage of sampling, all villages within the boundaries of these 27 parganas were listed parganawise—their total number being 6268. A sample of three villages was selected at random from each of the sample parganas with probability proportional to the square root of the product of the area of the village and population thereof. We had thus 81 sample villages—the size of the sample being 1.3% of the total number of villages in the sample parganas.

After sample had thus been drawn, the project area was visited to identify the sample villages and it was reported that villages in 2 parganas, viz. Rath and Jalalpur in Jhansi division and Fatehpur-Chaurasi in Lucknow division were inaccessible due to floods and that *zamindari* had not been abolished in Agori pargana in the Varanasi division. Therefore, these parganas and these villages were substituted by fresh sample drawn within their respective divisions.

A census of all households was then taken in each of the sample villages. This gave information about the principal tenurial status of the head of each household in the village. All households were then classified into four categories, according to the principal tenurial status of the head, viz. (i) *bhumidhars*, (ii) *sirdars*, (iii) others with land including share-croppers or *asamis* and (iv) the rest without any land. A consolidated list of households of all sample villages belonging to each strata was then prepared.

In all 14,062 households were listed—1,967 of *bhumidhars*, 7,176 of *sirdars*, 124 of others with land right, 4,769 of those without any land rights and 26 such whose tenurial status was not known. Excluding these latter there were left 14,036 households. A sample of 10% of *bhumidhars* and 5% of the *sirdars* was drawn from the respective stratum on a random basis for intensive household survey. An additional sample of 20% of the sample number of *bhumidhars* and 15% of that of *sirdars* was further drawn to allow for failures in responses. This resulted in a sample size of 237 *bhumidhars* and 414 *sirdars*. To this were added the entire number of 124 households classified as 'others'. For final analysis 2 cases of *bhumidhars* and 8 of *sirdars* had to be rejected due to non-response or incomplete information. The total sample size thus consists of 765 households among whom 235 are *bhumidhars*, 406 *sirdars* and 124 'others', i.e. *asamis* and landholders without rights. It represents 8.26% of the total households with interest in land, 11.94% of the *bhumidhars*, 5.66% of the *sirdars* and cent per cent of others. As compared to the total number of households with or without land interest the size of the sample is 5.45% of the total households.

The sample for intensive households study falls in 79 out of the 81 villages. The net cultivated area of the 81 sample villages was reported for 1959-60 as 51,117.98 acres or 0.013% of the net cultivated area of the State in the nine divisions under survey (roughly 40 million acres). Twenty-seven out of 81 sample villages are in the Western region, 18 in Central, 9 in Bundelkhand and 27 in the Eastern region.

1.5. PILOT SURVEY, SCHEDULES AND TABULATION

A pilot survey was undertaken in August, 1960, for pretesting the schedules in 6 villages in Sadar Tehsil of the Lucknow district. The original schedules were then revised and finalised for the main enquiry and detailed instructions were also given to the investigators in the light of experience gained during the pilot survey. Various terms and concepts that have been used were defined precisely so as to leave no doubt while filling in the questionnaires. Two types of schedules have been prepared, one in which information has been collected from individual households and the second to record information and particulars about the village as a whole. In each case the questionnaires have been filled in by the investigators on the basis of interviews at spot. Secondary data has been recorded from the village records. In each case supervisors were responsible for a field check and follow up of a minimum of 15% of all the schedules filled in by the investigators and a check up of all the schedules for internal inconsistencies and recording mistakes. These schedules were then verified and coded and particulars from there were transferred to basic data tables. Summary tables have been prepared from this basic data. The different schedules used in the investigation are as follows:

1. Census of village households
2. Details of village area
3. Structure of proprietors' holding before Z.A. 1951-52
4. Structure of *bhumidhars'* holding after Z.A. 1959-60
5. Area held as *sir* and *khudkasht* by zamindars before *zamindari* abolition and extent to which it was let, 1951-52
6. Area of *sir* and *khudkasht* held by zamindars classified according to slabs of land revenue before Z.A. 1951-52
7. Distribution of cultivated holdings
8. Cultivation by sub-tenants
9. Village revenue and rent etc.
10. Transfer of land through sale or gift after Z.A. (from 1951-52 to 1959-60)
11. Statement of ejectments after Z.A. (from 1951-52 to 1959-60)
12. Agriculturist's household enquiry and
13. Village particulars

A list of sample districts, parganas and villages is given in the Statistical Appendix along with two tables indicating the size and distribution of the sample (Tables 1, 2 & 3)

1.6. PERIOD

The survey covers a period of 12 months from June 1960 to May,

1961. The first two months were utilised for the selection of sample and for identifying the sample villages. One month was taken by pilot survey and training of the field staff. The field enquiry was conducted during September, 1960 to February, 1961. The remaining period has been used for the tabulation of data and preparation of the final report.

CHAPTER II

BASIC PURPOSES OF LAND REFORMS

2.1. A CASE FOR LAND REFORMS

There can be little doubt that in economies where an overwhelming majority of the people live by agriculture, raising of agricultural productivity is a necessary condition of economic growth and improvement of the standard of living of the masses. Agricultural productivity per acre and per capita is often circumscribed and limited by the prevailing land system. Hence land reforms occupy a pivotal position in any programme of planned development of agricultural communities and underdeveloped economies. This is particularly so if the prevailing land system inhibits all initiative, stifles all effort and prevents any enlargement of inputs due to insecurity, rack-renting, the practice of sub-letting and a feudal or feudalistic structure of land rights.

It has been pointed out in a recent ECAFE paper that "In a number of countries of the region, defective land tenure systems stultify the farmers' initiative for the improvement of production and deaden the impact of economic plans. Agricultural development throughout the world is strongly motivated by the incentives of farmers, which may take the form of pride of ownership, security of occupancy and the expectation of a just division of farm income between landlords and tenants. These factors have everywhere proved to be stimulants for land improvement."[2] It is explained that in many cases the production decisions of the cultivators have to be taken in an environment under which they are not certain that they would receive the additional benefits due to extra efforts. This is so primarily on account of landlord-tenant relationship under conditions of acute land hunger. In many other cases the land system is such that it leaves the cultivators so impoverished that he can seldom put any extra input, howsoever, little the demand may be. The only spare input with such cultivators is unskilled labour, and its productivity in the prevailing agricultural organisation is almost zero.

[2] *U.N. Economic Bulletin for Asia and the Far East*, Vol. XI, No. 1, June 1960, p. 8

This aspect was very much highlighted in the Report of the Working Party on Economic Development and Planning (Third Session) to the Economic Commission for Asia and the Far East (Fourteenth Session). Discussing the incentives and institutional factors influencing the rate of agricultural development the Secretariat of the F.A.O. reported as follows:

"Unsatisfactory forms or conditions of land tenure may constitute a major impediment to development by creating or perpetuating social unrest, as well as by hampering the modernization of agriculture. Out-of-date cropping systems, for instance, may be propped up by tenancy laws or customs. The application of modern methods may be impossible because farmers' incomes are depressed by exorbitant rents to an extent which leaves no margin for saving or investment. The tenant may lack the minimum security of tenure which would encourage him to invest savings in improvements or would encourage a creditor to grant the cultivator a loan. The tenant's bargaining position may be further weakened by the host of intermediaries between the cultivator and the legal owner of the soil. Under unsatisfactory conditions of land tenure, it is doubtful whether subsidies or efforts by extension services to encourage development will be fully effective because the tenant may receive only a small share of any increases in production due to his own efforts or investments, and so has little incentive to make them."[3]

The importance of land reforms has been felt so acutely in the underdeveloped countries that in China (Mainland) this was given top priority after the revolution of 1949. Article 27 of the Common Programme stated: "Agrarian reform is the indispensable condition for the development of the productive forces and the industrialization of the nation".[4] Experience of post-war Japan and China (Taiwan) confirms the same hypothesis. At home, the Congress Agrarian Reforms Committee reported in 1949 that "there cannot be any lasting improvement in agricultural production and efficiency without comprehensive reform in the country's land system.... The Committee is strongly of the opinion that in the agrarian economy of India there is no place for intermediaries and land must belong to the tiller."[5]

In the State of Uttar Pradesh, where the British land revenue settle-

---

[3] *U.N. Economic Bulletin for Asia and the Far East*, Vol. VIII, No. 3, November 1957, p. 73
[4] Adler, S., *The Chinese Economy*, Routledge & Kegan Paul, London 1957, p. 27
[5] *A.I.C.C. Report of the Congress Agrarian Reforms Committee*, p. 7

ments in the last quarter of the eighteenth century and early nineteenth century disturbed the even tenure of the village communities by implanting a feudal system, the necessity of land reforms had become so urgent that almost the very first act of the newly elected U.P. Legislative Assembly was to pass the following resolution on August 8, 1946:

"This assembly accepts the principle of the abolition of the zamindari system in this Province which involves intermediaries between the cultivator and the state and resolves that the rights of such intermediaries should be acquired on payment of equitable compensation and that Government should appoint a Committee to prepare a scheme for this purpose." This was one year before Independence and nearly five years before the adoption of the First Five Year Plan.

The U. P. Zamindari Abolition Committee built up a case for *zamindari* abolition along the following lines.[6] The organisation of agriculture and its efficiency depend very much on the system of land tenures and a cultivator "will not work to his full capacity nor will he invest his resources in improving his land, unless he is certain that he will enjoy the fruits of his labour and the benefits accruing from his investment." The history of landlord rights in the State has been associated with a progressive increase in the rights and security of the tenant. At the same time there has been an increase in the landlord's share and a gradual reduction in the state's share. In general, the *zamindari* system retards agricultural efficiency and "makes it impossible to effect technological improvements in production." The landlords or the zamindars do not contribute anything and are thus functionally useless. They have done nothing to improve the land and have reduced the tenantry to a "plight worse than before". Further, land being nature's gift is vital to the community and cannot be looked upon as property owned and possessed by individuals.

The *zamindari* system, argued the Committee, originated in the creation of an office for collection of rent. It is in this sense that the term is used in *Aeen-i-Akbari*. For this purpose the machinery has become too expensive at present. The figures for 1954-55 disclosed that to collect a land revenue of Rs. 7.5 crores including local rates the State had to forgo not less than Rs. 10 crores in maintaining the landlord system. Moreover, it had resulted in an extreme form of land concentration in the hands of a few and apart from its economic disadvantages it "meant the degradation" of the many. The bigger landlords constitu-

[6] *Report of the U.P. Zamindari Abolition Committee 1948*, Vol. 1, Ch. XIII, pp. 336-358

ting only 1.49 per cent of the total owned nearly 57.77% of the land while 98.55% of them owned only 42.23% of it. At the top 804 landlords out of a total of 2 million owned anything between one-third and one-fourth of the entire agricultural land of the state. They constituted .0014% of the total population and were an index of the extreme concentration of land and agricultural wealth. Not only were the zamindars without an economic function of a positive character, they had been responsible, according to the Committee, for a steady impoverishment of both the land and man behind the plough. Further, in its words: "They have indulged in rack-renting and illegal exactions."

The State's share in the total rental demand was found by the Committee to have decreased from 90% in 1793 to 39% in 1946 while the rental demand had increased by about 45% since 1893 alone as against an increase of 15% in land revenue. It is obvious that there had been as much as 70% increase in the margin of the profits of the intermediaries or the zamindars and this had by no means been ploughed back into the land. Rack-renting had been associated with decrees, ejectments and relinquishments and the tenants had been drawn continuously to the law courts. Cases were not infrequent when zamindars had resorted to the auctioning of the pitiful belongings of their tenants such as "household utensils, cots, frame-work of doors, thatched roof" (p. 349). The scramble for land had continuously intensified as a result of large-scale evictions and ejectments on the one hand and little increase in the cultivated area in spite of increasing population, on the other.

The Committee has further observed that one of the basic causes of food crisis was the outmoded system of landlordism since it dampened the cultivators' incentives and prevented intensive cultivation. "It has become a drag on the development of the productive forces of the country. It hinders every sensible scheme of large scale operation for rehabilitating the collapsed economy of the country. Abolition of parasitic landlordism along with the simultaneous development of industries can alone draw away the population unproductively engaged in agriculture— the landless labourers and the occupiers of uneconomic holdings—and make possible the reorganisation and regrouping of those who remain on land into cooperative enterprises and, thereby, increase the national wealth and income. No solution within the existing framework of the land system being possible, the landlord must go." (Ibid. p. 357).

In brief, the Committee built a case for *zamindari* abolition more on economic than on social grounds although the latter were not altogether ignored. Among the former, much emphasis was laid on increasing agricultural productivity and output and its equitable distribution. At the same time the Committee envisaged that removal of the intermediary is not the end of the matter, as cooperativisation of agricultural production will have to be adopted to increase wealth and income. It also envisaged that *zamindari* abolition alone will not bring about economic growth since the latter depends equally on industrialisation. What it pointed out was that *zamindari* abolition was a necessary condition— the first step for the release of the productive forces of the economy.

2.2. OBJECTIVES OF LAND REFORMS

Measures of land reform have been introduced in different parts of of the world to meet different requirements and these incorporate as many different programmes as the varying needs of individual countries. According to a survey by the United Nations[7] programmes of land utilisation and control of land use are included as much in the policies of land reforms, e.g. in Canada and Australia, as conferment of ownership rights on tenants and redistribution of land. Everywhere, however, the emphasis is on increased productivity and output. In many cases this has demanded structural and institutional changes in the agrarian economy although in certain others no such changes have been attempted or found necessary. In any case the scope of land reforms has become increasingly wider and is not simply restricted to the improvement of the land tenure system. According to one view the term 'land reform' means "the improvement of agricultural economic institutions, for example agricultural land ownership and tenancy, land rents, taxation of agricultural land or income from land, and also agricultural credit and producer marketing. It includes agricultural technology, physical problems of land utilization and development, conservation of resources, methods and levels of productivity and problems of rural industries in so far as they are relevant to the institutional problems enumerated above."[8] On the other hand the Italian Government introduced measures of land reforms "to remedy or at least obviate the social situation, both for moral and civil reasons as also for economic and technical considerations."[9] In Spain, land reforms policy "has instead embraced a wider field in which may be included all those measures modifying agrarian conditions with a view to the improvement of the economic conditions both of farming and of far-

---

[7] *U.N. Progress in Land Reforms*, New York, 1954
[8] Ibid. pp. 6-7
[9] Ibid. pp. 13-14

mers, the social and cultural aspects of rural life not being forgotten".[10]

The above discussion brings to light the plurality and range of measures that are included in the conception of land reforms. Yet, the United Nation's survey emphasises that in spite of these contrasts there are some common policy objectives. The most important of these is "family-farm ownership". This has been almost the first step everywhere. "The policy of establishing and maintaining peasant ownership, which in Western Europe is now essentially conservative, in Asia, under the slogan of 'the land to the tiller' is inevitably revolutionary."[11] Thus establishment of family-farms appears to be the main operative tool of land reforms policy although by itself it does not assure a high living standard to the farmer. The latter depends on the size of the farm or the holding. Hence land reform measures have also included programmes of land redistribution. Finally, land reforms include all those measures which aim at optimum land use, higher productivity and maximisation of agricultural output.

In brief, we may list four distinct but not necessarily exclusive or alternative objectives of land reform policy. Firstly, there is the problem of low agricultural productivity and output. Any measures at an institutional level that tend to remove obstacles towards *maximisation of agricultural output and productivity* or that promote it directly have often received the top priority in shaping land reforms. Security of tenure, improvement of tenurial status, ownership rights to the tillers of land and even schemes of land redistribution and consolidation of holdings are all designed to achieve this goal. These include promotion and strengthening of incentives, removal of obstacles to technological advance and maximisation of farm inputs.

Secondly, land reforms have been undertaken to bring about *a fair or equitable distribution of agricultural income*.

Thirdly, a basic problem of most underdeveloped and agricultural countries is that of vast underemployment in agriculture. Land reforms, therefore, may be directed to achieve *an increase in employment*. A case for land redistribution is often built on this ground. An I.L.O. Report states that "a wider distribution of ownership can certainly stabilise and increase the volume of farm employment and production, since it allows a fuller employment of the family labour force. Large estate systems in the less developed countries aim at reducing the costs of labour by employing hired workers only at peak seasons, so that for long periods of

[10] Ibid. p. 14
[11] Ibid. p. 49

the year the workers are unemployed. If, however, farm workers are settled on independent holdings they have an incentive to work more regularly; they will tend to diversify cropping and keep livestock so as to spread labour requirements and employ their families; their skill in management and initiative can be developed. Where redistribution of ownership is accompanied by public investment in land improvement or reclamation, the gains in production will be all the greater."[12] Such redistribution of land may not assure economic holdings to all but even then independent family holdings provide better incentive to work, to diversify cropping, to put larger labour inputs and to improve skills as well as to intensify cultivation and to develop mixed farming. An achievement of this objective requires the elimination of hired labour, for whom there may be a reduction of employment if the landless are not the recipients of land in any scheme of land redistribution.[13]

Finally, land reforms have a *social or ethical purpose* as well. In agricultural countries land has not only an economic value but possesses a prestige value too. People and families without land in the villages are the *declasse* of the rural society. They have little social status and always suffer from a sense of injury. Ethical considerations alone demand that all those who subsist on land must have a piece of land, howsoever small it may be. Social tensions and conflicts can seldom be avoided and a sense of 'we feeling' can hardly be promoted in villages or little communities unless each family has land like any other.

To sum up, the broad objectives of land reforms are mainly four, viz., maximisation of output and productivity, fair and equitable distribution of agricultural income, increasing employment opportunities and ethical order. Its instrumentalities are ownership rights, wider land distribution and settlement, private and public investments in agriculture and technological and institutional changes leading to scientific farming and higher standard of farm cultivation and living.

2.3. Programme of Land Reforms in the Country

As stated earlier land reforms were envisaged in the country long

---

[12] I.L.O., *Why Labour Leaves the Land*, Geneva, 1960, p. 226

[13] "Agrarian reform undertaken in Asian countries has consisted of granting ownership of the holding or of offering secure conditions of tenancy to occupying tenant farmers. In such cases there is likely to be no increase in employment, although the incomes of cultivators may improve, and more capital be invested. Hired workers may not be included in the distribution of ownership, and employment may be concentrated in the families of the recipients, resulting in a reduction of employment among the landless." Ibid. p. 227.

before the adoption of planning. There were attempts to improve the land tenure system almost from the very beginning of the present century and in certain cases even earlier. But these were confined to legistative measures designed to improve the tenurial status of the tenants and did not go deep into the roots of the system that was basically feudalistic and anachronistic. These left the agrarian structure sterile, rigid and unresponsive to agricultural development or improvement in the condition of the peasantry. In its wake agararian unrest was deepening and a demand for the abolition of the system, as distinct from its "mending", was growing stronger and stronger. It was under these circumstances that a Land Revenue Commission was appointed in Bengal in early forties and Committees were appointed in several other provinces in the late thirties to examine the system in all its bearings. The spade work was all done during this period. Immediately, therefore, after independence far-reaching land reforms began to be envisaged in several parts of the country. The abolition of the *zamindari* system in Uttar Pradesh formed part of this phase. These reforms, however, were not on a uniform pattern nor linked to any unified scheme for the country as a whole.

It was in this background that the Planning Commission applied itself to this task. It pointed out that land policy has to be conceived in terms of a balance between the different interests in land on the one hand and the effects on production of each measure on the other.[14] The different interests to be taken into account are (i) intermediaries, (ii) large owners, (iii) small and medium owners, (iv) tenants at will and (v) landless workers. With regard to intermediaries legislation by this time had already been adopted in many States to abolish their rights. The only issue in this respect was with regard to the mode of payment of compensation and improvement of village record. In respect of the large owners the Commission favoured the principle that there should be an upper limit to the amount of land that an individual may hold. It, however, distinguished between (a) a limit for future acquisition and (b) a limit for resumption for personal cultivation. The Commission further emphasised that the limit be fixed in each State with reference to its own problems and history and land management legislation be passed to lay down and enforce standards of cultivation and management. For the small and medium owners the Commission recommended programmes for consolidation of holdings and gradual transition towards cooperative farming. The Commission favoured the idea of defining the rights of

[14] Planning Commission, *The First Five Year Plan*, Ch. 13, pp. 184-198

tenants who cultivate the land of small and middle owners and suggested
a security of tenures of 5 to 10 years that should be renewable. The
problem of landless workers was however found by the Commission to
be more intractable since in its opinion schemes of land distribution
were not likely to benefit them substantially as the first claim to any
land available for distribution was to be that of tenants. The only solution according to the Commission was in the adoption of "a cooperative system of management in which the land and other resources of a
village can be managed and developed so as to increase and diversify
production and to provide employment to all those who are able and
willing to work."[15] Its long-term objective is obviously the establishment
of cooperative farming societies on a voluntary basis and the adoption
of cooperative land management through the agencies of the village
Panchayats.

By the time of the Second Five Year Plan the Commission's emphasis
on maximisation of output and productivity had become even more
marked. It pointed out that the objectives of land reforms were two-
fold: (i) to remove such impediments upon agricultural production as arise
from the character of the agrarian structure and (ii) to create conditions
for evolving, as speedily as may be possible, an agrarian economy with
high levels of efficiency and productivity.[16] The emphasis on land redistribution in excess of a ceiling also gained further weight. The same was
true about cooperativisation of agricultural economy. The Commission
pointed out that during the Second Five Year Plan, "it is proposed to
take a series of measures which will lay the foundation for cooperative
reorganisation of the rural economy".[17] Detailed suggestions were made
for land reforms. Personal cultivation was to be defined more accurately
and resumption for personal cultivation was to be limited to the area
which the adult workers in the family could bring under cultivation.
Particular emphasis was placed on (*a*) determining a ceiling on family
holding, (*b*) consolidation of holdings and (*c*) extension of cooperative
farming. For this latter purpose surplus lands and other lands available
in a village were to be regrouped into cooperative farming units and
small cultivators were to be encouraged to pool their land for cooperative farming. Administration of land reforms programmes was considered
necessary for implementation of the land policy.

The main task during the Third Plan is reported to be "to complete

[15] Ibid. p. 193
[16] Planning Commission, *The Second Five Year Plan*, p. 178
[17] Ibid. p. 179

as early as possible the implementation of policies evolved during the Second Plan and embodied in the legislation which States have recently undertaken in pursuance of the accepted policies."[18]

2.4. Broad Purposes of Land Reforms in U. P.

The major land legislations that have been introduced in U.P. in recent years are (i) the U. P. Zamindari Abolition and Land Reforms Act, (ii) the U. P. Consolidation of Holdings Act and (iii) the U. P. Imposition of Ceiling on Land Holdings Act. The last was notified as late as Jan. 3, 1961 and the first received assent of the President on Jan. 24, 1951. Within a period of these ten years far-reaching changes have been made in the land system of the state. But all of them have had a common broad purpose, viz. increased output and productivity. Thus it was stated in the Statement of Objects and Reasons for introducing the Bill for Zamindari Abolition that the abolition of *zamindari* and its replacement by a new land system was necessary "to ensure agricultural efficiency and increased food production, to raise the standard of living of the rural masses and to give opportunities for the full development of the peasants' personality." Similarly, the Preamble to the U. P. Consolidation of Holdings Act 1953 stated that "it is expedient to provide for the consolidation of agricultural holdings in Uttar Pradesh for the development of agriculture." The Uttar Pradesh Imposition of Ceilings on Land Holdings Act 1960 has the same objective, viz. "to ensure increased agricultural production". It is thus obvious that recent land legislation in Uttar Pradesh has been undertaken mainly with a view to increase agricultural output and productivity.

Subservient to this broad purpose of maximum output are the detailed provisions in regard to the following:

1. Abolition of the *zamindari* system which involves intermediaries between the tiller of the soil and the State.
2. Replacement of the multiplicity of land tenures by a simple and uniform scheme under which the vast majority of cultivators will become *bhumidhars* or owners of their holding.
3. Restriction of sub-letting.
4. Avoidance of multiplication of uneconomic holdings by prohibition of partition of holdings below a certain level.

[18] Planning Commission, *The Third Five Year Plan: Draft Outline*, p. 94

5. Restriction on future acquisition of holdings to a maximum of 30 acres in the beginning and 12.5 acres at present.
6. Restrictions on ejectment and elimination of rack-renting.
7. Encouragement and rapid growth of cooperative farming.
8. Vesting of certain land in *Gaon Samaj* and land management and control by *Gaon Sabha*.
9. Consolidation of holdings.
10. Imposition of ceiling on land holdings at 40 acres of 'Fair Quality Land' plus 8 acres for every additional member of a family in excess of five members subject to a maximum of 24 such additional acres.
11. Redistribution of surplus land to cooperative farmers and particularly its settlement with a cooperative society of landless agricultural labourers.

Provision was made for the first eight of the objects in the Main Act abolishing *zamindari*, while the remaining three were provided for in subsequent legislations. In so far as we have excluded from our design the impact of consolidation of holdings, and the imposition of land ceilings is only very recent, the land reforms for purposes of this study have to be judged in the light of the first eight programmes only. These provided a sort of yardstick with which we can measure the success of the main scheme for *zamindari* abolition in the State.

CHAPTER III

LAND SYSTEM BEFORE ZAMINDARI ABOLITION

Section A

3.1. PROPRIETORS AND INTERMEDIARIES

Before the abolition of *zamindari* in the State the various tenure holders could broadly be divided into two classes, viz. (*a*) proprietors and (*b*) tenants. The land was owned and held by the proprietors while the tenants generally cultivated it. These proprietors included zamindars as well as *taluqdars* and they acted mainly as intermediaries between the state and the actual tiller of the soil. Their rights were permanent, hereditary and transferable so that they had the right to hold land in perpetuity which was theoretically vested in the State subject to the payment of land revenue that was determined at the time of settlement. This right was extremely comprehensive and entitled them to use the land in any way that they liked. They were free to cultivate it themselves or to let it to tenants, to use it for an agricultural or non-agricultural purpose or to keep it vacant, to manage it well or to let its resources be depleted. In other words, the only obligation imposed on them was that of the payment of land revenue. Their rights were so extensive as to include all village land including *abadi* (inhabited sites), culturable and unculturable land as well as the village common land.

It was only to a small extent, not exceeding 1/5 of the total area under cultivation at the time of *zamindari* abolition, that the land was cultivated by the proprietors themselves. The bulk of it was cultivated by their tenants who were subject to ejectment by them under certain conditions depending on their tenure. Holdings were let out mostly on a cash rental basis although the system of share-cropping was also in vogue. Rents had continuously increased as pressure on land increased and rack-renting had become such a marked evil of the system that the government had to adopt legislation several times particularly since the beginning of the present century to protect the tenants against enhancement of rents and ejectments. Besides the rent the zamindars used to collect a number of illegal exactions or *nazrana* under one pretext or the other.

Besides the proprietors, there were other intermediaries between a principal tenant and a zamindar. These included an "under-proprietor", "sub-proprietor", "permanent tenure holder" or a "permanent lessee". Their rights were guaranteed under the terms of settlement and were permanent, hereditary and transferable like those of the zamindars. The latter had no right to resume land under the occupation of these inferior proprietors from whom they received a share out of rental income. There was thus a long chain of sub-infeudation and the burden of it all fell on the tiller of the soil, who was a tenant. This chain was sometimes lengthened by permanent or temporary leases or mortgages of their land by the zamindars or under-proprietors in favour of *thekedars* or mortgagees. In certain other cases the tenants themselves leased out or sub-let their holdings and added to this process.

3.2. REVENUE SETTLEMENTS

Land revenue was permanently fixed in Banaras Division, part of Azamgarh and certain areas in Gonda and Bahraich. The rest of the State was temporarily settled. Under permanent settlement land revenue was fixed in perpetuity and under temporary settlement it was subject to periodical revision. Besides, there were those who had land free of revenue and also those with whom settlement was not made. The permanent settlement was introduced in Banaras under the Regulation of 1795. A few minor changes were made later in 1833, 1841 and 1882. The temporary settlements were made in the first instance for a period of 30 years in different districts in different years. In 1929 the period of settlement was extended from 30 to 40 years. The main argument against permanent settlement had been that land revenue could not be increased and so profits on land due to its development and maturity and extension of cultivation went to private proprietors. At the same time the hope that it will result in security of tenure and fair rent for cultivators did not materialise.[19] On the other hand revenue was increased at each successive revision under temporary settlement. Immediately this increased the Government's share and reduced that of the zamindars in the increased rental demand. Each enhancement of land revenue was, however, followed by an attempt that was often successful, by the zamin-

---

[19] "It is a matter of common knowledge that though the burden of revenue fixed upon the zamindars themselves grew lighter and lighter with the extension of cultivation it did not prevent them from continuously increasing the burden of rent upon cultivators, or making illegal exactions and ejecting them whenever another person offered a higher rent." *Report of the Zamindari Abolition Committee,* Vol. 1, p. 95.

dars to increase the total rental demand and rack-rent the tenants, particularly those who had little security of tenure.

It is reported that there were no set rules or principles in the early settlements of land revenue. This was the case at least up to 1822 and the revenue demands were revised after brief periods and progressively increased. For instance, the first settlement in Kanpur was probably in excess of the whole rental of the district. Some system was, however, introduced with the enactment of Regulation VII of 1822.

Regulation of 1822 laid down rules for the assessment of revenue and for determining and recording of land rights. It also provided for joint settlement in case of coparceners under *pattidari* or *bhaichara* system with one person as their representative who was called the *sadar malguzar* or *lambardar*. This regulation made provisions for sub-settlement on fixed rents in the case of persons holding heritable and transferable right in land or hereditary occupancy right. It further laid down rules for cadastral surveys and determination of revenue on the basis of soil classification and productivity. Land revenue was fixed at 80% to 83% of the *net produce*. Revenue courts were established to decide cases pertaining to land rights. In 1833 another Regulation was passed according to which land revenue was reduced to 66% of the net assets (net produce).[20] The period of the settlement was fixed at 30 years. It also revised rules relating to all cultivators residing and engaged in cultivation in the village. In the light of experience gained through the working of these Regulations, directions for Revenue Officers were drawn up in 1844. These Directions "laid down comprehensive rules regarding the procedure of settlement, calculation of net produce and assessment of revenue." These were revised in 1855 so as to restrict land revenue to 50% of the net assets (net produce). The N.W.P. Land Revenue and Oudh Revenue Acts were enacted in 1873 and 1876 to consolidate the the existing legislation and to bring about greater uniformity in the revenue systems of the two broad divisions of the State, viz. Agra and Oudh. The Land Revenue Act of 1901 was aimed at removing this distinction and enlarging the power of settlement officers. It also provided for greater accuracy in the preparation of land records and separation of records of rights from settlement proceedings.

The U.P. Land Revenue Act of 1929 reduced the burden of revenue further from 50% to 40% of the net assets (net produce). A concession of 15% to 30% of the land revenue was also allowed to zamindars in

[20] According to usage the terms net and gross assets are used for the annual net or gross produce of the soil.

respect of their *sir* and *khudkasht*. The Act also extended the period of settlement from 30 to 40 years.

3.3. TENANTS AND THEIR RIGHTS

There were several kinds of tenants in the State before the abolition of *zamindari* system such as fixed-rate tenants, tenants holding on special terms in Oudh, ex-proprietary tenants, hereditary tenants, occupancy and non-occupancy tenants and others like grantees and grove-holders. Besides, there were sub-tenants and trespassers. Thus the rights and conditions of tenures showed wide variations. A fixed-rate tenant enjoyed heritable right and he had also unlimited right to sub-let land. The interest of tenants holding on special terms in Oudh was heritable but not transferable: they enjoyed certain special privileges because they were previously the owners of their land. In other respects they had the same rights and liabilities as those of the occupancy tenants. Ex-proprietary rights accrued in *sir* and *khudkasht* land when a proprietor lost his proprietary rights by voluntary alienation or by operation of law such as foreclosure or sale in execution of a decree. He held such land at a rent rate which was two annas in a rupee less than the rent rate of an occupancy holder. Occupancy rights were acquired ordinarily by continuous cultivation for a period of twelve years before the tenancy reforms of the twenties. The occupancy rights were hereditary although not transferable. The occupancy tenants could, however, sub-let their holdings. The hereditary tenants came into existence after the passing of the U.P. Tenancy Act of 1939. They included a large number of ordinary tenants who did not have any permanent rights before the passing of the above legislation and, therefore, were always under the fear of ejectment. The non-occupancy tenants were largely the inferior right-holders such as sub-tenants, or tenants of *sir* on which tenancy rights could not be acquired.

Tenancy reforms to protect the tenants had to be introduced rather early after settlement with the zamindar. In Agra, occupancy rights were given to certain types of tenants by order of the settlement officer at the first regular settlement between 1833 and 1849. Act X of 1859 which was enacted for the protection of tenants in Bengal was also extended to the then North-Western Provinces. It gave occupancy right to every tenant in respect of every field which he had occupied continuously for 12 years. This act was amended several times and was replaced by Act XII of 1881 which among other changes gave occupancy rights in their home-farm (*sir*) to those who parted with their proprietary rights. Further protection was given by the Tenancy Act of 1901, which put restriction upon ejectments of ordinary tenants. In Oudh no restrictive action was taken to protect the rights of the tenants in the beginning. The Oudh Rent Act of 1886 created occupancy rights in their home-farms in favour of ex-proprietors. This was amended by the Rent Act of 1901.

The last comprehensive tenancy legislation before the abolition of *zamindari* system was the U.P. Tenancy Act of 1939. Under this Act all tenants who formerly had no permanent right were granted permanent and heritable rights, the only exception being the sub-tenants and tenants of *sir*. Further, tenants were given right to make improvements on their holdings with the consent of their landlords and if the court allowed them, could do so even if the landlords did not agree. They could also claim compensation in the case of ejectment. The Act imposed restrictions upon the enhancement of rent which could be enhanced either due to increase in area or because of increase in productivity. The rules framed under the Act provided that rent could not be revised for a period of 20 years or till the next settlement was due. Provision was also made for the remission or suspension of rent.

3.4. PATTERN OF LAND OCCUPATION

Although all agricultural land was owned and held by the zamindars, the area under their direct cultivation or occupation was small. The table on page 26 shows the area occupied and operated by various classes of occupants according to their tenures.

From the table it is seen that more than 20% of the total area in the State was under the direct occupation of the zamindars as their *sir* and *khudkasht*. The whole of it, however, was not under their direct cultivation. (The U.P. Zamindari Abolition Committee estimated[21] that in 1945-46 out of a total of 42,50,000 acres of *sir*, 9,33,000 acres, i.e. nearly 22% was let out, and out of a total of 31,30,000 acres under *khudkasht*, 2,02,000, i.e. nearly 6.5% was let). Another 2% was under the occupation of *thekedars* and mortgagees, etc. and about 1.5% was occupied by sub-proprietors and under-proprietors. The rest, i.e. about 80% of the total was occupied by tenants among whom the largest occupation was that of the hereditary tenants who occupied more than two-fifths of the total agricultural land. The occupancy tenants occupied another 28%. These two classes of tenants whose rights were permanent

[21] *Report*, Vol. I, p. 174.

TABLE No. 1

CLASSIFICATION OF HOLDINGS BEFORE ZAMINDARI ABOLITION
(1951-52)

Type of Tenure	All Villages (Area in acres)[1]	Percentage	Sample Villages (Area in acres)[2]	Percentage
1. *Sir* and *Khudkasht*	74,36,701	16.55	11,089.25	20.06
2. *Thekedars*, mortgagees in possession and ex-proprietors	9,31,232	2.07	2,119.87	3.83
3. Sub-proprietors and under-proprietors	6,71,545	1.49	—	—
4. Permanent tenure holders	2,191	—	—	—
5. Fixed-rate tenants	8,21,748	1.83	—	—
6. Tenants on special terms in Avadh	7,409	0.02	—	—
7. Occupancy tenants and tenants of not less than 12 years in 1333 Fasli	1,25,76,638	27.99	17,900.92	32.38
8. Hereditary tenants and hereditary tenants with special rights	1,89,39,407	42.15	18,473.12	33.42
9. Non-occupancy tenants	4,48,069	1.00	438.84	0.79
10. Occupiers of land without consent	19,73,923	4.39	2,772.02	5.01
11. Grove-holders	7,36,779	1.64	2,043.23	3.70
12. Grantees	3,89,108	0.87	445.62	0.81
Total	4,49,34,750	100.00	55,282.87	100.00

[1] These figures are for the year 1951-52 and have been worked out from the Annual U.P. Land Revenue Administration Report.

[2] The figures for sample villages have been worked out on the basis of average area for 3 years, viz. 1948-49, 1949-50 & 1950-51.

and hereditary occupied among themselves 70% of the total area in agricultural holdings in the State. The area under non-occupancy tenants was insignificant aggregating to about 1% only although land occupied without the consent of proprietors was much larger amounting to 4% to 5% of the total.

The pattern of occupation was more or less the same in our sample villages. A few differences that may be noted are that the area in the sample villages recorded as *sir* and *khudkasht* was 20% as against 16.55% in the State as a whole. Correspondingly, the area under the occupation of tenants with permanent heritable rights was less at 66% in the sample villages as against a figure of 70% for the State.

It is interesting to note that nearly 5% of the area in the sample villages as well as in the State was recorded as occupied by 'occupiers of land without consent'. This provided the potential for many land disputes and it has been suggested that this land was often actually occupied by tenure holders whose rights were not correctly recorded.

Section B

3.5. STRUCTURE OF ZAMINDARI HOLDINGS

According to the data collected by the U.P. Zamindari Abolition Committee there were 20,16,783 zamindars in U.P. in 1947. They paid an aggregate amount of Rs. 6.81 crores as land revenue. Most of them (85%) were petty land-owners paying each a land revenue of Rs. 25.00 or less. In fact as many as 98.5% of the total number of zamindars paid a land revenue of Rs. 250.00 or less each and only 30,142, i.e. 1.5% of the total paid a land revenue of more than Rs. 250.00. But these latter held land assessed at 68% of the total land revenue of the State. In other words the small zamindars paying a land revenue not exceeding Rs. 250.00 possessed among themselves only two-fifths of the total land area although they constituted 98.5% of the total whereas an insignificant minority (1.5% of the total) possessed nearly three-fifths of the total land. The extreme inequality in the distribution of land among zamindars themselves is revealed further by the fact that only 390 zamindars out of a total of more than 2.0 million paid nearly 23% of the total land revenue and 29 among these nearly 10% of the total.

3.6. ZAMINDARI IN SAMPLE VILLAGES

In the 81 villages under survey there were in all 4,340 zamindars. They owned 75,400.08 acres of land in 1951-52. The distribution of zamindars and the area owned by them according to size of holding is given in the following statement:—

TABLE No. 2

DISTRIBUTION OF ZAMINDARS AND THE ZAMINDARI AREA ACCORDING TO AREA
OWNED IN SAMPLE VILLAGES IN 1951-52

Area owned	No. of zamindars	% to Total	Total area held (Acres)	% to Total	Average area per zamindar (Acres)
Less than 5 acres	2,869	66.11	3,722.86	4.94	1.30
5 to 10 acres	455	10.48	3,534.98	4.69	7.77
10 to 25 acres	434	10.00	6,948.92	9.22	16.01
25 to 50 acres	292	6.73	10,328.23	13.70	35.37
50 to 100 acres	145	3.34	10,378.16	13.76	71.57
100 to 200 acres	79	1.82	10,977.31	14.56	138.95
200 to 500 acres	45	1.04	13,323.59	17.67	296.08
500 to 1000 acres	18	0.41	12,277.03	16.28	682.06
1000 & above acres	3	0.07	3,909.00	5.18	1,303.00
Total	4,340	100.00	75,400.08	100.00	17.37

These figures disclose that more than three-fifths (66.11%) of the zamindars were small land-owners holding less than 5 acres each–their average holding was 1.3 acres and they owned among themselves less than 5% of the total *zamindari* area in these villages. As against this more than half (53.69%) of the land was owned by 3.3% of the zamindars holding 100 acres or more each. No less than 22% of the total area was owned by 0.5% of zamindars each holding 500 acres or more.

The inequality in the distribution of land among the zamindars themselves was marked in all regions. It was, however, at its extreme in the eastern districts where a little more than 1% (1.20%) of the zamindars owned nearly half of the village area. For all regions taken together the average holding of a zamindar works out at 17.37 acres. It is, however, as small as 7.89 acres in the eastern districts, where 85% of the zamindars had less than 5 acres each. Yet, the broad pattern is the same all over, i.e. 40% to 60% of the total area was owned by less than 5% of the zamindars, and 40% to 85% of them had 4% to 12% of the total area. The medium zamindars owning 25 to 100 acres each accounted for 10% of the total number of zamindars and owned 27% of the total area. Their proportion was, however, as small as 3.6% in the eastern districts although they constituted nearly 22% of the total zamindars in Bundelkhand, 14% in western districts and 10% in the central region. By regions it was found that the degree of inequality was relatively less in the western districts and in Bundelkhand than in the central and eastern districts. One obvious reason is that in the former there were mostly small and medium zamindars under the *bhaichara* land tenures while the latter had many big zamindars under their *taluqdari* system. Diagram No. 1 indicates the extreme concentration of *zamindari* areas among the former zamindars. The relevant data are given in Table Nos. 4 & 5 in the Statistical Appendix.

DISTRIBUTION CURVE OF ZAMINDARI

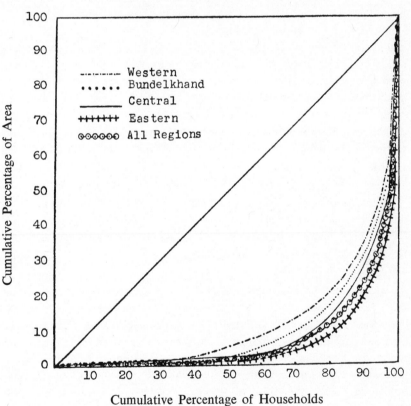

Cumulative Percentage of Households

Diagram No. 1

3.7. ZAMINDARI OF THE SAMPLE HOUSEHOLDS

Out of a total of 765 sample households selected for intensive study 145 reported having *zamindari* before its abolition. Apparently this indicates that nearly one household in every five (18.9%) was a zamindar. This would, however, be erroneous since the sample was drawn on a fixed basis from each stratum and not in proportion to its weight in the total. This sample is, however, useful for studying the internal structure of the group and the changes brought about in it by the *zamindari* abolition. Our data disclose that land-ownership under the *zamindari* system was seldom confined to the boundaries of a village where a person resided. The larger the holding of a zamindar the larger was the area of his holding outside his own village. The total holding of the 145 former zamindars in the sample amounted to 6,778 acres of which 58% was within the villages where they lived and 42% outside the village of their residence. Most of the big zamindars seldom lived in a village and had been living in nearby towns or cities giving rise to the evil of absentee landlordism. Since our sample was confined to villages this feature is not reflected sharply by our data. Even then it is obvious from figures in table No. 6 of Statistical Appendix that whereas land of 47% of the *zamindari* households owning more than 40 acres each was outside the villages of their residence, 96% of the owned land of zamindars having less than 3 acres each was within the villages of their residence.

These figures reveal the same marked inequality in the distribution of *zamindari* area as revealed by the revenue records of the State and of the sample villages—one-fifth of the zamindars held more than 82% of the total *zamindari* area while nearly three-fifths of them had only about 13% of the land.

By occupation the households of the ex-zamindars reported to be predominantly peasants (61.38%), i.e. those who cultivated their holdings with their own labour. Another 30% were reported as farmers, i.e. those who let out their holdings or cultivated it through hired labour or share-cropping. The remaining 9% were distributed in various miscellaneous occupations including agricultural labour. The sample household data reveals that 69% of the area was owned by the farmers as their *zamindari* and 30.5% by the peasants. Persons engaged in other occupations held little *zamindari*. The relevant figures are given in the following table:

TABLE No. 3

DISTRIBUTION OF ZAMINDARI AREA OF THE SAMPLE HOUSEHOLDS BY PRESENT
OCCUPATION OF THE EX-ZAMINDARS

Present Occupation	Number of Households	Percentage to the Total	Area Owned (Acres)	Percentage to the Total
1. Farmers	44	30.35	4,679.00	69.03
2. Peasants	89	61.38	2,069.00	30.53
3. Agricultural Labourers	3	2.07	1.58	0.02
4. Miscellaneous	9	6.20	28.45	0.42
Total	145	100.00	6,778.00	100.00

3.8. ZAMANDARI BY CASTE AND COMMUNITY

Zamindari rights were vested mostly in the upper and the intermediate caste Hindus or in the Muslims. The lower caste Hindus were seldom admitted to it. According to the data pertaining to the 145 ex-zamindars in our sample 57% of the *zamindari* area belonged to the upper caste Hindus and only 0.09% which is practically insignificant to the scheduled caste. The remining area was shared by the intermediate caste Hindus and the Muslims.

A little less than half of the total number of households holding *zamindari* rights belonged to the upper caste Hindus and they held 57% of the land, 38% belonged to the intermediate caste and they possessed 32% of the area, only 2% of them belonged to the scheduled caste and they owned 0.09% of the land. Besides them 10% of the households having *zamindari* were Muslims and they owned 11% of the total area. The detailed figures are given in Table No. 7 of the Statistical Appendix.

Section C

PROPRIETORS' CULTIVATION

3.9. SELF-CULTIVATION AND LETTING OUT

Not only were *zamindari* rights very unequally distributed among the zamindars themselves but the small and large land-owners differed considerably in respect of self-cultivation and renting out of their land. The smaller a zamindar the larger was the proportion of owned land which he cultivated himself and the bigger the zamindar, the larger the proportion of the *zamindari* area that he let out to the tenants. It is obvious from the fact that whereas smaller zamindars paying a land revenue not exceeding Rs. 250.00 owned only about two-fifths of the total *zamindari* area in the State, they held nearly 83% of the total *sir* and *khudkasht* (proprietor's home-farm land). Further, whereas in 1947 only 13% of the *sir* and *khudkasht* land of these smaller zamindars was let out, the corresponding ratio was 25 per cent in case of the bigger zamindars. Most zamindars, however, cultivated some land as out of 2.168 million zamindars in the State 1.998 million (87.5%) were reported to be having *sir* or *khudkasht*. The area of their cultivated holding was usually small since in 83% cases their *sir* or *khudkasht* did not exceed 5 acres. Only a very small minority (0.1%) had a home-farm exceeding 100 acres and the total area in such holdings was not more than 6.37% of the total area under *sir* and *khudkasht*.

Nearly one-fourth (24.5%) of the total area in these large home-farms of zamindars was let out to tenants. In 1945 17.8% of the total agricultural land was recorded as their *sir* and *khudkasht* but 15% out of this also was let out to tenants. Direct cultivation by zamindars, i.e. the area of their *sir* and *khudkasht* minus the area let out of it by them covered only 14.6% of the total area.

The village records of 1951-52, the last year of *zamindari*, reveal that in the sample villages only 66.94% of the zamindars (2,905 out of 4,340) had *sir* and *khudkasht* land and taken together their proprietary cultivation accounted for only 16.33% of the total. Further, the petty and small zamindars had *sir* and *khudkasht* to a larger extent in the sense that a larger proportion of them had home-farm lands and a larger proportion of their proprietary area was under their own cultivation than was the case with the larger zamindars. This is obvious from the following table:

TABLE No. 4

EXTENT OF *Sir* AND *Khudkasht* IN THE SAMPLE VILLAGES

Size of Proprietary Holding	Percentage of Zamindars having *Sir* & *Khudkasht* to Total in the Class.	Percentage of *Sir* & *Khudkasht* Land to Total Area Owned.
Less than 5 acres	82.52	69.58
5 to 10 acres	55.16	51.36
10 to 25 acres	45.85	42.25
25 to 50 acres	19.52	21.25
50 to 100 acres	13.79	13.20
100 to 200 acres	10.13	10.23
200 acres and above	1.52	0.95
All Groups	66.94	16.33

3.10. DISTRIBUTION OF *Sir* AND *Khudkasht*

Most of the zamindars (81.55% in the sample villages and 83.2% in the State) having *sir* and *khudkasht* had less than 5 acres each as *sir* and *khudkasht*. The total area of *sir* and *khudkasht* under the occupation of these small holders was, however, small, i.e. 21% of the total *sir* and *khudkasht* in the sample villages and 39% in the State as a whole. Only a few zamindars who had *sir* and *khudkasht* (less than 3% of them in the sample villages and 1.7% in the State) had a home-farm of 25 acres or more. But they had among themselves 25% to 40% of the total area of *sir* and *khudkasht*. There was thus the same extreme inequality in the distribution of *sir* and *khudkasht* rights as in the ownership rights over agricultural land. The relevant figures about the sample villages are given in the following two tables:

TABLE No. 5

DISTRIBUTION OF *Sir* AND *Khudkasht* AREA IN SAMPLE VILLAGES
(FIGURES FOR 1951-52)

Sir and *Khudkasht*	Zamindars having *Sir* and *Khudkasht*		Total Area of *Sir* and *Khudkasht* Held		Average *Sir* and *Khudkasht* per Zamindar (Acres)
	No.	Percentage	Area (Acres)	Percentage	
Less than 5 acres	2,369	81.55	2,590.18	21.04	1.09
5 to 10 acres	251	8.64	1,815.54	14.74	7.23
10 to 25 acres	199	6.85	2,935.60	23.85	14.75
25 to 50 acres	57	1.96	2,194.99	17.83	38.51
50 to 100 acres	20	0.69	1,369.72	11.13	68.45
100 to 200 acres	8	0.28	1,123.47	9.13	140.43
200 acres & above	1	0.03	280.05	2.27	280.05
Total	2,905	100	12,309.55	100	4.24

TABLE No. 6

DISTRIBUTION OF *Sir* AND *Khudkasht* LAND IN SAMPLE VILLAGES BY REGIONS
(FIGURES FOR 1951-52)   *(Acres)*

Sir and *Khudkasht* Holding	Western Region	Central Region	Bundelkhand Region	Eastern Region	Total
Less than 5 acres	997.15 (25.72)	479.59 (54.89)	617.44 (12.49)	496.00 (18.97)	2,590.18 (21.04)
5 to 10 acres	751.18 (19.38)	191.17 (21.88)	554.34 (11.21)	318.85 (12.19)	1,815.54 (14.75)
10 to 25 acres	1,205.66 (31.08)	143.32 (16.41)	900.47 (18.21)	687.15 (26.28)	2,935.60 (23.85)
25 to 50 acres	600.69 (15.50)	—	1,097.48 (22.20)	496.82 (19.00)	2,194.72 (17.83)
50 to 100 acres	322.62 (8.32)	59.53 (6.82)	766.23 (15.49)	231.34 (8.45)	1,369.72 (11.13)
100 to 200 acres	—	—	1,008.47 (20.40)	115.00 (4.40)	1,123.47 (9.13)
200 acres & above	—	—	—	280.05 (10.71)	280.05 (2.27)
Total	3,876.30 (100)	873.61 (100)	4,944.43 (100)	2,615.21 (100)	12,309.55 (100)

Note: Figures within brackets indicate percentages to the total.

3.11. INCREASE IN AREA UNDER *Sir* AND *Khudkasht*

The area under *sir* and *khudkasht* increased in the few fateful years immediately preceding *zamindari* abolition. It was reported at 73.54 lakh acres in 1944-45 by the U.P. Zamindari Abolition Committee and at 74.37 lakh acres in 1951-52, the last year of *zamindari* abolition. For the sample villages it increased from 11,325 acres in 1948-49 to 12,309 acres in 1951-52. There was, however, little increase in the area under *sir* and *khudkasht* in relation to the total area comprised in agricultural holdings as this stood at 17.8% in 1944-45 and 16.6% in 1951-52. A detailed break-up of our sample reveals that the area under *sir* and *khudkasht* increased unmistakably in certain districts and regions whereas it declined in others as indicated in the following table:

TABLE No. 7

AREA UNDER *Sir* AND *Khudkasht* IN SAMPLE VILLAGES BY REGIONS

(In Acres)

Year	Western Region	Central Region	Bundelkhand Region	Eastern Region	All Regions
1948-49	2,518	781	5,392	2,634	11,325
1949-50	2,566	831	5,427	2,618	11,441
1950-51	2,635	845	4,411	2,610	10,502
1951-52	3,876	874	4,944	2,615	12,309

These figures reveal that in the years immediately preceding *zamindar* abolition, the area under *sir* and *khudkasht* tended to increase in the western and central regions although a reverse trend was registered in the Bundelkhand and the eastern regions. It appears that this increase was confined to those areas and regions where the area under the direct cultivation of zamindars was little. It is significant to note that according to our sample survey the *sir* and *khudkasht* area increased only in the western and central regions and it is in these regions that it accounted for only 13.85% and 8.97% of the agricultural area respectively. In the eastern and the Bundelkhand regions where such area was 24.55% and 30.05% respectively there was an actual decline in the last year of the *zamindari*, i.e. 1951-52, while there was an increase under *sir* and *khudkasht* in all the regions as compared to the previous year, i.e. 1950-51. It is, therefore, suggested that the increase that took place in the area under *sir* and *khudkasht* in the years immediately preceding *zamindari* abolition was for purposes of resumption of cultivation or for establishment of farms by the zamindars to retain as much land as possible.

Section D

THE REVENUE SYSTEM

3.12. RECENT DEVELOPMENT OF THE SYSTEM

Initially under the British rule the land revenue was simply levied at the highest sum which anybody would offer. In 1788 Mr. Jonathan Duncan was authorised to amend the system in Banaras division on the basis of fixed standard rates for different classes of soil after obtaining valuation of the produce. Thus he made a summary settlement on the basis of this revised procedure and after some revision this was made permanent fixing the revenue demand in perpetuity by Regulation of 1795. In the rest of the ceded and conquered districts temporary settlements were made in the beginning on the basis of unsatisfactory and inadequete data. Some improvements were introduced subsequently by Regulation 1 of 1821 and Regulation VII of 1822. This last provided for a complete record of rights, a full account of the rate of cash rents, the method of division of produce for grain rents, a survey and the maintenance of village records and establishment of revenue courts. Land revenue was fixed at 80% of the receipts of zamindars. The system was, however, found to be unworkable and replaced by Regulation IX of 1833 which laid down a new procedure for fixing the revenue demand on the basis of a general knowledge of the aggregate cultivated area of the State, village maps, field books and rent rolls. The first regular settlement was made between the years 1833 and 1849 and confirmed for a period of 30 years. Its results have been summarised as follows:

"(1) Settlement was made wherever possible with village proprietors; and the *ryotwari* system of Bundelkhand was replaced by a *zamindari* system with joint responsibility. In the eastern districts the subordinate proprietors or *Birtias* where given full proprietary rights. The *taluqdar* generally disappeared save in rare cases where the village proprietors desired the connection to continue, in which case their payments to him were fixed; elsewhere the *taluqdar* received a rent charge or *malikana*, originally fixed at 18 per cent on the assets. The *taluqdari* system is now rare in Agra.

(2) Hereditary tenants, and tenants who had resided and culti-vated in the same village for 12 years, were given rights of occupancy when they claimed them, or even when they did not claim them, if the local officer thought they might have done so.

(3) The assessments were on the whole moderate; though they amounted on an average to 66 per cent of the rental assets."[22]

When the Saharanpur settlement was made in 1855 the proportion of the assets to be taken as revenue was reduced to 50% instead of 66% and the assets were defined as the net average assets.

In the second regular settlement in the former province of Agra the assessment was based upon the average rental assets and since the *patwari's* papers were still unreliable these assets were calculated by enquiry into the rates of rents actually prevailing in an area. The soils were classified and standard rates of rents were fixed for each class. The assessment was thus based neither on the basis of rents as recorded in *patwari's* papers nor on actual rents realised by the zamindars but on the estimated rental which was considered to be the sum which could be realised.

In the third regular settlement the circle rent rate was determined on the basis of enquiry and rent rate that was formerly the basis of assess-ment was replaced by the actual rent rate and the circle rent rate was simply used as a check.

Oudh was annexed only in 1856 and although the first settlement ignored the *taluqdari* right, the second summary settlement was made with *taluqdars* in 1858 and they were given full proprietary rights.

The main features of land revenue settlements under the British rule varied little after that except that the revenue demand was reduced to ordinarily 40% of the net assets. This was, however, the maximum as the assessment could be as low as a rate between 25% and 35% where the number and circumstances of proprietors in a *mahal* justified it. Secondly, the term of settlement was raised to 40 years.

With the abolition of the *zamindari* the basis of assessment has been changed to the estimated average produce of the holding after deducting the ordinary expenses of the cultivation although the village will remain the unit of assessment and cultivators will continue to have a joint res-ponsibility for the payment of land revenue. Such an assessment will, however, take place only after a period of years from the date of *zamindari* abolition. For the time being the land revenue has been fixed at the rates

[22] Ray, S. C., *Land Revenue Administration in India*, p. 124.

of rents payable by different classes of tenants. The net assets or rents have thus been the basis of revenue assessment rather than the net produce or rental value. We have reproduced in Appendix III the main features of revenue settlement in State as reported by the Taxation Enquiry Commission (1953-54, Vol. III), while we give below an account of the operations as reported by Sir Edward Blunt in his monograph on the Indian Civil Service.

"In the United Provinces, the first step is to assign to each soil a value, which is obtained by consideration of relevant data, for instance, the rents actually recorded, as paid for each class of soil; crop-cutting experiments, which consist in measuring out exactly a given area, and ascertaining the yield of that area; a comparison of the value of the crops actually grown in each soil; and also generally inquiries from the cultivators themselves. The second step is to arrange the villages in circles, which are homogeneous in respect of such characterstics as climate, communications and agricultural conditions. The recorded rent-rolls of the village in a circle are then examined, and all fraudulent, inadequate, excessive and other abnormal rents are excluded. The incidence of the remaining rents is then calculated for each class of soil, and a set of standard rates for each circle is worked out. These Circle rates are then compared for each village with the recorded rent, in other words, the rent-roll as it is, is compared with the rent-roll as it ought to be. If, after making allowance for any local peculiarities, the two approximate, then the recorded rent-roll will be accepted as the basis of assessment. If the two diverge greatly without any ascertainable justification then the assessment is based on the valuation at circle rates. To the rent-roll or rental valuation, is added a valuation at circle rates of unrented lands, which usually consist of the landlord's own holding, from which a deduction, usually 25 per cent, is made to allow for the landlord's cost of production. To the total of these two figures are added any other assessable items, in the nature of manorial dues, and the total forms the net assets of the village.

After the Settlement Operations are over the Settlement Officer writes out the Report. The report is submitted to the Board of Revenue and the Legislative Council. The Legislative Council is given an opportunity to discuss it. Ordinarily, minor alterations are proposed which are usually adopted and the Report is accepted."

3.13. NET ASSETS AND ECONOMIC RENT

The basis of assessment in U.P. was the value of the net assets in the sense of an annual net income from the soil but it did not necessarily mean the surplus produce of a holding, i.e. the economic rent. It was already provided in the rules issued after 1886 that, (a) the net assets should exclude any considerations of prospective increase in value and (b) concession be given for improvements made by individual proprietors. Subsequently the U.P. Land Revenue Act 1901 laid down a detailed procedure for the settlement of revenue and revision of assessment while the U.P. Tenancy Act of 1939 made provision for the determination and modification of rent. The latter Act provided that rent rate officers shall propose separate rates for each circle and for each class of soil. The rates of the occupancy tenants were to be lower than those applicable to the hereditary tenants for whom the Act provided that the proposed rates shall be based on genuine and stable rents paid by such tenants with substantial holdings without hardship over a series of years. To find out whether the rents were paid without hardship the rent rate officers had to take into account (a) the level of rents paid by tenants admitted at different times, (b) prices of agricultural produce prevailing at such times, (c) changes in crops grown and in the yield and (d) the value of the produce so that the rate does not exceed one-fifth of such value, (e) expenses of cultivation and (f) the cost to the cultivator of maintaining himself and his family. In actual practice the contractual rents paid by the tenants have been the main basis of assessment of revenue. These have differed according to the pressure of population on soil in various parts of the State, the tenures of cultivators, and the time or period during which individuals were admitted to tenancy. In brief, there was little uniformity in rents paid by tenants before *zamindari* abolition and tenants within the same village often paid different rents for the same type of land. Under the circumstances there was little nexus between rents and surplus produce. Nonetheless the total rental demand in the State increased little during the twenty-five years immediately preceding the abolition of *zamindari* system.

According to revenue records the rent collected in any year was seldom equal to the total rental demand. Very often it has been only 50% to 60% of the demand and if this is true it is obvious that large arrears of rent must have accumulated. During the Great Depression the total rent collection was reported to be only about 36% of the annual rental demand and only 58% at its best during the Second World War. It appears that there has been considerable under-reporting of rent collections; otherwise the evictions and ejectments would have been on a very vast scale. Even when allowance is made for this factor it is obvious that the net receipts of the zamindars after deducting the amount of land revenue increased little between 1926 and 1951. At the same time there was a sharp price increase during the decade 1941-1951. This must have affected adversely the real income of the zamindars. Between 1931 and 1939 when prices had declined and remained at a low level any increase in the real income of the zamindar was neutralised by the system of rent remissions. In so far as the rents were not linked to price variations there was an inherent weakness in the rental system of the State that was particularly marked on account of the upward rigidity or insensitivity of the rent rates to increases in agricultural prices. Certain figures with regard to the annual rental demand and rent collections are given in the following table:

TABLE No. 8

RENTAL DEMAND AND COLLECTION IN THE STATE

(Figures in Lakhs of Rupees)

Period	Annual Rental Demand	Rent Collected & its % to Total Demand	Revenue Demand	Zamindars' Surplus of Rent Collected over Revenue Demand	Percentage of Surplus over Rent Collected, i.e. % of 5 to 3.
1	2	3	4	5	6
1926-31	1,929	1,010 (52.36)	698	312	30.89
1931-36	1,880	681 (36.22)	711	−30	—
1936-41	1,812	791 (43.65)	702	89	11.25
1941-45	1,733	1,007 (58.11)	682	325	32.27
1946-51	1,848	942 (50.97)	706	236	25.03

Source: Z.A.C.R., Vol. II, p. 87 and Revenue Administration Reports.

3.14. PER ACRE RENT AND REVENUE

Before *zamindari* abolition in 1950-51 the average rent per acre in the State as a whole amounted to Rs. 5.45 on cash rented holdings and Rs. 6.81 on crop-shared holdings. The average rental demand on all types of holdings worked out at Rs. 5.46 excluding *sayar* and Rs. 5.66 including *sayar*. The revenue demand per acre amounted to Rs. 1.8 in 1950-51 and Rs. 1.9 in the preceding quinquennium.

A significant fact, however, is that the rent per acre varied by tenures. In Oudh in 1951-52 the non-occupancy tenants paid a rent three times as high as that for the occupancy tenants and the hereditary tenants paid a rent which at an average was twice as high as that of the latter. The differences were not so marked in the rest of the State where the non-occupancy tenants were paying a little less than Rs. 6 per acre and the hereditary tenants paid more or less the same rate. The occupancy tenants and the ex-proprietary tenants paid about 20% to 25% less than that paid by the hereditary tenants. On the whole the occupancy tenants in Oudh paid less than those in the former province of Agra and the non-occupancy tenants paid nearly twice as much as those of the latter. The relevant figures are given in Table 8 of the Statistical Appendix.

There were similar marked variations in the rent and revenue per acre in the different parts of the State. Land revenue per acre was the highest (Rs. 2.45) in the division of Meerut and lowest in Jhansi (Rs. 1.06). Average rent per acre was the highest in Lucknow division at Rs. 6.23 and the lowest in Jhansi at Rs. 2.60. The zamindar's margin was the highest in Lucknow at Rs. 4. 32 per acre and lowest in Jhansi at Rs. 1.54 per acre. Again, the *zamindari* net receipts after payment of land revenue were highest in Lucknow at Rs. 2.16 per rupee of land revenue paid by zamindars and lowest in Gorakhpur at Rs. 0.98 per rupee of land revenue.

The variations in rent per acre by administrative divisions cannot all be explained by differences in soil fertility. Out of the nine divisions excluding the hill areas the rent per acre varied between Rs. 5 and Rs. 6 in six divisions, was about Rs. 3.5 in two divisions and only Rs. 2.6 in one division. But the average rent rate in the division of Meerut which includes the most fertile parts of the State was less than that in Lucknow. The yield per acre in the eastern districts comprised in the divisions of Banaras and Gorakhpur is not very much less than that in Lucknow and Faizabad divisions and yet the average rent per acre in the former case was nearly 40% less than in the latter. To a large extent these variations in rent per acre were the result of the relative security or insecurity enjoyed by tenants in different parts of the State on account of the differences in the tenurial and land revenue system and secondly on account of the differences in the time of the introduction of regular settlements. Rents were low under the system of permanent settlement in Banaras and highest under the *taluqdari* system. Under the *mahalwari* system particularly under *bhaichara* land tenures as prevailing in the western districts the rents were not so high or under the *taluqdari* system although higher than that under the permanent settlement. The land revenue demand per acre was also the lowest under permanent settlement. Under temporary settlement it did not form a uniform fraction of the rent per acre. Broadly speaking, it was relatively low in the *taluqdari* areas and high elsewhere. The relative figures are given in Table 9 of Statistical Appendix.

CHAPTER IV

CULTIVATORS' HOLDINGS AND LAND USE
BEFORE ZAMINDARI ABOLITION

Section A

4.1. CULTIVATORS' HOLDINGS BY TENURES

According to the information collected by the U.P. Zamindari Abolition Committee there were 25.68 million cultivators in the State in
1944-45. Out of these 21.56 million were direct tenure holders[23] and 4.12
million were sub-tenants or tenants under the tenure holders.[24] This
total, however, exceeded the number of cultivators as the same person
holding more than one class of interest in land was counted more than
once. None the less these figures are a fair indication of the proportion
of direct tenure holders and cultivators with inferior rights. These figures
indicate that 1 in every 5 cultivators was a tenant under a tenant, a
tenant of *sir* and *khudkasht*, sub-tenant or occupier of land without
consent. In any case he enjoyed little security of tenure and could be
ejected from land by the principal tenure holder. The area cultivated
by these inferior tenure holders aggregated to 36,62,443 acres out of a
total cultivated area of 4,13,29,440, i.e. 8.87% of the total.

Among the principal tenure holders by far the most numerous were
hereditary tenants (32.7% of the total) and they operated the largest
area (39.5%). They were followed by occupancy tenants who constituted
28% of the total number of cultivators and held 30% of the land area.
The third place in order of numerical strength was occupied by *sir* and
khudkasht cultivators, i.e. zamindars cultivating their own land. These
accounted for 13.1% of the total number of cultivators and held 17.8%
of the total area. Another 5% came under the category of ex-proprietary
tenants or *thekedars* or mortgagee cultivators and fixed-rate tenants.
These held 4.3% of the total area. Numerically strong were those who
occupied land of the zamindars without their consent. They formed
11.2% of the total number of cultivators and occupied 3.4% of the total

[23] Tenure holders entered in Part I of *Khatauni*.
[24] Tenants and Sub-tenants entered in Part II of *Khatauni*.

area. Another 5.6% of the cultivators were grove-holders and they occupied 1.7% of the land. The same proportion of land was occupied by sub-proprietors who accounted for only 1.2% of the total number.

Among the inferior tenure holders who were holding land from the tenants or were tenants of *sir* and *khudkasht* the most numerous were the sub-tenants, i.e. 38.7% of the total. These were cultivating 44% of the total area under the occupation of inferior tenure holders. The next numerous class was that of tenants of *sir* and *khudkasht* accounting for 29% of the cultivators among the inferior tenure holders and holding an equal proportion of such land. They were followed closely by occupiers or tenants of land without consent (28.0% of the total) and among themselves they held 23% of the area in the occupation of inferior tenure holders.

In the sample villages one-fifth of the total area was under *sir* and *khudkasht*, two-thirds was occupied almost in equal proportion by occupancy and hereditary tenants, 5% by occupiers of land without consent, 3.8% by ex-proprietary tenants, *thekedars* and mortgagees and 3.7% by grove-holders.

4.2. *Sir* AND *Khudkasht* (PROPRIETORS' CULTIVATION)

Nearly one-fifth of the total land was under the cultivation of proprietors as their *sir* and *khudkasht*. The average size of their cultivated holding works out at 2.60 acres according to the data of the U.P. Zamindari Abolition Committee and 4.24 acres according to the data of our sample villages. In both cases it proves that most of the *sir* and *khudkasht* cultivators had petty holdings under their cultivation although as pointed out in the previous chapter the *sir* and *khudkasht* land was very unequally distributed among such tenure holders. There were also certain marked regional differences. In the sample villages a little less than 9% of the total area, was under *sir* and *khudkasht* in the central districts, 13.85% in the western, 24.55% in the eastern and 30.05% in Bundelkhand region. The corresponding figures for the State for the year 1944-45 as collected by the U.P. Zamindari Abolition Committee are 11.33%, 15.8%, 22.85% and 26.80% respectively. It is obvious that there was little proprietors' cultivation in the central districts while it covered no more than one-fourth of the total area under cultivation in Bundelkhand. More or less the same was true about eastern districts although it covered only 14% to 16% in the western districts.

4.3. CULTIVATION BY PERMANENT TENANTS

By permanent tenancy is meant a permanent and hereditary tenancy right with or without the right to transfer. This includes the rights of fixed rate, ex-proprietary, occupancy and hereditary tenants as well as of the sub-proprietors, under-proprietors, *thekedars* and mortgagees. In 1944-45 nearly three-fourths of the total area under holdings in the State was under permanent tenancy varying from 70% in Bundelkhand and eastern districts to nearly 80% in the western and central districts. Immediately before *zamindari* abolition (average for the years 1949-52) the area held by permanent tenants in sample villages was a little less than 70% in all the districts taken together and varied between 61% in Bundelkhand to 79% in the western districts. The relevant figures are given below:

TABLE NO. 9

PERCENTAGE AREA UNDER HOLDINGS OF PERMANENT TENANTS IN
DIFFERENT REGIONS BEFORE ZAMINDARI ABOLITION

Regions	Sample Villages (Average 1949-52)	All Villages* (1944-45)
Western Districts	78.73	79.48
Central Districts	71.98	79.11
Bundelkhand Districts	60.75	69.82
Eastern Districts	65.86	70.07
All Districts	69.63	75.60

*Compiled from Statement 15 of the *Report of the U.P. Zamindari Abolition Committee*, Vol. II.

Permanent tenants apparently held less area in the sample villages than revealed by the revenue records of all villages. If, however, we combine the area held by proprietors as their *sir* and *khudkasht* and the area held by permanent tenants it is found that nearly 90% to 94% of the total area in the sample villages as well as in the States as a whole was held by tenure holders with permanent rights. Simultaneously, wherever the proportion of *sir* and *khudkasht* was high as in Bundelkhand and eastern districts the area held by permanent tenants was relatively less than the area held by them in the central and western districts where the area under *sir* and *khudkasht* was low. Yet, the fact remains that at the time of *zamindari* abolition most of the cultivated area (90% to 95%) was held by tenure holders with permanent and hereditary rights.

4.4. CULTIVATION BY TEMPORARY TENANTS

For determining the extent of temporary tenancy before *zamindari* abolition we have taken together the area occupied by the non-occupancy tenants and that in the possession of occupiers of land without consent. According to the revenue records of the year 1944-45 that were analysed by the U.P. Zamindari Abolition Committee 11% of the cultivators were occupying land without consent, and 1.1% were non-cocupancy tenants. They held 3.4% and 0.6% of the total area respectively or a total of 4%. In 1951-52 the area under the occupation of non-occupancy tenants was 1.0% and that occupied by occupiers of land without consent 4.4%, i.e. a total of 5.4%. In the sample villages the area in their possession had been worked out at 5.01% and 0.79% respectively, or about 6%. It is significant to note that it is not the proportion of area under non-occupancy tenants that has registered any substantial increase but it is that under wrongful occupation which has increased considerably from 13.99 lakhs in 1944-45 to 19.74 lakhs in 1951-52. This measures an increase of nearly 40%. A part of this may be explained by incorrect entries in revenue records and a part by actual wrongful occupation to acquire certain rights in land after *zamindari* abolition. Complaints were made that revenue record entries were at times manipulated to prevent certain individuals from getting their due land rights or to make it possible for others without any rights to make their claim. The position appears to be at its worst in the eastern districts where 7.2% of the land in our sample villages was occupied without consent. Bundelkhand followed next with 5.8% of such land. The proportion of such land was only 3.7% in western and central districts.

4.5. GROVE-HOLDERS AND GRANTEES

In 1945, 5.6% of the cultivators were recorded as grove-holders and 2.5% as grantees holding a rent-free land in lieu of service or otherwise. They occupied only 1.7% and 0.9% of the total area respectively. In 1951-52 the respective figures were 1.64% and 0.81%. In the sample villages the average for the three years preceding *zamindari* abolition (1948-49, 1949-50 and 1950-51) works out at 3.7% of the total area under grove-holders and 0.8% under grantees. Obviously, the area occupied by grantees did not change but there appears to have occured an increase in the land under the occupation of grove-holders. Acutally there might not have been any increase even in the area under the grove-holders and the discrepancy is perhaps due to the size of our sample. This supposition is strengthened by the fact that in our sample villages in the central districts 13.8% of the total area is shown in the occupation of grove-holders whereas according to the revenue records of 1332 *fasli* less than 0.25% of the area in central districts was in their occupation.

4.6. CULTIVATION BY SUB-TENANTS

Among the sub-tenants are included not only sub-tenants proper but tenants of *sir* and *khudkasht*; tenants under rent-free grantees and occupiers of land without the consent of the tenants. They may be taken as constituting nearly one-fifth of the total cultivators before *zamindari* abolition although they held only 8.86% of the total area.[25]

According to the data of the sample villages for the three years preceding *zamindari* abolition the area under sub-tenancy cultivation was 4,449 acres out of a total of 55,282 acres of cultivated area, i.e. 8.04%. The proportion of sub-tenancy in different regions is indicated in Table 10 of Statistical Appendix. Its data indicate that the extent of sub-tenancy cultivation was as high as 11% in the the eastern districts and 9% in Bundelkhand although it was only about 6% in the western and central districts. A major portion of such area (36% in all districts) 54% in Bundelkhand and 40% in eastern districts was held by tenants of *sir* and *khudkasht*. In the western and the central districts the position was a little different as only 17% and 14% respectively of the area under sub-tenancy cultivation was comprised of the holdings of tenants of *sir* and *khudkasht*. Nearly one-fourth of this area was in the occupation of sub-tenants proper and nearly one-third in the occupation of sub-tenants holding land without consent from the principal tenants.

It has been calculated that *sir* and *khudkasht* were let out to tenants to the extent of 8% to 9% in the western and central districts, 17% in Bundelkhand and 19% in the eastern districts. For all the sample villages taken together the proportion works out at 14.5%. About 6% of the area occupied by permanent tenants was sub-let to either sub-tenants or occupied by persons without consent in all regions except the eastern districts where it works out at more than 10%. This high ratio in the latter is presumably due to a considerable area being held without consent

[25] *Report of the U.P. Zamindari Abolition Committee*, Vol. II, Statement 6, p. 8.

rather than being regularly let to sub-tenants. Sub-letting, however, was most common among rent-free grantees. More than half of their area was in the occupation of their tenants. Many of them perhaps were in non-agricultural occupations and the area held by them as grant was so small that very often they found it more convenient and economical to sub-let it rather than cultivate it themselves.

There were marked regional differences in the extent of sub-tenancy. It was recorded highest in the eastern and Bundelkhand region being 11.53% and 9.23% and only about 6% in the western and central districts.

4.7. SIZE AND DISTRIBUTION OF CULTIVATED HOLDINGS

The average size of cultivated holding and the distribution of the area among cultivating households by size of holdings has been estimated from the results of intensive sample household survey. The total sample consisted of 765 households with cultivating interest in the year of enquiry. These were selected, as explained earlier, out of a total of 9,267 households found to be cultivating at the time of enquiry in the sample villages. Out of these sample households only 734 had a cultivated holding before *zamindari* abolition. Further, as against a population of 81,399 at the time of enquiry the sample villages had a population of only 72,513 according to the census of 1951. Assuming that the size of household, and the occupational distribution in villages have not changed since 1951 we have estimated that the number of cultivating households has increased between 1951 and 1960 in the same proportion as population of these villages. On this basis we have arrived at an estimate of 8,285 cultivating households in the sample villages on the eve of *zamindari* abolition as calculated in Table 11 of Statistical Appendix.

The results of the intensive sample households enquiry give us the frequency distribution of the cultivating households by size of holdings. In so far as the sample was drawn separately from the various tenurial strata of households at the time of enquiry and its proportion to the universe varied in each tenurial class, the pattern of distribution for all cultivating households could not obviously be the same as for the total sample households. We, therefore, estimated the distribution of the cultivated holdings in each tenurial stratum directly from the distribution of the sample households of that stratum. But for the overall picture we adopted the technique of blowing up the estimates for all households of *bhumidhars, sirdars* and 'others' separately from the sample data and then adding them up to estimate the distribution of cultivated holdings and cultivating households by size-group of holdings.

The average size of cultivators' holding in the sample villages has been worked out at 7.73 acres. There are, however, considerable differences from region to region—the smallest size at 5.25 acres being in the central districts and the largest in Bundelkhand at 11.42 acres. The average size is 8.37 acres in the western districts and 7.14 acres in the eastern. The differences by tenures and castes are even more marked. The present *bhumidhars* cultivated before *zamindari* abolition a holding which was on an average twice as large (12.36 acres) as that cultivated by the present *sirdars* (6.49 acres). Similarly the high caste Hindus had under their cultivation an average holding (11.93 acres) which is nearly 2.8 times the average holding of the scheduled caste Hindus (4.36 acres) and about 1.8 times that of 'others' consisting of intermediate caste Hindus and Muslims (6.52 acres). There is ample evidence in these figures to indicate that the average size of cultivators' holdings was small but within this limit certain groups had an advantage over others. Generally speaking the less protected a class or a caste was the smaller was the size of the area that its members cultivated before *zamindari* abolition. The regional variations on the other hand were an index of the relative development of agriculture and land use as well as the pressure of population on the soil. Table No. 10 on the following page gives the relevant estimates.

The average size of holding does not by itself bring to light the marked inequality in the distribution of land among cultivating households before *zamindari* abolition which is brought out by the break-up of the households and the cultivated area by size of holdings. Such data disclose that nearly 30% of the households had a cultivated holding of less than 3 acres each and had only 6.51% area among themselves. More than half of the cultivating households (51.53%) had only one-sixth (16.95%) of the total cultivated holdings area and had less than 5 acres each. The holdings of some 11% of the cultivating households were of 15 acres or more although they had in their holdings more than two-fifths (42.88%) of the total area. A little more than 3% of the cultivating households had a holding of 30 acres or more but these had among themselves more than one-fifth (28.91%) of the total area. The data pertaining to the distribution of cultivated holdings is summarised in Table No. 11 on the following page.

An analysis of the data of sample households reveals that the inequality in the distribution of land among cultivating households existed

TABLE No. 10

AVERAGE SIZE OF CULTIVATED HOLDINGS IN THE SAMPLE VILLAGES
BEFORE ZAMINDARI ABOLITION

Cultivating Households	Area per Household (In Acres)
(A) *Present Tenure*	
i. *Bhumidhars*	12.36
ii. *Sirdars*	6.49
iii. *Asamis*	5.80
iv. Non-Tenure Holders	3.53
(B) *Regions*	
i. Western	8.37
ii. Central	5.25
iii. Bundelkhand	11.42
iv. Eastern	7.14
(C) *Caste & Community*	
i. Upper Caste Hindus	11.93
ii. Scheduled Caste	4.36
iii. Others	6.52
(D) *All*	7.73

TABLE No. 11

PERCENTAGE DISTRIBUTION OF ALL CULTIVATING HOUSEHOLDS AND THE
AREA IN THEIR HOLDINGS BEFORE ZAMINDARI ABOLITION IN THE SAMPLE
VILLAGES

Size Group	Percentage		Cumulative Percentage	
	Households	Area	Households	Area
Less than 1 acre	3.80	0.29	3.80	0.29
1— 3 acres	26.35	6.25	30.15	6.54
3— 5 ,,	21.38	10.41	51.53	16.95
5—10 ,,	25.54	22.75	77.07	39.70
10—15 ,,	11.73	17.42	88.80	57.12
15—20 ,,	3.86	8.29	92.66	65.41
20—30 ,,	3.79	11.68	96.45	77.09
30—40 ,,	2.03	8.82	98.48	85.91
40 acres and above	1.52	14.09	100.00	100.00

throughout the State before *zamindari* abolition although it was more marked in the eastern and central regions than in the western districts or in Bundelkhand. In the eastern districts 47% of the cultivating households had a holding of less than 3 acres each and they cultivated less than one-tenth (9.66%) of the total area while only about 5% had a holding of 30 acres or more possessing more than two-fifths (41.53%) of the total area. In the central region 41% of the cultivating households had a holding of less than 3 acres each and cultivated among themselves only about one-seventh (14.37%) of the total area. Only about 2% had a holding of 20 to 30 acres and the land comprised in such holdings was a little less than one-fifth (9.97%) of the total. In Bundelkhand where the average size of holding has been found to be the largest only some 9% of the cultivating households had a holding of 3 acres or less although a little more than 23% of the cultivating households had a holding of less than 5 acres each and they cultivated not more than 5% of the total. But as much as 43.7% of the total area was distributed in the holdings of only about 10% of households, each with a holding of 80 acres or more and actually the largest slice of the area (34.28%) was under some 6% of the households, each with a holding of 40 acres or more. In the western districts a little less than one-fifth (19.53%) of the cultivating households had a holding of less than 3 acres each and had only about 3.8% of the area. About 4% of the cultivating households had each a holding of 30 acres or more but they had less than one-fifth (18.48%) of the total area among themselves.

Estimating the distribution of cultivated area among households by their tenurial status separately we arrive at the same conclusion, viz. that cultivated land was very inequitably distributed among households belonging to different tenures (See Diagram 2). The relevant data are given in Tables 12 and 13 of Statistical Appendix.

Section B

PERSONAL CULTIVATION AND SHARE-CROPPING

4.8. Personal Cultivation and Cultivation Through Outside Labour

Cultivation may be carried on by a household either through its own labour or through hired labour. In both cases it falls within our defini-

CONCENTRATION CURVE FOR CULTIVATED HOLDINGS OF ALL HOUSEHOLDS IN THE SAMPLE VILLAGES ACCORDING TO THEIR PRESENT TENURIAL STATUS, BEFORE ZAMINDARI ABOLITION

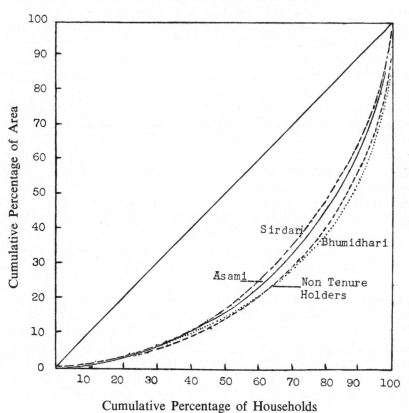

Diagram No. 2

tion of household cultivation—the main element of which lies in the control and direction of cultivation with or without labour participation. A household and its holding has been classified as personally-cultivated if the household cultivated it mainly through its own labour although it may have also employed temporary or casual outside labour. On the other hand a household has been classified as cultivating through outside labour if the holding has been cultivated mainly through hired labour engaged usually on a permanent or seasonal basis. Besides such households there are others who manage their cultivation by giving their holdings to share-croppers. They share in the farm produce without direct labour participation although they may be supplying certain other inputs besides land, e.g. seeds or manure. There are thus three types of cultivating households, viz. (a) households cultivating mainly through their own labour and that of their family members; (b) households cultivating mainly through hired or outside labour; and (c) households giving their land to share-croppers. The first two types alone can be regarded as cultivating directly and the last as indirect cultivators. In addition to this a cultivator may also be sub-letting his holding—a feature that we have already discussed in the previous section. All that we propose to discuss in this section is the extent of direct cultivation and share-cropping before *zamindari* abolition.

An objective assessment of the extent of share-cropping is, however, most difficult since the tenure holders may hide the fact of share-cropping to prevent any accrual of rights in favour of share-croppers over their land. In several cases, when enquired, they might state that the land given to a share-cropper is being cultivated by them directly through hired labour and might thus identify share-cropping with cultivation through hired labour. Hence it is obvious that information on the extent of share-cropping collected from the tenure holders will tend to underestimate it. An alternative method could be to get information from the cultivators about the land leased-in by them on a share-cropping basis. This method is likely to give a more reliable result as those who have taken land on share-cropping basis would obviously be interested in showing it to be so. Here the difficulty lies, however, in the fact that even they might not always declare it to be so for fear of such land being taken away from them by the principal tenure holders in the absence of any record of their rights in the village papers. For this enquiry we have utilised both these sources of information and the latter method revealed the extent of share-cropping to be more than twice as arge as by the first method. Even then there appears to be an under-

estimate as some share-cropping is concealed under the category of cultivation through hired and outside labour. We can, therefore, be more
definite about personal cultivation mainly through one's own labour
than about the extent of cultivation through the remaining two categories, i.e. hired labour and share-cropping. The latter two categories
often overlap each other and it is best to treat them together. Our subsequent analysis is, therefore, subject to these limitations.

Before *zamindari* abolition 62 out of a total of 734 sample cultivating
households were found to be employing permanent farm servants. They
constituted 8.5% of the total cultivating households and engaged among
themselves 139 labourers, i.e. a little more than 2 per household. The
proportion of cultivators engaging permanent farm servants varies from
region to region, i.e. from 16.0% in the eastern districts to 11.7% in
Bundelkhand, 6.4% in the western districts and 1.2% in the central
districts. Households cultivating mainly through their own labour accounted for as many as 87.3% of all cultivating households—87.2%
in the western districts, 95.0% in the central, 87.0% in the Bundelkhand
and 81.4% in the eastern districts.

The rest of the cultivators let out their holdings to share-croppers.
It is estimated that 4.2% of the total cultivating households were giving
their land to share-croppers before *zamindari* abolition—6.4% in the
western districts, 3.8% in central districts, 1.3% in Bundelkhand and
2.6% in the eastern region.

Thus it is found that most of the households cultivated their land
directly. Such households accounted for nearly 96% of the total in all
the sample villages—99% in the villages of Bundelkhand, 97.4% in
those of the eastern districts, 96.2% in the central and 93.6% in the
villages of the western districts.

This, however, does not imply that the same proportion of the cultivated area in the holdings of the sample households was cultivated directly.
Actually, before *zamindari* abolition only 69% of the cultivated area
in the holdings of the sample households was personally cultivated,
27% was cultivated through hired labour and a little less than 4.0%
through share-croppers.[26] This was so since households who were cultivating through their own labour and that of their family members had
smaller holdings than those who were cultivating through hired labour.
The average size of the personally cultivated holdings works out at 6.36

[26] For all households in the sample villages, 71.97 per cent of the total cultivated
area was calculated to be in the holdings of those who personally cultivated their
holdings; 24.68% in those cultivating mainly though hired labour; and 3.35% in those
cultivating though share-croppers (See Table No. 31 in Statistical Appendix).

acres as against 26.2 acres for the hired labour cultivated holdings. In fact, most of the area comprised in smaller holdings of less than 10 acres was personally cultivated. As the size of holding increased the area under personal cultivation declined so that most of the area (88.2%) of the total comprised in holdings of 40 acres or more was cultivated through hired labour. The size of holding, however, was not a significant factor in determining the extent of share-cropping.

Another factor that determined the extent of cultivation through outside labour was cultivation by the zamindars, who usually employed outside labour to cultivate their land. Less than 44% of the home-farm land of zamindars, i.e. their *sir* and *khudkasht* was personally cultivated while only one-fifth of the land held by tenants was cultivated through hired labour. Even within the smallest size group of holdings of less than 3 acres only 34.2% of *sir* and *khudkasht* was personally cultivated while more than 94% of the area in such holdings of the tenants was cultivated by them through their own labour. As far as holdings of 40 acres and above are concerned both the zamindars and tenants cultivated holdings mainly through hired labour.

Classifying the cultivating households by the size of their holdings into small (less than 5 acres), medium (5-15 acres), large (15-40 acres) and very large (40 acres and above), it is found that the small cultivators cultivated their holdings mostly with their own labour while the very large-size holdings were cultivated mainly through hired labour as is obvious from the following summary data:

TABLE No. 12

PERCENTAGE DISTRIBUTION OF THE AREA OF CULTIVATED HOLDINGS OF THE SAMPLE HOUSEHOLDS BY FORM OF CULTIVATION AND BY SIZE OF HOLDINGS

Size Group	Personally Cultivated	Labour Cultivated	Share-Cropped	Total
1. Small (less than 5 acres)	94.78	1.86	3.36	100.00
2. Medium (5-15 acres)	84.85	12.52	2.63	100.00
3. Large (15-40 acres)	74.26	23.19	2.55	100.00
4. Very Large (40 acres and above)	3.30	88.24	8.46	100.00
Total	68.84	27.39	3.77	100.00

A further break-up by the present principal tenure of the cultivating households and by regions and size of cultivated holdings is given in Table 14 of Statistical Appendix.

The above figures reveal that while 49% of the area in the holdings of the present *bhumidhars* was personally cultivated the corresponding figure was as high as 81% in the case of *sirdars* and 100% for the others. To some extent this can be explained by larger size of the holdings of the *bhumidhars*. But this is not all since in each size-group we find that the *bhumidhars* cultivated relatively less of their holdings personally than the *sirdars* and employed labour to a larger extent. This might have been due to the feudalistic practices under the *zamindari* system under which the land-owning cultivating households felt it undignified to culti-vate their holdings by their own labour. The present *sirdars* are those who were formerly the tenants of the zamindars and they cultivated their holdings through their own labour.

There are to be found some regional differences also that are parti-cularly marked in the western and the eastern districts. In the latter, in spite of relatively smaller size of average holdings than in the western districts, only about 41% of the total area was personally cultivated and 54% was cultivated mainly through hired labour. Traditionally the high caste Hindus, particularly *Brahmans*, did not touch the plough and yet they had considerable amount of land under their holdings to culti-vate. Very often they carried on their cultivation through hired labour. There was no such practice in the western districts and it is this which explains to a large extent the regional differences in the relative propor-tion of personally- and labour-cultivated holdings. To illustrate, in the size-group of 10-20 acres of holdings only 45% of the area was person-nally cultivated in the eastern districts and 50% was labour-cultivated as against 41% and 7% respectively in the western districts.

4.9. SHARE-CROPPING

Although only 31 out of the 734 sample households engaged in culti-vation before *zamindari* abolition were reported to have given their holdings for share-cropping as many as 126 households, i.e. 17.1% of the total reported to be cultivating some land of others on a share-crop-ping basis. The total area of land cultivated by them as share-croppers aggregated to 534.55 acres as against a total area of 5,931 acres culti-vated by them, i.e. 9.01% of the total. Our earlier figures revealed that only 3.72% of the area comprised in the holdings of the sample households was share-cropped while these figures reveal that no less than 9% of the total area under the cultivation of the sample households was helds by them as share-croppers. Share-cropping seems to have been practised on a much wider scale than revealed by the earlier figure of the area given by the sample households for share-cropping. The latter figure gives a more correct idea of the situation but even this, as explained earlier, appears to be an under-estimate.

Section C

LAND UTILISATION

4.10. PATTERN OF LAND USE

The land-use figures for the entire State show that before *zamindari* abolition about 69% of the total area was under cultivation and that about 14% was not available for agricultural purposes. Table 13 on p. 58 gives the distribution of land according to use in the State and in sample villages.

The proportion of cultivated area in sample villages varies from one region to another as shown in Table No. 13(a) on p. 58.

It will be observed from the above table that the proportion of cultivated land is the highest in eastern (78.85%) and lowest in the Bundelkhand region (50.95%). Similarly, the proportion of land not available for cultivation, viz. area under the last four groups is the highest in Bundelkhand region (28.17%) of the total area obviously because of the nature of soil in that division.

It is equally significant to note that whereas the culturable waste including old fallow is about 6% in the sample villages of the eastern region, it is as high as nearly 21% in those in Bundelkhand, 11.36% in the central districts and 15.24% in western districts.

4.11. POPULATION DENSITY AND CULTIVATION

According to the census of the year 1951 the State had an average density of 557 persons per sq. mile ranging from 130 persons per sq. mile in the Himalayan region to 850 persons per sq. mile in East Plain.

TABLE No. 13

LAND UTILISATION BEFORE ZAMINDARI ABOLITION IN THE STATE AND IN
THE SAMPLE VILLAGES (IN ACRES)

Averages for the year 1948-49 to 1950-51

Land Use	Uttar Pradesh	Sample Villages
1. Cultivated area including current fallow	4,04,54,554 (68.81)	51,942 (64.44)
2. Old fallow	7,13,710 (1.21)	1,032 (1.28)
3. Cultivable waste	79,76,128 (13.57)	11,141 (13.82)
4. Groves	13,22,717 (2.25)	2,168 (2.69)
5. Underwater	26,66,881 (4.55)	2,845 (3.53)
6. Non-agricultural land used as sites, roads, railways, canals, buildings etc.	18,86,845 (3.21)	2,078 (2.58)
7. Graveyards and otherwise barren	37,67,237 (6.40)	9,397 (11.66)
Total	5,87,88,072 (100)	80,603 (100)

Source: The figures for the State have been worked out from the *Area Statistics Register*. Figures in brackets are percentages to total.

TABLE No. 13(a)

PERCENTAGE DISTRIBUTION OF LAND IN SAMPLE VILLAGES ACCORDING TO
USE AND REGION

Land Use	Western	Central	Bundel-khand	Eastern	Total
1. Cultivated area including current fallow	71.14	64.66	50.95	78.85	64.44
2. Old fallow	0.81	0.25	2.50	0.53	1.28
3. Cultivable waste	14.43	11.11	18.13	5.54	13.82
4. Groves	1.07	12.37	0.25	3.25	2.69
5. Under water	1.99	3.72	4.59	4.41	3.53
6. Non-agricultural land used as sites, roads, railways, etc.	2.64	4.56	1.39	3.33	2.58
7. Graveyards	0.09	0.10	—	0.01	0.25
8. Otherwise barren	7.83	3.23	22.19	4.08	11.41
Total	100.00	100.00	100.00	100.00	100.00

The following table reproduced from the Census Report for U.P. for 1951 indicates that the intensity of land-use cultivation was very largely a function of density of population:

TABLE No. 14

DENSITY AND CULTIVATION IN VARIOUS REGIONS OF THE STATE

Natural Division	Density of Population	Percentage				
		Cultivable to Total	Cultivated to Total	Cultivated to Cultivable	Irrigated to Cultivated	Double-cropped to Cultivable
Uttar Pradesh	557	61.8 (70.6)	53.2	86.1 (75.3)	29.3	21.2 (18.5)
Himalayan	130	17.9 (17.9)	12.1	67.4 (67.4)	10.4	13.1 (13.1)
East Plain	850	77.2 (83.6)	68.9	89.4 (82.5)	36.0	28.2 (26.1)
Central Plain	717	70.0 (81.8)	61.6	87.9 (75.3)	29.0	22.7 (19.5)
West Plain	657	75.5 (83.6)	66.9	88.5 (80.0)	31.4	20.5 (18.5)
Hills and Plateau	248	53.3 (74.0)	41.0	76.9 (55.4)	14.1	9.9 (7.2)

"The cultivable area is the sum of the cultivable waste, fallow and the cultivated area. But all cultivable waste cannot be brought under cultivation for it includes percentage of *usar*, also threshing floor, village paths, well-runs, pastures, etc. Messrs. Blunt and Turner both estimated that only about five per cent of the recorded cultivable waste was really cultivable and calculations in the table have been made on this basis. Figures on the basis of the recorded cultivable waste also have been calculated and shown in the brackets". (*U.P. Census Report p. 22*)

These figures disclose that in the eastern districts where the density was highest the percentages of the cultivated to the cultivable area as well as the percentage of the irrigated to the cultivated area and that of the double-cropped to the cultivable area was also the highest. The Himalayan region had the lowest density and the intensity of cultivation was the lowest here. Next come the hills and the plateau that include the region of Bundelkhand and the district of Mirzapur. The density of population here is less than half of the average in the State and less than one third of that in the eastern districts. Here the percentage of the cultivated to the total area is only 41.0 (51.0 in the sample villages) and that of the irrigated to cultivated area 14.1% and that of the double-cropped to cultivable area 9.9%.

It we take into account the gross cultivated area, i.e. the net cultivated area plus the double-cropped area, the Census Commissioner reported that in 1951 the percentage of gross cultivated to cultivable area was 107.3 in the State as a whole, 117.6 in the East plain, 110.6 in Central Plain, 109.0 in Western Plain and 86.8 in the hills and plateau. Again we find a close correspondence in the density of population and intensity of cultivation.

4.12. CROP PATTERN

The crop pattern as revealed by the major crops cultivated by the sample households before *zamindari* abolition is given in the following table:

TABLE No. 15

PERCENTAGE DISTRIBUTION OF AREA UNDER MAJOR CROPS CULTIVATED BY SAMPLE HOUSEHOLDS BY REGIONS BEFORE ZAMINDARI ABOLITION

Crop	Western	Central	Bundel-khand	Eastern	Total
1. Sugar-cane	4.81	0.51	—	11.84	4.66
2. Wheat	41.75	23.27	19.56	22.48	30.41
3. Paddy	7.06	7.79	4.47	35.22	12.76
4. Barley	6.65	22.21	18.68	12.18	12.91
5. Pulses	7.20	14.51	16.85	11.04	11.02
6. Millet	21.51	30.28	40.28	4.76	22.70
7. Maize	6.11	1.01	—	2.36	3.32
8. Oil seeds	2.27	0.42	0.16	—	1.08
9. Potato	0.14	—	—	0.02	0.07
10. Fibres	1.80	—	—	—	0.76
11. Miscellaneous	0.70	—	—	0.08	0.31
Total	100.00	100.00	100.00	100.00	100.00

It follows from the above table that the various crops are given varying importance in different regions, e.g. wheat claimed nearly 42% of the total area in the western region while it is only about 20% in the Bundelkhand region.

It is obvious that while wheat covered the largest proprotion of the cultivated area in all the villages taken together (30.41%) its importance was not the same in all the regions. It was only in the western districts that wheat cultivation occupied the most dominant position with nearly 42% of the area under it. In Bundelkhand it occupied less than 20% of the total cultivated area and in the central and eastern districts about 23%. Paddy covered less than 13% of the cultivated area of the sample households although its proportion was as high as 35% in the villages of the eastern districts. Elsewhere it occupied only 4% of the cultivated area in Bundelkhand, about 8% in the central and western districts. Sugar-cane is an important commercial crop of the cultivator and accounted for nearly 4.7% of the total cultivated area in all villages taken together. Its cultivation was, however, confined mainly to the western and eastern districts.

Commercialisation of farming may be measured by the extent of cultivation of the commercial crops consisting of sugar-cane, wheat, oil seeds, potato and fibres. These are the main commercial crops although quite a substantial proportion of wheat is retained by the cultivator for his own consumption and use. The extent of cultivation of the commercial crops was as follows:

TABLE No. 15(a)

PERCENTAGE AREA UNDER COMMERCIAL CROPS TO TOTAL CULTIVATED AREA OF SAMPLE HOUSEHOLDS BY REGIONS BEFORE ZAMINDARI ABOLITION

Crops	Western	Central	Bundel-khand	Eastern	All Villages
1. Commercial Crops	50.77	24.20	19.72	34.34	36.98
2. Other Crops	49.23	75.80	80.28	65.66	63.02

The crop pattern of the sample households may be compared with the crop pattern of the State and of its various parts before *zamindari* abolition. The relevant figures are given in the following table:

TABLE No. 16

CROP PATTERN IN THE STATE BEFORE ZAMINDARI ABOLITION BY REGIONS
(1951-52)

Crop	Regions				
	Western	Central (Lucknow Division only)	Bundel-khand	Eastern (Banaras & Gorakh-pur only)	Total
1. Sugar-cane	10.63	6.44	0.41	4.97	6.24
2. Wheat	22.03	18.56	18.67	8.86	16.50
3. Paddy	6.90	16.26	4.70	32.83	17.31
4. Barley	6.47	11.28	2.53	15.09	9.35
5. Pulses	10.61	9.40	34.09	6.02	12.07
6. Millet	15.51	9.51	20.24	2.19	10.85
7. Maize	4.15	4.13	0.59	3.33	4.23
8. Oil seeds	2.10	2.97	6.94	0.76	2.28
9. Potato	0.35	0.51	0.05	0.54	0.47
10. Fibres	1.45	0.75	0.63	0.79	0.98
11. Miscellaneous	19.80	20.19	11.15	24.62	19.78
Total	100.00	100.00	100.00	100.00	100.00
1. Commercial Crops	36.56	29.23	26.70	15.92	26.47
2. Others	63.44	70.77	73.30	84.08	73.53
Total	100.00	100.00	100.00	100.00	100.00

Source: *Season and Crop Report for 1951-52.*

The crop pattern for the State as a whole is not identical to that of the sample households. The former is based on the record of crops as given in the Season and Crop Report, district by district. This record is prepared from the village records as kept by the *Lekhpals* who are supposed to report field by field. With regard to the sample households the estimates are not based on all the crops grown by them but in three most preferred crops cultivated by them before *zamindari* abolition. Consequently, the two are not strictly comparable although these reveal the relative importance of different crops in various regions. According to these data commercialisation of farming for all parts of the State taken together had not gone beyond 26% to 37% of the cropped area. It was most developed in the western districts where the commercial crops occupied nearly 37% of the cultivated area. Other parts of the State were relatively less developed. We have measured commercialisation by the extent of cultivation of five crops only and have left paddy out of account. Paddy is largely grown for direct consumption by the cultivator and cannot be treated at par with wheat. Our figures disclose that the basic character of agriculture in the State before *zamindari* abolition was subsistence farming.

SECTION II

CHAPTER V

LEGISLATIVE MEASURES

The Uttar Pradesh Zamindari Abolition and Land Reforms Act 1950 (U.P. Act No. 1 of 1951) received the assent of the President on January, 24, 1951 and came into force on January, 26, 1951 although the vesting order was issued as late as July 1, 1952. It provided for the abolition of the *zamindari* system that involved intermediaries between the tiller of the soil and the State and for the acquisition of their rights, title and interest and reformed the law relating to land tenures and made provision for other matters connected therewith.

5.1. OBJECTS & REASONS

Its necessity was explained in the Statement of Objects and Reasons for introducing the bill that formed the basis of the Act in the following terms:

"The United Provinces Legislative Assembly recorded on August 8, 1946 its acceptance of the principle of the abolition of the *zamindari* system which involves intermediaries between the cultivator and the State and resolved that the rights of such intermediaries should be acquired on payment of equitable compensation. The Zamindari Abolition Committee, appointed in pursuance of the Assembly resolution, after careful consideration of the various aspects of this complex problem, submitted its report containing a detailed scheme for the abolition of *zamindari* and its replacement by a land tenure suited to the genius and traditions of our country. The subject aroused keen public interest and there was a great deal of discussion in the press and on the public platform both of the general issues involved and since the publication of the Committee's report, of its recommendations. It is now widely recognised that without a radical change in the existing land system no co-ordinated plan of rural reconstruction can be undertaken to ensure agricultural efficiency and increased food production, to raise the standard of living of the rural masses and to give opportunities for the full development of the peasants' personality. The landlord-tenant system established by the British for reasons of expediency and administrative convenience, should, with the dawn of political freedom, give place to a new order which restores to the cultivator the rights and the freedom which were his and to the village community the supremacy which it exercised over all the elements of village life.

"The bill provides for the acquisition of intermediaries' rights on payment of compensation at eight times of their net assets. It will yield an income to the bigger zamindars sufficient for a reasonable standard of living. For rehabilitation of the smaller zamindars who constitute the overwhelming majority, it further provides for the payment of a graded rehabilitation grant ranging from 2 to 20 times of the net assets, being largest for low incomes and smallest for those with comparatively large incomes. To overcome financial and legal difficulties the tenants are being asked to make voluntary contributions of ten times their rent. This will provide finance for the speedy abolition of *zamindari*, check inflation and utilise the peasant's savings for a productive purpose. The tenants who make this contribution will be entitled to transferable rights in their holding, and will be called *bhumidhars* who will pay as land revenue fifty per cent of their existing rent.

"It is considered necessary to substitute the bewildering variety of the existing land tenures.by a simple and uniform scheme. Accordingly it has been provided that there will be in future only two main forms of land tenure. It is expected that the vast majority of cultivators will become *bhumidhars*. The present intermediaries in respect of their *sir*, *khudkasht* and groves will be classed as *bhumidhars*. So will also the tenants who pay an amount equal to ten times their rent. The remaining tenants will be called *sirdars* with permanent and heritable rights in land, the right to use their land for any purpose connected with agriculture, horticulture or animal husbandry, and to make any improvements.

"A minor form of land tenure called *asami* which will apply to but a small number of men includes non-occupancy tenants of land in which stable rights cannot be given such as tracts of shifting or unstable cultivation, and persons to whom land is let in future by *bhumidhars* or *sirdars* who are incapable of cultivating the land themselves. To prevent the re-emergence of the landlord-tenant system it is considered necessary to restrict the right of letting in the case of *bhumidhars* as well as *sirdars* only to disabled persons, such as minors, widows and persons suffering from physical or mental infirmity.

"It is also desirable to protect the interest of the considerable body of cultivators who do not at present enjoy any permanent rights in land, but whose displacement would lead to social injustice and grave economic difficulties. The general body of tenants of *sir* to whom hereditary rights do not accrue, and of the existing sub-tenants will be given security of tenure for a period of five years after which they can, on payment of 15 times the hereditary rate or the rent of their tenant-in-chief, acquire *bhumidhari* rights.

"To avoid multiplication of uneconomic holdings the restricted table of devolution laid down in the United Provinces Tenancy Act, 1939 has been maintained with minor variations, and future partition of holdings which would result in the creation of an uneconomic holding has been prohibited. To prevent accumulation of large holdings and the consequent exploitation of labour, no person will in future be permitted to acquire by sale or gift a holding of more than 30 acres.

"All lands of common utility, such as *abadi* sites, pathways, wastelands, forest, fisheries, public wells, tanks and water channels, will be vested in the village community or the *Gaon Samaj* consisting of all the residents of the village as well as the *pahikasht* cultivators. The *Gaon Panchayat* acting on behalf of the village community has been entrusted with wide powers of land management. This measure which makes the village a small republic and a cooperative community is intended to facilitate economic and social development and to encourage the growth of social responsibility and community spirit.

"In order to remedy the inefficiency and waste involved in the cultivation of the existing uneconomic holdings, the Bill makes provision also for the encouragement and rapid growth of cooperative farming suited to our conditions.

"It is proposed to extend its provisions to Government estates as soon as it becomes an Act. Separate legislation is under contemplation in respect of agricultural areas lying within the limits of municipalities, cantonments, notified areas and town areas. The question of scaling down the debts of intermediaries whose rights will be acquired will be so dealt with by a separate Bill."*

* *Government of U.P. Gazette Extraordinary*, June 10, 1949.

5.2. ORIGINAL ACT AND SUBSEQUENT LEGISLATION

Although the Principal Act (U.P. Act No. 1 of 1951) was very comprehensive it could not provide for all the contingencies and difficulties that were experienced in its implementation. Hence it had to be amended no less than ten times since its enactment—the last amendment being as late as in September, 1961. Besides a number of supplementary laws had to be adopted or amended and the process has perhaps not yet come to an end even after more than nine years of its implementation. All this seems to have been necessary due to three main reasons, viz. (i) the difficulties created by the former intermediaries in its implementation and the attempts made by some of them to evade certain of its provisions during the course of their enforcement; (ii) the colossal task of establishing a uniform system throughout the State that previously had different systems in several parts; and (iii) the confusion about the final pattern of land tenure and allied matters that still continues.

To begin with, the zamindars challenged the validity of the Principal Act and this delayed the implementation of the Act for some time during which they could abuse their rights. It was after the appeals by the zamindars against the Order of the Allahabad High Court attacking the validity of the Act were dismissed that the State Government declared its decision that the *zamindari* shall be abolished from the 1st day of July, 1952. The Government however apprehended that during the short period in which the intermediaries would still remain in possession, they would abuse their powers of land management under the U.P. Tenancy Act 1939. Hence it was considered necessary that certain leases and transactions made by them on or after 21st July, 1952 be declared void and it was for this purpose that the U.P. Tenures (Regulation of Transfer) Act 1952 was passed.

Further, as soon as the Act was enforced it was complained to the Government that a large number of persons who had been in cultivatory possession of land in the holdings of *bhumidhars* and *sirdars* had been forcibly evicted from the land. These were in fact the persons who were formerly admitted to the possession by the tenure holders themselves although they constituted the weakest and often the poorest section of village community. Hence a Bill was published on August 21, 1952 that was subsequently adopted as Uttar Pradesh Land Reforms (Supplementary) Act 1952. This was enacted to protect the rights of this class of persons by giving effect to their rights in land.

According to this supplementary Act persons in cultivatory possession in 1359 *fasli* in the holdings of a *bhumidhar* or *sirdar* became the *asamis*, if the original holder was a woman, a minor or physically incapable of personal cultivation. If, however, the original tenure holder was not such a person, then the occupant acquired *adhivasi* rights.

The U.P. Muslim Waqfs Act 1936 had to be amended in 1952 (Act No. IX of 1953) to enable the Central Boards of Waqfs to receive the contribution formerly paid by waqfs directly from the State Government.

During the winter preceding the vesting of estates in July 1952 Acharya Vinoba Bhave started the Bhoodan Movement and obtained land, both from zamindars as well as tenants, as donation for distribution among the landless. But these donations were defective since the zamindars were precluded from making any such transfers under the U.P. Zamindari Abolition and Land Reforms Act while the tenants had no right to transfer their lands. These legal difficulties were removed by the U.P. Bhoodan Yojna Act 1952 that came into force on March 5, 1953. Further, when the Cooperative Societies (U.P. Amendment) Act 1956 was passed (enforced from March 12, 1957) the *sirdars*, whose rights are not transferable under the Zamindari Abolition and Land Reforms Act 1950, were enabled to raise funds on the security of their holdings from a Cooperative Society.

Further, to facilitate final disposal of evacuee properties, the custodian and the Government of India were empowered to transfer *sirdari* interests and to give opportunity to certain occupiers to acquire superior rights, the U.P. Land Reforms (Evacuee Land) Act was enacted in 1957 and enforced since August 29 of the same year.

Besides the supplementary legislation of this type several other Acts had to be enacted or amended and the main Act extended on different dates to establish a uniform land system throughout the State as explained later. These are listed in Appendix IV by areas to which land reforms were extended and by the dates of such extension. In Appendix V are given extracts from the "Statement of Objects and Reasons" for the amendment of the Principal Act in chronological order. The main changes have been to either remove certain difficulties experienced in the implementation of the Principal Act or to reshape after a second thought the land system established after the abolition of the *zamindari* system. For instance, certain types of tenants of *sir* and sub-tenants were recognised in the beginning as tenants with inferior tenures and classified into a separate category of *adhivasis*. By a subsequent amendment they were merged into the category of *sirdars* and conferred a superior tenurial status or again, the ceiling on the future acquisition of *bhumidhari* that was originally fixed at 30 acres was later found to be too high and hence the Act was amended in 1958 to reduce it to 12½ acres. There have been similar changes with regard to the functioning of *Gaon Samajs*. It has already been noted as to how the *sirdars*, who constitute the bulk of the cultivators and do not enjoy any transferability of their rights under the Principal Act have now been given restricted transferable rights under the cooperative law.

5.3. Scope and Coverage of the Act

The U.P. Zamindari Abolition and Land Reforms Act 1950 as amended up to date extends to the whole of Uttar Pradesh except the areas included in a municipality, a notified area, a cantonment or a town area. For the purposes of the abolition of the intermediary rights in urban areas a separate piece of legislation has been passed in 1956 through the passing of the Uttar Pradesh Urban Areas Zamindari Abolition and Land Reforms Act, 1956, known as U.P. Act No. IX of 1957. In these areas the operations are still in progress and by the end of June 1961, *zamindari* had been abolished in 172 such local bodies out of more than 400 of them. Similarly the Act of 1950 does not apply to the area known as Kumaun and Uttarakhand region, for which also the U.P. Legislature has passed a separate Act.

It was realised at the time of the passing of the Act that due to certain special circumstances it may not be possible to implement it immediately in certain areas to which it was to be extended later.

Such areas were the areas specified in the 1st Schedule to the U.P. Tenancy Act of 1939; the estates owned by State and Central Government or local authorities, areas held and occupied for public purposes or for a work of public utility, etc. and a few particular places like pargana Kaswar Raja of Banaras district; newly merged former States of Banaras, Rampur and Tehri and Garhwal; as well as the Enclaves, and pargana Jaunsar-Bawar of Dehradun district. So far as the areas specified in the first schedule of the U.P. Tenancy Act 1939, including the Tarai-Bhawar and government estates with intermediaries are concerned they have not yet been covered; similarly all the estates owned by the Central Government have not been covered. The areas held and occupied for public purposes and works of public utility remain still uncovered by the Act of 1950.

In the pargana Kaswar Raja of Banaras district, *zamindari* has been abolished through a notification dated August 28, 1952. In what was formerly known as Banaras State the U.P. Zamindari Abolition and Land Reforms Act, 1950 has been extended on June 30, 1953. Similarly in Rampur estate, the *thekedari* and *pattedari* system was abolished through the passing of an Act in 1953 known as U.P. Act No. X of 1954, and the *zamindari* system was abolished here with effect from June 30, 1954 when the U.P. Government issued a notification on the above date with a view to extend the U.P. Act I, 1951.

So far as the region Tehri-Garhwal, now known as Kumaun and Uttarakhand, is concerned, it still remains uncovered by the Act of 1950. But at the same time *zamindari* has been abolished in the pargana of Jaunsar-Bawar of Dehradun district. In Jaunsar-Bawar formerly the Government adopted a number of tenancy reforms in 1941, 1948, 1949 and 1953, and because of the peculiarities of the land pattern of this area the U.P. Zamindari Abolition and Land Reforms Act, 1950 was not applied as it is in spite of the provision in Section 2(f) of the said Act. The Government therefore decided to introduce a Bill in 1955, which received the assent of the President on March 25, 1956 and has subsequently been applied.

Similarly the portion of the Mirzapur district south of Kaimpur range has been covered under the Act of 1950 through a Notification dated June 30, 1953.

5.4. Main Provisions of the Act:

A. Changes in Land System

(i) *Vesting of Estates in the State*

One of the main provisions of the Zamindari Abolition and Land Reforms Act 1950 is with regard to the vesting of all estates in the State from the date of vesting, which was later notified on July 1, 1952. An estate was defined as an area recorded under one entry in any of the registers maintained under the U.P. Land Revenue Act and thus all agricultural land, cultivated or otherwise, was vested in the State.

In consequence of this vesting all rights, title and interests of all the intermediaries were terminated and ceased from the date of vesting. An 'intermediary' of an estate was defined as a proprietor, under-proprietor, sub-proprietor, *thekedar*, permanent lessee in Avadh and permanent tenure-holder of such estate or part thereof. The only rights of the inter-mediaries that were preserved were those of working any mines, of ease-ment as a *bhumidhar*, *sirdar*, *adhivasi* or *asami* of any land, and rights to recover any arrears. Groves and buildings belonging to an intermediary also continued to belong to him. Further, land in the cultivation of an intermediary as his *sir* or *khudkasht* was converted after *zamindari* abolition into his *bhumidhari*.

(ii) *Simplification of Tenures*

After the abolition of *zamindari* a new and simple tenurial pattern has come into existence consisting only of three types of tenures in place of a bewildering variety of about forty types of various land interests. Out of these two are principal tenures known as *bhumidhar* and *sirdar* while the third known as *asami* is rather an inferior type of tenure. In the Act of 1950 there was a provision for accrual of yet another temporary right known as *adhivasi* created for a transitional period.

(a) BHUMIDHAR

Under this tenure all the land under personal cultivation of the ex-zamindars consisting of their *sir* and *khudkasht* and groves and the land under the tenants possessing the right to transfer the holding by sale, which might be occupancy or hereditary, and tenant on *patta dawami* or *istamarari* has been recognised as their *bhumidhari* by conversion. All the ex-zamindars as grove-holders have been declared *bhumidhars* of their groves. There have been imposed restrictions with regard to sub-lease.

Besides, the Act provided for the acquisition of *bhumidhari* rights by any tenant, sub-tenant and occupiers without consent under the former law, by paying ten times of their annual rent if paid in lump sum, or equal to 12 times if paid in instalments as provided for in the Act.

A *bhumidhar* has a permanent heritable and transferable right to his holding. No *bhumidhar* is liable to ejectment. He can use the land for whatever purposes he likes. The land revenue of the *bhumidhars* who have acquired the right by paying ten times land-revenue has been fixed at 50 per cent of the rent paid by them. Others continue to pay the land revenue as fixed under the settlement.

(b) SIRDAR

The vast body of cultivators consisting of tenants, sub-tenants and occupiers of land without consent have been declared as *sirdars* of the land under their cultivatory possession. All the tenants including those holding on special terms in Avadh, ex-proprietary tenants, occupancy and hereditary tenants, non-occupancy tenants of tea-estates, grantees at a favourable rate of rent, and tenants of leased out *sir* have thus acquired the *sirdari* rights.

Sirdari interest is permanent and heritable but not transferable. A *sirdar* is entitled to use the land for agriculture, horticulture or for animal husbandry but not for any other purpose. A *sirdar* pays as land revenue to the State directly the amount he formerly paid as rent to the zamindars. He is liable to be ejected in case of void transfers, for use of land in contravention of the provisions of law and from land of public utility, i.e. common pasture land, cremation or burial grounds, tank, pathway or *khaliyan*, etc. A limited right to transfer has been given subsequently to the *sirdars* under the Cooperative Societies Act 1956 which provides for the sale of the holding of a *sirdar* in execution of a decree for money due to a society.

(c) ASAMI

The tenure of an *asami* has been created in order to provide a new status to tenants who had so far a temporary and unstable right upon the holdings they cultivated. They mainly consist of former tenants of intermediaries grove land, sub-tenants of grove land, sub-tenants of mortgagees, those who held land from disabled *bhumidhars* or *sirdars* or those who held pasture land or land covered under water etc. from the *Gaon Samaj* or any other local authority. The *asami*'s rights are heritable but not permanent and transferable. He cannot bequeath his holding by will. The Act provides for ejectment of *asami* under certain circumstances. On being admitted to the occupation of land an *asami* is liable to pay such rents as may be agreed upon between him and his landholder or the *Gaon Samaj* as the case may be.

(d) ADHIVASI

Tenants of *sir* land, sub-tenants and occupants of land other than grove land who previously did not enjoy any security of tenure were declared as *adhivasis* under the Principal Act and were thus enabled to retain possession of their holdings subject to the payment of rent. An *adhivasi* was entitled to become a *bhumidhar* after a period of 5 years from the comencement of the Act or within that period with the consent of the landholder, on payment of sum equal to fifteen times the rent computed at hereditary rates. By an Amendment of the Act in 1954 the right, title and interest of landholders in the land held by *adhivasis* were acquired and *sirdari* rights were conferred on *adhivasis*.

(iii) *Provision against Sub-division and Fragmentation*

The Act has fixed a floor below which a holding cannot be divided. It lays down that a holding that does not exceed 3.1/8 acres cannot be partitioned by a Court of law. Instead of dividing such a holding the land would be sold off in favour of one of the partners and the other co-tenure holder may be awarded compensation in lieu of the share of the holding and for the admission by the Land Management Committee of such co-tenure holder to land. In the event of two or more co-tenure holders having an equal preferential right and severally asking for leave to buy, the land would be sold to one who offers the highest price. There is no restriction on the area that may be sold if the purchaser is an adjoining landholder. For the areas under consolidation operations, it has been further provided that if the land is sold to a person other than an adjoining tenure holder and the seller's holding of which the land forms part consists of less than 3.1/8 acres, the holding would be sold in its entirety. In order to prevent any further fragmentation of consolidated holdings, the Act puts restrictions on transfers. For instance it has been provided for that "...no person shall transfer whether by sale, gift or exchange any fragment situate in a consolidated area except where the transfer is in favour of tenure holder who has a plot contiguous to the fragment or where the transfer is not in favour of any such tenure holder, the whole of the plot to which the fragment pertains is thereby transferred." If any transfer is made contrary to this rule, it shall be void and the transferee shall be ejected from such a land.

(iv) *Restriction on Sub-letting*

The Act has prohibited sub-letting except under certain specific circumstances. A *bhumidhar sirdar* or *asami* may however sub-let to a recognised educational Institution for a purpose connected with instruction in Agriculture, Horticulture or Animal Husbandry. Sub-letting is permissible under the Act only in the case of the following types of tenure holders:

    (*a*) An unmarried, divorced or separated woman or widow or a woman whose husband is a lunatic or idiot or is otherwise incapable of cultivating because of physical invalidity.

    (*b*) A minor whose father has either died or suffers from lunacy or idiocy.

    (*c*) A lunatic or idiot.

(*d*) A person incapable of cultivation because of physical infirmity or blindness.

(*e*) A bonafide student below 25 years in age, and whose father has died or suffers from lunacy or other physical infirmity.

(*f*) A person in defence services.

(*g*) A person under detention or imprisonment.

Although the law has restricted the free sub-letting of holdings, it has provided for a kind of "arrangement whereby a person is entitled to a right merely to share in the produce grown on the land in consideration of such person assisting or participating with a tenure holder in the actual performance of agricultural operation...." Thus it may be stated that indirectly the system of share-cropping has been permitted under the garb of partnership.

(v) *Restrictions on Future Acquisition of Holding*

At the time of passing of the Act 1950, a restriction on future acquisition of holding up to 30 acres was made. But this limit has been subsequently reduced to 12½ acres through an amendment in 1958. The Act does not aim at putting any ceiling on the existing holdings, for which purpose a separate Act has now been enacted. But it has been made clear that land cannot be transferred to any person (other than an institution established for a charitable purpose), where he would come to possess in all, i.e. his own holding as well as this new land, more than 12½ acres in U.P. Similarly as a result of a lease in contravention of the rules against sub-letting, if any lessee gets land which together with his own holding exceeds 12½ acres, he would be ejected from the surplus land.

(vi) *Restriction on Ejectment and Elimination of Rack-renting*

Out of the three principal tenures established after *zamindari* abolition, the rights of a *bhumidhar* are permanent and a *bhumidhar* cannot be ejected from his *bhumidhari* holding. *Sirdars* have also been given permanent rights but a *sirdar* may be ejected on the following grounds:

(*i*) Transfer in contravention of the Act, on the application of the *Gaon Samaj.*

(*ii*) Use of land in contravention of the Act, for purposes other than agriculture and horticulture, etc.

(*iii*) any person who after August 8, 1946, has planted a grove or has brought under his cultivation any land which is a land of public utility such as a common pasture land, cremation or burial ground, tank, pathway or *Khalian etc.*

An *asami,* however, enjoys a very limited right of fixity of tenure and is liable to ejectment on several grounds, e.g. unlawful transfer, misuse of land, extinction of *asami* rights, etc.

Even after ejectment takes for whatever reason, a tenure holder is entitled to get back any ungathered crops and his trees. If any tenure holder has been ejected wrongfully, he may sue for the possession of his holdings and claim compensation for wrongful dispossession.

All tenure holders whether *bhumidhars, sirdars* or *asamis* are liable to ejectment if they have occupied land without title. At the same time when an *asami* has not been sued for ejectment or a decree obtained in such a suit is not executed within a prescribed period, the *asami* shall become a *sirdar* of the holding on the expiry of this period.

As far as rent is concerned *bhumidhars* and *sirdars* have come into direct contact with the State. Their land revenue has been fixed at the revenue and rent paid by them respectively at the time of *zamindari* abolition. It cannot be increased unless the next settlement takes place for which the prescribed date is not earlier than 40 years from the commencement of the Act.

Only *asamis* pay their rents to their landholders. Their rents too have been regularised and it has been provided for in the Act that an *asami* will pay a rent that has been agreed upon between him and the landholder or the *Gaon Samaj* as the case may be. Normally this rent shall not be varied. The rent may also be fixed through a suit and payment may be made either directly or through a postal money order.

Adequate provision for writing off the arrears of rent by a *Gaon Samaj,* or remission for calamity has been made in the Act to give relief to the *asamis* when they are in adverse circumstances. On failure of the payment of the rent, a detailed procedure has been laid down through which arrears of rent can be recovered from the *asami.* There is now little scope for any rack-renting.

(vii) *Encouragement to Rapid Growth of Cooperative Farming*

According to the Act, "Any ten or more members of a *Gaon Samaj* holding between them *bhumidhari* or *sirdari* rights in 30 acres or more in the circle and desiring to start a cooperative farm, may apply in writing...for the registration thereof." (Section 295). After the farm has been registered, all land held in the circle by a member, whether a *bhumi-*

dhar, sirdar or an *asami*, would be deemed to have been transferred to a cooperative farm. There is, however, no element of compulsion in this.

But a cooperative farm of all the uneconomic holdings in a circle can be established under the Act if two-thirds of the total number of persons holding *bhumidhari* or *sirdari* rights in uneconomic holdings and holding between them not less than 2/3 of the aggregate area comprised in all such holdings apply for it. In other words, all land in the uneconomic holdings is liable to be transferred to a cooperative farm if the majority (not less than two-thirds) so desires. The holdings of the minority (not more than one-third) can thus be transferred to a cooperative even if they are not willing to join it. But there is no compulsion on the part of any individual to join a cooperative and provision has been made for payment of compensation to the holder of an uneconomic holding who is not willing to join a cooperative farm but whose holding is transferred to it under the Act.

When a landholder has agreed to join a cooperative farm and has contributed his land to the farm, his interest in land would continue to vest in himself. After the farm has been constituted it would be responsible for the payment of land revenue and other charges. After the death of a member his natural heirs become the members of the cooperative farm.

In order to encourage the establishment the Act has provided certain incentives and priorities by way of various kinds of help given to them in the matters of reduction in land revenue, free technical advice, reduction of or exemption from agricultural income tax, financial aids and grant of subsidy and loans with or without interest and priority in irrigation from State irrigation works.

B. COMPENSATION AND REHABILITATION GRANT

The U.P. Zamindari Abolition Committee held the view that "Abolition of landlordism without compensation would, in the existing state of affairs, in our opinion, create a dangerous economic and social situation. Apart from the questions of social stability we cannot look with equanimity on the suffering and national waste involved in the forced pauperisation of a section of people....abolition without compensation, we are afraid, will create, for the State and the society, problems no less difficult and dangerous than abolition with full compensation."[27]

[27] *U.P. Zamindari Abolition Committee Report, op. cit.,* p. 399.

Being prompted by the above considerations the U.P. Legislature made a provision in the Act for compensation to "every intermediary whose rights, titles or interest in any estate were acquired under the provisions of this Act."[28]

Similarly, the Act provides for making a payment of Rehabilitation Grant to an intermediary other than a *thekedar* whose estate or estates have been acquired under the provisions of this Act provided his annual land revenue did not exceed ten thousand rupees.

(a) *Compensation*

(i) DETERMINATION: Compensation is determined on the basis of entries made in the record of rights and a payment would be made at a uniform rate of eight times of the net assets. For the purposes of determination of the net assets an Assesment Roll is prepared after the determination of gross assets. The net assets have to be calculated after deducting from the gross assets, any amount due to agricultural income tax, cost of management and irrecoverable arrears of rent equal to fifteen per cent of the gross assets, the rent of the *sir and khudkasht* or grove computed at the ex-proprietary rates and average of the income tax payable in respects of royalties from mines etc.

(ii) PAYMENT OF COMPENSATION: The compensation payable under this Act may be given in cash or in bonds or partly in cash or partly in bonds. It is to be paid in cash where the total amount payable does not exceed Rs. 50. On the amount paid or to be paid in cash an interest at the rate of $2\frac{1}{2}$ per cent shall be paid in cash from the date of vesting to the date of determination of compensation. Besides such amounts in cash the rest is to be paid in negotiable bonds known as Zamindari Abolition Compensation Bonds. The bonds bear an interest at the rate of $2\frac{1}{2}$ per cent per annum from the date of vesting, and the amount along with interest is paid in equal instalments within forty years beginning from the date of vesting. In redeeming the bonds priority is to be given to intermediaries entitled to small amount of compensation.

(iii) THE STOCK CERTIFICATE: *Waqfs*, trusts and endowments for religious or charitable purposes which were intermediaries are paid compensation in the form of the stock certificate bearing interest at the rate of $2\frac{1}{2}$ per cent per annum. These certificates are redeemable after the expiry of forty years after the date of vesting. The amount of compensation is to be deposited with the bank or such authority as may be prescribed. So long as these certificates are not being issued to these

[28] *U.P. Zamindari Abolition and Land Reforms Act, 1950*, Sec. 27.

institutions, they are being paid interim interest at the same rate and the amount so paid will be deducted from the interest accruing on the Stock certificate when issued.

(b) *Rehabilitation Grant*

The Act provides for a Rehabilitation Grant to all ex-intermediaries whose land revenue did not exceed Rs. 10,000. According to the estimates of the Zamindari Abolition Committee the total number of intermediaries in U.P. was 20,16,783 in 1947 out of whom only 390 paid as land revenue of Rs. 10,000 or more.

(i) DETERMINATION: The grant is fixed at a graduated rate as a multiple of the net assets on the following scale:

Class of the intermediaries according to land revenue				Multiple of net assets
1. Up to Rs. 25				20
2. Exceeding Rs.	25 but not Rs.		50	17
3. ,, ,,	50 ,,	,, ,,	100	14
4. ,, ,,	100 ,,	,, ,,	250	11
5. ,, ,,	250 ,,	,, ,,	500	8
6. ,, ,,	500 ,,	,, ,,	2,000	5
7. ,, ,,	2,000 ,,	,, ,,	3,500	3
8. ,, ,,	3,500 ,,	,, ,,	5,000	2
9. ,, ,,	5,000 ,,	,, ,,	10,000	1

(ii) PAYMENT: The amount of Rehabilitation Grant is paid in cash if the total amount is Rs. 50 or less, where the amount exceeds Rs. 50 it is paid in bonds of various denominations as in the case of compensation, the residual amount over and above a bond is also paid in cash. The bonds are in the form of negotiable promissory notes redeemable in 25 yearly equal instalments. No interest is paid on rehabilitation grant.

C. LAND MANAGEMENT

After the abolition of *zamindari*, the land which used to vest in the zamindar, vested in the State. For the purpose of the superintendence, management and control of land, the Act makes provision for the establishment of *Gaon Samaj*, having perpetual succession and as a corporate body for each village consisting of all the adults residing in a village. The *Gaon Samaj* so constituted has been vested with certain types of lands and property as given below:

(*i*) All land whether cultivable or otherwise except the land under any holding or grove for the time being;

(*ii*) all forest within the village boundary;

(*iii*) all trees (other than trees in a holding or on the boundary thereof or in a grove or *abadi*);

(*iv*) Fisheries;

(*v*) *Hats, bazars* and *melas* other than those under the *Zila Parishads;*

(*vi*) Tanks, ponds, private ferries, water channels, pathways and *abadi* sites.

The Land Management Committee has been charged on behalf of the *Gaon Samaj* with the duties of general supervision, management, preservation and control of all such lands and properties. The main duties of the *Gaon Samaj* would be as below:

(*a*) The development and improvement of agriculture;

(*b*) The preservation, maintenance and development of forest and trees;

(*c*) The maintenance and development of *abadi* sites and village communications;

(*d*) The management of *bazars, hats* and *melas*;

(*e*) The development of cooperative farming;

(*f*) The development of animal husbandry;

(*g*) The consolidation of holdings;

(*h*) The development of cottage industries;

(*i*) The maintenance and development of fisheries and tanks, and

(*j*) Such other matters as may be prescribed.

The Land Management Committee in this connection will let out land vested in it to *asamis* and realise rent from them. The *sayar* will also be collected through the Committee. The Committee will collect land revenue where the *Gaon Sabha* of the circle has been charged with the duty of collecting the same by the State Government and rendering assistance in the collections in all other cases.

D. Land Revenue

(i) *Initial Demand and Future Revision*

The Act lays down that *bhumidhars* and *sirdars* shall pay land revenue for their holdings to the State Government. The land revenue payable by *bhumidhars* has been fixed (i) equal to the amount of revenue or rent paid by them at the time of *zamindari* abolition or their holdings over which they acquired *bhumidhari* rights by conversion, and (ii) equal to one-half of the rent paid by them on holdings over which they acquired *bhumidhari* rights by payment to ten times the rental demand. For *sirdars* land revenue has been fixed equal to the rent payable by them to the intermediaries immediately before the vesting of an estate in the State.

Further, "All *bhumidhars* and *sirdars* in any village shall be jointly and severally responsible to the State Government for the payment of the Government revenue for the time being assessed thereon, and all persons succeeding, whether by devolution or otherwise, to the interest of such *bhumidhars* and *sirdars* shall be responsible for all arrears of land revenue due at the time of their succession." (Section 243).

The *bhumidhars* and *sirdars* are required to pay along with their land revenue as *abwab* or cess, or local rates if any which were previously paid by zamindars. Except on the ground of increase or decrease in the area of holding the amount of land revenue paid by a *bhumidhar* or *sirdar* would not be varied within forty years after the commencement of the Act. According to this Act the land revenue would ordinarily be assessed on the aggregate holdings area of the *bhumidhars* and *sirdars* in a village in a year of record excluding the land occupied by buildings, *khalihans*, graveyards, and cremation grounds, etc.

At the time of settlement the following principles will be observed:

(1) "In assessing the revenue payable for a holding in an assessment circle the Settlement Officer shall have regard to the estimated average surplus produce of such holding remaining after deducting the ordinary expenses of cultivation as ascertained or estimated in such manner as may be prescribed; and the revenue shall be such percentage of the surplus produce as may be fixed by a resolution of the Uttar Pradesh Legislature passed after considering the recommendations of the State Government, which shall be laid before the Legislature at any time after the expiry of one month of their publication in the Gazette and in the assessment circle in such other manner as may be prescribed.

(2) "The percentage of revenue to the surplus produce shall vary according to a graduated scale prescribed by State Government, being largest on holdings with the highest surplus produce and smallest on holdings with lowest surplus produce.

(3) "The percentage applicable to a *bhumidhar* shall not exceed one-half of the percentage applicable to a *sirdar*." (Section 264).

The land revenue shall not be enhanced or abated during the currency of the settlement except for an increase or decrease in the area of holding, or, in the productivity of the land comprised therein by fluvial action or other natural cause.

(ii) *Collection of Land Revenue*

It appears that the framers of the Law were not quite clear about the machinery that they intended to establish for the collection of land revenue. Hence the Act provided that "the State Government may make such arrangements and employ such agency for the collection of land revenue as it may deem fit." (Section 275).

At the same time it makes provision for the collection of land revenue by *Gaon Panchayat* (Land Management Committee) whenever the Government so decides. The Land Management Committee (*Gaon Sabha* until the amendment of the Act in 1958) will be entitled to certain prescribed commission in the collection of land revenue.

An arrear of land revenue may be recovered (*a*) by serving a writ of demand on citation to appear, (*b*) by arrest and detention of a defaulter, (*c*) by attachment and sale of his movable property including produce, (*d*) by attachment of the holding in respect of which the arrear is due, (*e*) by sale of the holding, and (*f*) by attachment and sale of other immovable property of the defaulter. Whenever a *Gaon Panchayat* (Land Management Committee) is to be charged with the duty of collection of land revenue it shall have all these powers.

So far the *Gaon Panchayats* have not been used for this purpose and land revenue is being collected by the State Government directly through its revenue staff and in particular through *amins* who have been specially appointed for the purpose.

5.5. CERTAIN DISTINGUISHING FEATURES

The U.P. Zamindari Abolition and Land Reforms Act, 1950 as amended up to date has certain features that make the scheme of *zamindari* abolition in the State distinct from elsewhere. Firstly, it combined payment of compensation to the intermediaries with a rehabilitation grant and while the former is fixed on a flat rate for all the latter is graduated. Secondly, the two taken together tend to make the scheme of abolition a costly proposition for the State exchequer. Thirdly, the ex-intermediaries were given no right of resumption that has been responsible for large scale eviction of cultivators from land in certain other States. Fourthly, there is still a multiplicity of tenures and while the rights of *bhumidhars* are transferable the rights of *sirdars* who hold the bulk of land are not transferable. Even among *bhumidhars* some had to pay ten times their rental demand for acquiring their rights; others got it without any payment. Even land revenue per acre is not uniform for the same type of land and differs according to tenure and also the manner in which one acquires his tenure. Fifthly, the process of determination of compensation or rehabilitation grant has proved to be quite lengthy and all claims have not yet been finally settled whereas the liability of State Government for payment has been spread over a period of 40 years. Sixthly, certain provisions in the Act have been of little practical use. These relate to (i) establishment of cooperative farms of uneconomic holdings and (ii) revenue collection through *Gaon Panchayats*. Seventhly, the response to the provision for acquision of *bhumidhars'* right has not been as much as originally expected. Finally, land management through village communities is still in its infancy and the *Gaon Samaj* has not yet acquired that status that it is expected to have under the Act. To some extent this has been due to the confusion about the role and constitution of the various village agencies, viz. the *Gaon Sabhas, Gaon Samajs, Panchayats* and Land Management Committees. The *Gaon Sabhas* and *Gaon Panchayats* have now nothing to do with land management for which Land Management Committees are being established. It was only after the Amendment Act of 1958 that a 'consolidated *Gram Samaj* Fund' has been created and put at the disposal of the Land Management Committee to discharge its funtions. Similarly, in each district there will now be a consolidated *Gram Samaj* Fund to which every *Gaon Samaj* will contribute 15 per cent of its annual income. The two amendments in the Principal Act made in 1961, simplified the procedure for collection of land revenue and further extended the powers of *Gaon Samaj*.

Chapter VI

ADMINISTRATIVE MACHINERY AND ORGANISATION

6.1. Vesting of Estates and Administrative Reforms

The U.P. Zamindari and Land Reforms Act provided that all estates with certain minor exceptions shall vest in the State from the date of vesting. A *Gazette Extraordinary* was issued on July 1, 1952 fixing the date of vesting on the same day, i.e. July 1, 1952. The detailed implementation of land reforms has since then been a major responsibility of the Revenue Ministry. The Revenue Secretariat headed by the Revenue Secretary has 6 different sections two of which deal exclusively with matters connected with land reforms and *zamindari* abolition. The control of all judicial matters pertaining to land and revenue settlement is vested with the Board of Revenue which has a specific department within it dealing with land reforms.

Due to temporary settlement the State had already a well-developed and organised revenue administration system not only at the central level but equally at the district, *tehsil* and village levels. This very machinery was strengthened to implement the scheme of land reforms and additional staff was appointed particularly for determination of compensation and rehabilitation grants as well as for collection of land revenue directly from cultivators. The Act itself provided for the appointment of a compensation staff consisting of (*i*) a Compensation Commissioner, (*ii*) Asstt. Compensation Commissioners, (*iii*) Compensation Officers and (*iv*) Rehabilitation Grant Officers. Their duties were prescribed under the rules:

"The Compensation Commissioners and the Asstt. Compensation Commissioners, subject to the general control of Compensation Commissioner, shall exercise power of supervision and superintendence over the work of the Compensation Officers and Rehabilitation Grant Officers and in particular may give directions regarding the distribution and programme of work, the appointment of staff, the preparation of statements required by or under the Act, their verification and correction, and other administrative and disciplinary matter relating to the staff employed for the purposes of the Act and the duties entrusted to them."[29]

Broadly speaking the Compensation Officers were made responsible for preparing a Draft Compensation Assessment Roll for every intermediary. These Drafts were finalised after the hearing of objection if any. Similarly, the Rehabilitation Grant Officers were appointed to entertain applications of the ex-intermediaries in connection with the rehabilitation grant as provided in the Act.

6.2 COMPENSATION AND REHABILITATION GRANTS

(a) Compensation Rolls

The Draft Compensation Assessment Roll of every intermediary in respect of his interest in one or more *mahals* contained the following information:—

(*a*) Gross and net assets; (*b*) arrears of land revenue, cess and other dues; (*c*) land revenue payable by the intermediary in the previous agricultural year.

After its publication the parties concerned could make objections that were considered and decided by the Compensation Officers. An appeal, however, could be made to the district judge against the order of the Compensation Officer. Appeal could also be made to the High Court provided there was a difference of Rs. 2,500/- or more between the net assets claimed by the intermediary and those entered in the Roll. After the objections were disposed of the final Compensation Assessment Rolls were prepared by the Compensation Officers and a copy of the same supplied to the intermediary.

(b) Determination of Compensation

Compensation was then determined at a uniform rate of 8 times the net assets of each intermediary. The net assets were deduced from the gross assets in each case. The latter were calculated as the gross income of an intermediary's land or estate on the date of vesting. It comprised (*a*) rents, including cesses and local rates payable by the tenants in cash or kind, (*b*) rents computed at the ex-proprietary rate for the land in the personal cultivation as *sir* and *khudkhast* or grove of the intermediary, (*c*) *Sayar* including income from *hats*, *melas*, *bazars* and fisheries, etc. as entered in the *Khatauni*, and (*d*) average annual income during

[29] *U. P. Zamindari and Land Reform Rules, 1952.* Rule No. 341, Chapter VII.

the last 4 agricultural years from rents of building sites, average annual income from the forests for the last 20 to 40 years, average amount of royalties, if any, for the mines, during the last 12 years and average annual income from such mines if no royalty was received and the mine was worked by the intermediary himself.

The net assets were calculated by deducting from the gross assets (a) land revenue, (b) agricultural income tax, (c) cost of management and irrecoverable arrears of rent equal to 15% of the gross assets, (d) the rent of the *sir* and *khudkhast* or groves computed at the ex-proprietary rates, and (e) average of the income tax payable in respect of royalties from mines, etc.

(c) *Provision for the Payment of Compensation*

The compensation payable under the Act was to be paid in cash or in negotiable bonds or partly in cash and partly in bonds as prescribed in the Rule.[30] It was to be paid in cash where the total amount payable to an intermediary did not exceed Rs. 50. On the amount paid or to be paid in cash an interest was also paid in cash, which was calculated at $2\frac{1}{2}\%$ per annum from the date of vesting to the date of determination of compensation.

Besides such cash amounts, the rest of the compensation was paid in negotiable bonds, known as Zamindari Abolition Compensation Bonds. These bonds have been issued in denominations of Rs. 50, Rs. 100, Rs. 200, Rs. 500, Rs. 1,000 Rs. 5,000 and Rs. 10,000 bearing an interest at the rate of $2\frac{1}{2}\%$ per annum from the date of vesting and are payable in equated instalments of 40 years.

The following table gives a clear picture about the denomination of bonds and the amount of equated instalments to be paid:

S. No.	Denomination of Zamindari Abolition Compensation Bonds (Rs.)	Value of Annual Equated instalments for the first 39 years (Rs.)	Value of the Residuary instalments for the 40th year (Rs.)
1.	50	2-0-0	1-7-0
2.	100	4-0-0	2-14-4
3.	200	8-0-0	5-12-9
4.	500	19-15-0	18-10-4
5.	1,000	39-14-0	37-4-1
6.	5,000	199-3-0	198-11-11
7.	10,000	398-6-0	397-8-6

[30] Rules, op. cit., from 62 to 68.

Compensation was paid directly to intermediaries or their heirs whose names appeared on the Rolls. But in certain cases, the amount of compensation was deposited with a Bank or some other authority. Thus, where the person entitled to receive the compensation was a *waqf*, trust or endowment or a minor or a person suffering from some legal disability or was a limited owner, the money was deposited for and on behalf of the person, with such authority or Bank as may be prescribed. If any person claimed any part of the compensation of an estate as a *Guzaredar*, he was paid the amount after he had proved his claim in a court of law within three months of the claim.

(d) *Payment of Interim Compensation*

A provision was also made for the payment of an interim compensation if the determination of final compensation took more than nine months. This could be paid only to a person in actual possession of the estate and whose name was entered in the *Khewat* as proprietor. The interim compensation so paid was a kind of advance payment to be adjusted against the total amount to be paid under the provisions of the Act. Interim compensation payments had been allowed till the indenting of bonds and were subject to a maximum of 50% of the total compensation. Such payments were made in cash half-yearly and the amount in each case was limited to the instalment of land revenue formerly payable by an intermediary.

Rehabilitation Grants

In addition to compensation rehabilitation grants were also paid to all intermediaries whose aggregate land revenue did not exceed Rs. 10,000. This grant was payable after the compensation amount had been determined. For this purpose an intermediary was required to apply in writing to the Rehabilitation Grant Officer for determination and payment of the grant together with copies of the Compensation Assessment Rolls. The Rehabilitation Grant Officers were then required to determine the amount of grant of each applicant after deciding objections, if any. The rehabilitation grant was a variable multiple of the net assets of an intermediary, the value of the multiple being inversely related to the amount of land revenue as can be seen in the Schedule on page 90.

6.3. LAND REVENUE COLLECTION

Under the *zamindari* system the intermediaries collected the rent from

SCHEDULE 1*

(*Section* 98)

Serial No.	Land Revenue assessed or deemed to be assessed on all the estates of the intermediary in the areas to which this Act applies	Multiple for purposes of section 98
1.	Up to Rs. 25	20
2.	Exceeding Rs. 25 but not Rs. 50	17
3.	Exceeding Rs. 50 but not Rs. 100	14
4.	Exceeding Rs. 100 but not Rs. 250	11
5.	Exceeding Rs. 250 but not Rs. 500	8
6.	Exceeding Rs. 500 but not Rs. 2,000	5
7.	Exceeding Rs. 2,000 but not Rs. 2,500	3
8.	Exceeding Rs. 2,500 but not Rs. 5,000	2
9.	Exceeding Rs. 5,000 but not Rs. 10,000	1

* Schedule No. 1 of the U. P. Zamindari and Land Reforms Act 1952.

the tenants and paid land revenue to the State Government. For each *mahal*, if there was more than one proprietor, all were made individually and jointly responsible for the payment of land revenue. In such cases the co-proprietors of a *mahal* had one of them as *Lambardar* who collected the revenue from each sharer and paid it to the Government. With the abolition of the *zamindari* system the Government had to collect land revenue directly from the principal tenure holders, whether *bhumidhars* or *sirdars*. Only sub-tenants and *asamis* pay rent to the chief tenure holders or the *Gram Samaj* as the case may be.

Several alternatives were considered as a suitable agency for such direct collections from some two crores of petty cultivators throughout the State. The various agencies considered in this connection were the *Lekhpals*, Land Management Committees, the *Pradhans* of *Gram Sabhas* and a specially appointed staff. The Act of 1950 provides for collection of revenue through *Gaon Panchayat* as the agency of the *Gaon Sabha*, but so long as the *Gaon Panchayats* do not attain maturity, it was thought much more expedient to create a special official machinery for land revenue collections.

The ultimate responsibility of collection in a district is that of the District Magistrate as the Collector; he is assisted in his duties by an officer of gazetted rank called the District Collection Officer who supervises the work of the staff employed at the *tehsil* level for the purpose and coordinates the scheme for the collection of the whole district. At the *tehsil* level revenue collection officials designated as *Naib-Tehsildar* (Collections) have been appointed who are responsible directly to *Tehsildar* of the *tehsil* concerned. The actual collection is made by the temporarily appointed functionaries called *Amins*, each of whom is required to collect Rs. 5,000 *per mensem*. These *Amins* are normally appointed for 3 months. The Collector, however, may reduce or extend their tenures according to the needs of efficient collection. Their work is supervised by the *Naib-Tehsildar* of Collections.

On receipt of the demand register the *Tehsildar* divides the *tehsil* into *Amin* Circles. The demand in each circle is approximately equal to the amount that could be collected by one *Amin* within 3 months. The *Amins* collect the land revenue directly from the tenure holders and deposit the same in the tehsil at regular prescribed intervals. Each tenure holder gets a receipt from the *Amin* for the amount he pays.

In case of default or arrears of land revenue certain coercive measures can be taken under the Act. These include issue and service of a writ of demand, arrest or detention of the defaulters and attachment or sale of his movable property and holding. An entire village may also be attached for arrears and placed under the management of a Collector for a maximum period of three years.

6.4. DECENTRALISED LAND MANAGEMENT

From the date of the abolition of *zamindari* system or the date of vesting all land has been vested in the State. But for the purpose of the superintendence, management and control of land, etc. the Act of 1950 made a provision for the establishment of *Gaon Samaj*, having perpetual succession and as a corporate body for each village consisting of all the adults residing in a village. The *Gaon Samaj* so constituted has been vested with certain lands and property, etc. in a village as given below:

(*i*) all land whether cultivable or otherwise except the land under any holding or grove for the time being;

(*ii*) all forest within the village boundary;

(*iii*) all trees (other than trees in a holding or on the boundary thereof or in a grove or *abadi*);

(*iv*) fisheries;

(*v*) *hats, bazars* and *melas* other than those under the *Zila Parishads;*

(*vi*) Tanks, ponds, private ferries, water channels, pathways and *abadi* sites.

The *Gaon Samaj* is to act through a *Gaon Sabha* that has been charged on behalf of the *Gaon Samaj* with the duties of general superintendance, management, preservation and control of all such lands and properties. The main duties of the *Gaon Sabha* would in this connection be as follows:

(*a*) Development and improvement of agriculture,

(*b*) the preservation, maintenance and development of forest trees,

(*c*) the maintenance and development of *abadi* sites and village communications,

(*d*) the management of *hats*, *bazars* and *melas*,

(*e*) the development of cooperative farming,

(*f*) the development of animal husbandry,

(*g*) the consolidation of holdings,

(*h*) the development of cottage industries, and

(*i*) the maintenance and development of fisheries and tanks.

In the discharge of these duties the *Gaon Sabha* would be helped by the *Gaon Panchayats*. The latter would carry on all these duties with the agency of a newly created body known as Land Management Committee, with the village *Lekhpal* as its secretary and normally the *Pradhan* as its chairman. All the members of the *Gaon Sabha* will be the members of the Land Management Committee. In order to eliminate any chance of negligence or causing loss, waste or misapplication of the money or property of the *Gaon Samaj*, committed by any member of the Land Management Committee or any joint committee, adequate penalty has been provided for in the legislation.

The Land Management Committee would be entitled, among other things, to let out land vested in *Gaon Samaj* to *asamis* and realise rent from them. The Committee may also collect land revenue where the *Gaon Sabha* of the circle has been charged with the duty of collection by the State Government and rendering assistance in the collections in all other cases.

6.5. RESURVEY AND SETTLEMENT OPERATIONS

A provision has been made in the Act of 1950, for undertaking an original settlement of the land revenue of any district or part thereof. The original settlement may be had at any time after 40 years of the commencement of the Act. A revision of such settlement may take place in any district or its part after 40 years from the date of original settlement. In case of precarious tracts and alluvial areas the State government may direct the settlement of the land revenue at any prescribed time or intervals even before the expiry of 40 years from the date of the commencement of the Act.

The original settlement is to take place after proper notification under the supervision of the Settlement Officers specially appointed for the purpose assisted by a number of other subordinate officers. During the period of the settlement operations, the duties of the Collectors pertaining to the maintenance of maps and the field books and preparing the annual register will be transferred to the Settlement Officers.

When a part of the land has been brought under settlement, the settlement officer shall inspect every village under settlement and divide the district into soil classes and assessment circles according to the rules and principles laid down for the purpose. This settlement would naturally require the resurveys of the land under settlement which would be undertaken by the settlement officers.

As regards the powers to make survey, it has been provided in Section 324 that subject to any condition or restrictions that may be prescribed, any officer appointed under the U.P. Zamindari Abolition Act 1950 may enter at any time upon any land, make a survey or take measurements thereof. There is no other provision for surveys.

6.6. Preparation and Maintenance of Records of Land Rights

Uttar Pradesh had an elaborate system even under the *zamindari* system for the maintenance of village records and the record of land rights, field by field and for each tenure holder. Each village was in charge of a *patwari* for this purpose and his work was supervised by *quanungoes* each one of whom was in charge of a *pargana*. There were often complaints of wrong entries in these records and their accuracy was often in doubt. The *patwari* has now been replaced by the *Lekhpal*, the opportunities for tampering with the record of rights have been minimised and the entire system of keeping the village land records has been simplified. The *Lekhpal* in particular has little authority to make any alterations in the record of rights.

Besides the *Khasra* or the record of holdings and the *Khatauni* or the record of the land rights which are still maintained as before, a *patwari* had to maintain several other records as well. There was the proprietors' *Khewat*, sub-settlement holders' and under-proprietors' *Khewat* in Oudh, list of mortgagees' property, *Siyaha* etc. It is no longer necessary to maintain the *Khewats*. But the *Khasra* and the *Khatauni* are still maintained. Besides there is a village map indicating the cadastral number of each plot.

For preparation of the *Khasra* a *Lekhpal* is expected to make a field to field visit three times a year while the *Khatauni* which lists all persons cultivating or otherwise occupying land in a village is prepared triennially. It is prepared in two parts—the first listing the principal tenure holders and the second the inferior tenure holders and gives detailed particulars about each holder. The Land Record Manual presents rules for the correction of entries.

These records are consolidated at the *pargana*, *tehsil* and district levels. The 'registrar' and 'supervisor', *qanungoes* are responsible for their maintenance and supervision and they are made responsible to the Sub-Divisional Officer. There has been a considerable strengthening of the supervisory staff and particularly after the campaign of 1960 for the correction of entries, village land records have considerably improved.

6.7. FIXATION OF TENURES AND FAIR RENTS

The original Act provided for four tenures, i.e. *bhumidhar*, *sirdar*, *asami* and *adhivasi*. By a subsequent amendment the last one has been dropped.

All land under the home farm of the former zamindars has been converted into their *bhumidhari*. Besides, the right of *bhumidhari* could also be acquired by a *sirdar* on payment of ten times the rent payable on the land on which he wants to acquire the *bhumidhari*. Under the original Act the payment was to be made in a lump sum, but an amendment of 1958 now provides for payment in instalments. In the latter case the amount required to be paid has been fixed at 12 times the rent payable. In all such cases a certificate is issued to the *sirdar* indicating his new title.

All land included in the holdings of former ex-proprietary, occupancy and hereditary tenants has been given to them as *sirdars*. The same has been the case in respect of the holdings of certain classes of sub-tenants of special tenants.

Asami on the other hand is a tenure applying to the land under the sub-tenants of the *bhumidhars* or *sirdars* or a tenant of the *Gaon Samaj*, or that of non-occupancy tenants.

Fixation of Revenue of Bhumidhars

A land revenue on *bhumidhari* land retained by a former intermediary by conversion has been fixed at an amount equal to the land revenue on such land on the date immediately preceding the date of vesting. If the person was a rent-free grantee and the grant was in lieu of service, he would pay land revenue at hereditary rates; and in all other cases of a grant at the occupancy rates.

In the case of *bhumidhari* accruing to a fixed rate tenant the land revenue has been fixed equal to the rent payable by him on the date of vesting. Further, the intermediary who has now become *bhumidhar* through conversion of those occupancy, hereditary and *patta dawami* or *istamarari* tenures in which the right to transfer was enjoyed by him, and also as a grove, the land revenue has been fixed equal to the rent payable by him for the land.

If, however, *bhumidhari* has been acquired by payment, land revenue has been fixed at an amount equal to one-half of the rent payable on such land on the date immediately preceding the date of vesting.

Revenue Payable by a Sirdar

Every *sirdar* will normally pay a land revenue equal to the amount of the rent he was paying formerly to the zamindar. In all such cases rent formerly paid to zamindars has been covered into land revenue to be paid to the government.

Rent Payable by the Asamis

An *asami*, on being admitted to the occupation of land, is liable to pay a rent which has been agreed upon between him and his landholder or the *Gaon Samaj* as the case may be. This rent paid by him will not ordinarily be varied. If any amount of rent remains unpaid, an *asami* will have to pay an interest at the rate of $6\frac{1}{4}\%$ per annum from the date rent becomes due. Provision has also been made in the Act to realise the rent from the *asami* through coercive methods if he at last fails to pay the same. The rent payable by an *asami* may be enhanced or abated on the application of the *Gaon Sabha* or the landholder or the *asami* on the ground of increase or decrease in the area of the holding.

Commutation of Rent

According to Section 218 of U.P. Zamindari Abolition Act "where the rent is payable in kind or on estimate or appraisement of the standing crop or on rates varying with crops sown or partly in one of such ways and partly in another or other of such ways the Assistant Collector in-charge of the Sub-division may at his own instance and shall at the instance of the *Gaon Samaj* or the person by or to whom the rent is payable commute the rent . . . " in a prescribed manner. In this case the rent shall be determined or commuted at double the amount applicable at hereditary rates, where there are no hereditary rates, the court shall calculate the rates after taking into consideration the rents payable by *sirdars*, holding land of similar quality and advantages in the vicinity of the land held by the *asami*.[31]

6.8. CEILINGS ON LAND HOLDINGS

The U.P. Zamindari Abolition Act of 1950 had imposed restrictions on the future acquisition of land according to which no one could acquire a holding in future beyond 30 acres. An amendment to this, however, was made in 1958, which restricts the future acquisition to $12\frac{1}{2}$ acres. There was no provision in this Act for the imposition of maximum limit on the existing holding, which has now been provided for under the Imposition of Ceilings on Land Holdings Act 1960.

According to the Act of 1960, the ceiling area of a tenure holder shall be 40 acres of "fair quality land". But in case of large size families having more than five members the ceiling is raised by an additional eight acres per member exceeding this size and subject to a maximum of additional twenty-four acres for a family. Thus a family having eight or more members may have a maximum holding of 64 acres of fair quality land. Land beyond this limit is regarded as surplus land.

Fair quality land has been deemed to be the land the hereditary rate of which is Rs. 6 per acre. Similarly a family means as consisting of the holder of a holding and any or all of his following relations not being tenure holders in their own separate rights:

    (*i*) Wife or husband as the case may be,
    (*ii*) Dependent parents,
    (*iii*) Unseparated son, son's son and their widows or wives,
    (*iv*) Unmarried daughter and unseparated son's daughter; where a son has got a separate holding, he will be treated separately.

6.9. DETERMINATION OF SURPLUS LAND

Under the Ceilings Act of 1960, a surplus land means "land held by a tenure holder in excess of the ceiling area applicable to him and shall

[31] Rule 180A (1), (2); 180B (1), (2).

include buildings, wells and trees existing thereon". The Ceilings Act of 1960 has been enforced with effect from July 1, 1961. To prevent evasion of the Act through anticipatory partition and transaction all partitions and transactions made after August 20, 1959 were to be ignored for the purposes of their determination of the surplus land unless it was a transfer in favour of the State Government, a partition in connection with the consolidation operations and a partition of the holding of a joint Hindu family made by a suit or proceeding pending on the date mentioned above.

The Act, however, provides for certain exemptions from the operation of land ceilings. These exemptions apply to (a) land under a grove, (b) land used for industrial purposes, (c) land up to 2 acres used for cattle shed, compost pits, etc., (d) land covered under a residential house, a cremation ground or a graveyard etc. Besides this all land under tea, coffee and rubber plantations or used for *pharmacological* and such herbal and other plantations and land held by religious or charitable *waqf*, trust or endowment before May 1, 1959, has also been exempted from the imposition of ceiling. There are certain other categories of exemption also, such as land held for the purposes of an educational institution, a *Gosadan* or *Goshala;* land vested in the *Gram Samaj* or a local authority, land which is the property of the Union Government, land held by a Bhoodan Committee, land held by a cooperative society in its own name for purposes of agriculture, horticulture, animal husbandry etc. and land covered under the farm roads used throughout the year. Finally, any land for the purposes of growing *pan, keora, bela, chameli* or *gulab*, etc. will also be exempted from the land ceiling provided the tenure holder of such land has no other land on which ceiling could be imposed.

After the promulgation of the Act, the tenure holders having surplus land were called upon to submit within 30 days a statement in respect of all their holdings in a prescribed form and also to point out the plots from which they claim exemption and those to which they would like the ceilings to apply. If, however, the tenure holders fail to submit such a statement, or submit an incorrect or incomplete one, they may be served with a notice calling upon them to submit a statement within a specified period. After the submission of the statement objections, if any, could be met with and ultimately the Prescribed Authority shall determine the surplus land. Adequate provision has been made for appeals, etc. in case of any grievances of the tenure holders.

6.10. Acquisition of the Surplus Land

It has been provided for in the Act that after the final determination of the surplus land the Prescribed Authority shall notify in the official Gazette the surplus land of a tenure holder. From the date of notification all the surplus land shall stand transferred to and vest in the the State free from all encumbrances and rights, titles and interests of all persons in such surplus land with effect from this date shall stand extinguished.

Any person claiming interest as a tenure holder or a lessee in possession of such surplus land may within 30 days file objections before a Prescribed Authority, which may be disposed of in accordance with the rules. Adequate legal remedy lies for an aggrieved person if any as a result of the orders of the Prescribed Authority in this connection.

After the publication of the notification the Collector shall take possession of the surplus land and may for that purpose use such force as may be necessary. If, however, any property has been left on the surplus land, the tenure holder will be permitted to collect the same within a specified period of time. If he fails to do so the Collector will get it auctioned and send the proceeds to the tenure holder.

A provision has also been made according to which 10% of the surplus land of a tenure holder may, subject to a maximum of 10 acres, be settled with him on his giving an undertaking in writing to plant a grove on this land within a certain period.

6.11. Determination and Payment of Compensation

Every tenure holder whose surplus land has vested in the State will be entitled to a compensation. All proceedings relating to the assessment and payment of the compensation shall be conducted by a compensation officer appointed by the State Government for the purpose.

The amount of compensation for the surplus land will be calculated at much higher rates than those applied for the abolition of *zamindari* rights. Secondly, such compensation will vary according to the tenure of the holder. A *bhumidhar* shall be paid 40 times the land revenue determined at hereditary rates applicable or 80 times the land revenue payable, whichever is greater; and where the land revenue payable is less than that determined at hereditary rates applicable an additional amount equal to 20 times the difference between the two.

In case of a *sirdar* the compensation will be determined at the rate of 20 times the land revenue assessed at the hereditary rates applicable and where the land revenue payable is less than that determined at hereditary rates applicable an additional amount equal to 20 times the difference between the two will be the amount of compensation.

Asami of a *Gaon Samaj* will get five times the rent payable by him by way of compensation. Similarly, if he is an *asami* of a *bhumidhar*, in lieu of the maintenance allowance as under Section 11 of the U.P. Zamindari Abolition and Land Reforms Act of 1950, he will get compensation in varying degrees according to the nature of his tenure. For instance, if he is an *asami* in perpetuity, he will get 7/8 of the amount of compensation of a *bhumidhar* mentioned above; if he is an *asami* for his own life-time, he would be entitled to 3/8 of the amount of the *bhumidhar's* compensation and finally, if he is an *asami* for a specified period, half of the land revenue determined at hereditary rates applicable for each year of the unexpired period of the base, subject to a maximum of 35 times the land revenue so computed, will be paid to him by way of compensation.

A provision for the imposition of land ceilings and payment of compensation for surplus land has also been made for those parts of the State, where *zamindari* has not yet been abolished. In such areas the compensation with respect to the occupancy, ex-proprietary, hereditary tenants and grantees at favourable rate of rent shall be calculated at the same rates as admissible for the *sirdars* and for other tenants at rates applicable to the *asamis* of *Gaon Samaj*.

Compensation at varying rates will also be paid to the lessees of Government, on buildings, masonary wells, tube wells, etc., trees and timber, etc.

The Compensation Officer shall prepare a draft compensation assessment roll with respect to all those entitled to receive compensation and this will be finalised after meeting objections, if any. The amount of compensation entered in the compensation assessment roll shall be paid in cash or in bonds or partly in cash or partly in bonds, as has been prescribed in the rules. This compensation will be due from the date of dispossession.

The State Government shall pay an interest at the rate of $3\frac{1}{2}\%$ per annum on the amount from the date on which compensation becomes due to the date of determination if the amount is to be paid in cash and in case it is to be paid in bonds then up to the date of redemption of the bonds. The compensation so paid will be full discharge of the liability of the Government for the surplus land.

6.12. REDISTRIBUTION OF THE SURPLUS LAND

All surplus land acquired by the State as a result of the imposition of land ceilings may not immediately be settled with or distributed to new claimants. This will be so since the Act provides that the surplus land of a mechanised farm may be converted by the Government into a State farm under a Manager who may preferably be the previous tenure holder himself. The period of such operation and management may be extended by the Government to any length. Further, the Government may instead of settling the surplus land with anybody may use temporarily or permanently whole or any part of such surplus land for any purpose it decides. During this interim period, that is, before the surplus land has been finally disposed of, the Collector may even let it out to any person for cultivation.

Final settlement of surplus land will, however, be made in the following prescribed order of priority:

(*i*) The first beneficiary will be the *Goan Samaj* which will be entitled to receive land for the purpose of planting trees, growing fodder or for any other community purpose if the land with it is less than 15 acres.

(*ii*) Out of the remaining land, if any surplus land had been held by a member of a cooperative society immediately preceding the date of vesting, such land, if the society so desires, may be settled with the society.

(*iii*) The remainder of the surplus land will then be redistributed in the following manner:
(*a*) To a cooperative society of small holders below $3\frac{1}{8}$ acres, if the surplus land is less than 15 acres;
(*b*) If the remaining land is more than 15 acres in the village, it will be settled with a cooperative society of landless agricultural workers provided each member does not get more than $3\frac{1}{8}$ acres.

(*iv*) If any land remains after giving to the landless labour, it is to be settled "with any cooperative society no member whereof prior to such settlement holds more than $3\frac{1}{8}$ acres of land in his own right."

6.13. AGENCY FOR PROMOTION AND ORGANISATION OF COOPERATIVE FARMING

Provision was made under the Zamindari Abolition and Land Reforms Act of 1950 for the establishment of cooperative farms (*i*) on an entirely voluntary basis by 10 or more persons holding among themselves 30 acres or more in a village; and (*ii*) by pooling land in uneconomic holdings if not less than two-thirds of the total number of persons holding uneconomic holdings as *bhumidhari* or *sirdari* and holding between them not less than two-thirds of the aggregate area of all such holdings in the circle apply jointly to the Collector for the purpose. The State Government was to fix the minimum area below which a holding was to be considered as uneconomic—the limit so fixed could be different for different parts. Further a cooperative farm is entitled under the Act to such concession and facilities as may be prescribed particularly in regard to (*a*) reduction of land revenue, (*b*) reduction of or exemption from agricultural income tax, (*c*) free technical advice from experts employed by the Government, (*d*) financial aid and grant of subsidy and loans with or without interest, (*e*) admission to land by the Land Management Committee, and (*f*) priority in irrigation from State irrigation works.

The Act, however, did not envisage the establishment of any special machinery for implementation of this part of the land reforms. The Registrar of the Cooperative Societies, the Collector and the Asstt. Collector in charge of the subdivision were and are expected to deal with the applications, if any, as these are made. It appears that even the preliminary task of declaring the minimum size of a holding below which it will be deemed to be uneconomic has not yet been undertaken. Nor it is clear whether any concession and facilities as envisaged in the Act have yet been presented for the cooperative farms. Any campaign for the establishment of such farms or for the publicity of relevant legal provision was neither envisaged in the Act nor has been undertaken at any level.

The State Government was empowered to make rules for the purpose of carrying into effect the provisions of the Act in regard to cooperative farms. These were among others to provide for "the model form of bye-laws of cooperative farms to be registered" under these provisions. The Rules framed by the State Government under the Act do not yet contain any such bye-laws. All that is provided for under these Rules is that the following matters may be governed by the bye-laws of the farms:

(*i*) The contribution of land, funds and other property by member, their valuation and adjustment,

(*ii*) the remuneration and wages to be paid to the members working on the farm,

(*iii*) the payment of expenses and other dues of the farm,

(*iv*) the distribution of the produce and the profits of the farm,

(*v*) the conduct generally of the affairs of the farm and its working,

(*vi*) the liquidation of personal debts of members and the regulation of their credits.

Any cooperative farms established under the provisions of the Zamindari Abolition and Land Reforms Act will be registered under the Cooperative Societies Act and its management will be carried on by a Committee as provided under its bye-laws. The State Government has, however, the right to issue such directions to it from time to time as it may deem necessary in the interest of planned or controlled agricultural development. There has, however, been little progress in the establishment of cooperative farms under the provisions of the Zamindari Abolition and Land Reforms Act and this part of the Act has remained more or less a dead letter. A serious lacuna in this respect has been the absence of a special machinery responsible for the implementation of this part of the land reforms scheme.

6.14. CONSOLIDATION OF HOLDINGS

Soon after the *zamindari* abolition, provision was made for the compulsory consolidation of holdings under an Act passed in 1952. Consolidation operations have been taken in the State on a large scale and a separate Directorate of Consolidation has been established for the purpose. It has a large staff at the field level for conducting the operations while the Collectors act as Deputy Directors of Consolidation for their respective districts. Since our project is not concerned with the impact of consolidation of holdings it will not be relevant to discuss here the details of the consolidation machinery and its procedure.

6.15. AGENCY FOR CONFERMENT OF SIRDARI RIGHTS ON ADHIVASIS

According to the Act of 1950 generally the share croppers were put into a separate category of *adhivasis* and it was provided that except in certain conditions "an *adhivasi* shall continue to have all the rights and the liabilities which he possessed, or was subject to in respect of the land on the date immediately preceding the date of vesting." (Sec 231). This left his rights vague and the exceptions that were specified made his tenure insecure and rendered him liable to ejectment by the principal tenure holder. The U. P. Land Reforms (Amendment) Act 1954 corrected this situation by making provision for the acquisition of rights, title and interest of landholders in the land held by *adhivasis* and by conferring on them the *sirdari* rights. This took effect from October 30, 1954, the date of vesting under the Act of 1954 and required the assessment of payment of compensation to the landholders of such land. No new machinery was created for the purpose as the Compensation Officers who were engaged for the assessment of compensation for the zamindars could be entrusted with this responsibility as well. The amount of compensation was, however, determined differently than for the rights of the intermediaries and was all made payable in cash in one lump sum or in annual instalments.

To sum up, the State Government had not to create an entirely new agency for implementing its land reforms. Its detailed record of rights maintained in connection with land revenue administration provided the basic information while its experience of revision of land revenue settlements and machinery for collection of land revenue prevented the task of the implementation of land reforms from appearing as something entirely new or administratively too difficult.

CHAPTER VII

EXTENT AND COST OF ZAMINDARI ABOLITION

7.1. HOUSEHOLDS AND AREA INVOLVED

The U. P. Zamindari Abolition Committee estimated that there were 2.02 million zamindars in the state paying a total land revenue of Rs. 6.81 crores in 1947 and that there were no less than 21.56 million persons holding various interests in agricultural holdings covering an area of 41.33 million acres. Besides there were 4.12 million tenants of *sir* and *khudkasht*, sub-tenants and occupiers of land without consent having in their possession a total of 3.7 million acres. It was no easy matter to implement a legislation involving such vast numbers and changing a land system that had been established for more than 100 years and had become extremely complex in its details. Land reforms history had hardly another example where land rights had been changed over such a vast area within so short a period and in so peaceful a manner. The British rulers had to make several settlements at varying intervals before adopting their first regular settlements in the various parts of the State in the nineteenth century and their early settlements were often accompanied by much arbitrariness, agricultural dislocation, land desertion, misery and even violence.

The implementation of the Zamindari Abolition and Land Reforms Act over the entire state within a period of few years in a most peaceful and democratic manner is certainly a significant achievement of the U.P. State Government. It has already been noted as to how the Act in the beginning did not apply to certain special parts and areas which, however, were not significant as judged by size. Since then the Act has been extended to cover all such areas or fresh legislation has been enacted to deal with the special problems of certain parts, e.g. the hill area or the urban places.

Zamindari has already been abolished over 60.20 million acres out of a total State area of 72.60 million acres. This represents 83 per cent of the total area and covers nearly all village lands except those in the hill districts. The total area of holdings over which *zamindari* had been abolished by 1956-57 was 45.0 million acres and this constitutes 98.04%

of the total area under holdings to which the Zamindari Abolition Act applied. The elimination of intermediary rights over this vast area is all the more significant when it is realised that as against the number of 2.02 million zamindars as estimated by the U.P. Zamindari Abolition Committee the total number of intermediaries for whom rolls had actually to be prepared proved to be much larger at 6.64 millions.

Data pertaining to sample villages reveals that *zamindari* abolition affected 35.72 per cent of all village households and about 89 per cent of the total village area was comprised in the holdings or estates of the former intermediaries. The proportion of households holding intermediary rights was found to vary from 28.8 per cent in the sample villages of the western districts to 46.3 per cent in those of the eastern districts. Relevant figures are given in the following table:

TABLE No. 17

HOUSEHOLDS AND AREA COVERED BY ZAMINDARI
ABOLITION IN THE SAMPLE VILLAGES

Region	Total Number of House-holds	Households Affected by *Zamindari*	Percentage of 3 to 2	Village Area (Acres)	Area Covered by *Zamindari* Abolition (Acres)	Percentage of 6 to 5
1	2	3	4	5	6	7
Western	5233	1509	28.84	28233	23736	84.07
Central	3209	1027	32.00	11089	10709	96.57
Bundelkhand	1789	716	40.07	28182	24617	87.35
Eastern	3805	1762	46.31	13100	12744	97.28
All	14036	5014	35.72	80604	71806	89.09

7.2. PAYMENT OF COMPENSATION

According to the data on the implementation of the Principal Act up to Sept. 30, 1961, the total number of intermediaries for whom compensation rolls had to be prepared came to 6.64 millions. Rolls of nearly all of them except of 2057 intermediaries had already been finalised.

The total amount of compensation payable to those whose rolls have been finalised aggregate nearly Rs. 69.00 crores. Adding to this the estimated amount of compensation for unfinalised rolls the total compensation payable to the intermediaries amount to Rs. 69.32 crores. The average payment works out roughly at Rs. 15.4 per acre of the area comprised in the holdings of the former intermediaries. The margin of zamindar's revenue (rental demand minus revenue demand) worked out to about Rs. 11 crores annually for the period 1946-51. The total compensation thus amounted to 6.3 times this margin. Actually, however, the whole of the rental demand could seldom be collected by the zamindars and for the quinquennium preceding *zamindari* abolition their actual surplus, i.e. rent collected minus revenue demand was no more than Rs. 2.36 crores. Thus the compensation was nearly 30 times their realised surplus. These latter figures reveal that the rule of 8 times the net assets as compensation prescribed by law was very liberal.

Out of the total compensation payable amounting to Rs. 69.32 crores a sum of Rs. 54.24 crores or 80.5 per cent had been paid up to Sept. 30, 1961. The bulk of it (Rs. 48.76 crores) was paid in the form of special bonds issued for the purpose in favour of the claimants, and only a small part (Rs. 5.47 crores) amounting to a little more than 10 per cent of the total amount due was paid in cash. All payments up to Rs. 50 were made in cash and a little less than half of all the intermediaries were found to be entitled to a payment of Rs. 50 or less. They numbered 3.18 millions and received a total amount of Rs. 4.65 crores as compensation. A provision was also made for the payment of interim compensation. Only 4.83 lakh intermediaries applied for such interim payment and a total sum of Rs. 6.35 crores was so paid to them. *Waqfs* etc. were paid in the form of annuities valued at Rs. 1.84 crores. Besides a sum of Rs. 56 lakhs had been paid to them as interest on their compensation amount.

7.3. REHABILITATION GRANT

Intermediaries were also entitled to the receipt of a Rehabilitation Grant according to a progressive multiple as laid down in the Zamindari Abolition Act. Roughly calculated, the total amount of Rehabilitation Grant due to them is estimated by us at Rs. 56.46 crores. Actually the amount of such grant determined so far aggregates to Rs. 51.63 crores. In all 8.40 lakh intermediaries applied for such relief and while, 12000 applications were rejected the grant has been finally determined for 7.91 lakh persons. The amount paid in cash has again been only about 10 per cent. The bulk has been paid in the form of non-interest-bearing bonds to 6.02 lakh intermediaries.

7.4 COMPENSATION TO LANDHOLDERS OF ADHIVASIS

To deal with the non-occupancy tenants of the former intermediaries, i.e. tenants of their *sir* and *khudkasht* as well as to deal with the problem of sub-tenancy etc. a transitory tenure of *adhivasis* was created when *zamindari* was abolished. This gave a temporary security of tenure to these cultivators, who numbered more than 5.6 millions and had 2.39 million acres in their holdings in 1954. In this latter year it was decided to confer *sirdari* rights on all *adhivasis* and to compensate the main tenure holders by payment. As soon as a notification to this effect was made a large number of landholders applied for the ejectment of their *adhivasis* on the ground that the entries in revenue records were not correct. As a consequence, until Aug. 31, 1958, the date for which latest information is available, *adhivasis* holding 15% of the total area comprised in their holdings were ejected while *adhivasis* with 83 per cent of the holdings area secured *sirdari* rights. Cases of *adhivasis* having some 2 per cent of the total area were still pending in the courts.

This provision has resulted in the extension of permanent and heritable tenure over 1.72 million acres held by some 4.36 million *adhivasis*, who have all been given the *sirdari* rights. Quite many among them held land on a crop-sharing basis or occupied it without the determination of rent. Simultaneously with the conversion of *adhivasi* tenure into *sirdari* rent in kind has been commuted into money and wherever rent was not determined, assessment has been made.

The principal landholders of *adhivasi* tenure have been given compensation. Their total number up to Sept. 30, 1961 came to 4.03 millions. Compensation rolls of nearly all of them have already been finalised and a total amount of Rs. 12.06 crores has been determined as payable to them—mostly in cash. A total amount of Rs. 9.86 crores was reported to have already fallen due for payment out of which Rs. 7.76 crores was paid in cash and only Rs. 2.10 crores in bonds. Roughly estimated, compensation amounts to Rs. 70 per acre which is 4.5 times as high as for the abolition of intermediary rights without taking into account the rehabilitation grant. Even if the latter is taken into account the average compensation rate paid to tenure-holder is still more than 2.5 times that paid to the zamindars for their rights.

7.5. THE ZAMINDARI ABOLITION FUND

Simultaneously with the abolition of *zamindari*, the cultivators were given the opportunity to acquire permanent, heritable and transferable rights in the form of *bhumidhari* over the area under their tenancy rights by depositing ten times the rent of such land. This amount was to be credited to a special account known as the Zamindari Abolition Fund[32] and the Government hoped that it will be able to pay compensation to the ex-intermediaries out of this amount. It had calculated that even if four-fifths of the tenants applied for *bhumidhari* rights it will be able to collect Rs. 140 crores in this fund. There appears to have been considerable enthusiasm in the beginning among the peasantry to thus acquire *bhumidhari* rights and by the end of June 1952 no less than 4.09 million applications were received and nearly Rs. 33.16 crores were paid by the former tenants for the purpose. In consequence, 3.62 million *sanads* conferring *bhumidhari* rights had been distributed by that date.

But as the Principal Act was implemented and each tenant was made a *sirdar* without any payment, this enthusiasm waned and only a few cultivators applied subsequently for acquisition of *bhumidhari*. According to official data between June 1952 and December 1960 only some 7.5 lakh persons applied for acquisition of *bhumidhari*. The fresh deposits made by them amounted to a total of Rs. 7.5 crores only. The total amount thus deposited in the Zamindari Abolition Fund since its inception up to December 1960 amounted to Rs. 40.61 crores only. *Sanads* in respect of the amount of Rs. 38.15 crores have already been distributed giving *bhumidhari* rights to 4.26 million cultivators.

Now, it is obvious that this part of the *zamindari* abolition scheme has not succeeded as much as it was expected. The total amount collected so far under the Zamindari Abolition Fund has been less than one-third of the liabilities incurred by the Government in regard to the payment of compensation and rehabilition grant to the ex-intermediaries. If the liabilities on account of compensation to the landholders of land in the cultivation of *adhivasis* are also included, the total amount deposited in the Zamindari Abolition Fund hardly amounts to 30 per cent of the sum required. Further, the total number of *khata* holders, including former *adhivasis*, entitled to acquire *bhumidhari* rights was no less than 22 millions and only about one-fifth of them have actually acquired such rights. Again, nearly five-sixths of the total area under holdings was occupied by tenants before *zamindari* abolition. *Bhumidhari* rights could thus be

[32] The Zamindari Abolition Fund was created in 1949-50 by transferring an amount of Rs. 1 crore from the surplus of that year and even before the Zamindari Abolition and Land Reforms Act was put on the Statute Book, provision was made under the Agricultural Tenants (Acquisition of Privileges) Act 1949 for voluntary contribution to this Fund by tenants equal to 10 times their rent for acquiring *bhumidhari* rights.

acquired by payment over about 37 million acres or so. Actually, *bhumidhari* extends over some 15 million acres not more than half of which has been acquired by payment. In other words *bhumidhari* rights have been acquired by payment only on about one-fifth of the land over which these could be acquired.

The success in this respect has been limited in spite of a campaign by the Government in the countryside at the time of the *zamindari* abolition to enthuse the cultivators to acquire *bhumidhari*. It appears that the campaign was not continued in subsequent years whereas some political parties campaigned against it in later years on the ground that *bhumidhari* rights be granted to all cultivators without payment. In a subsequent section we have analysed the responses of the sample households for not acquiring *bhumidhari* rights. It may, however, be stated here that the incentive for acquiring *bhumidhari* has not been strong since the only major difference between *sirdari* and *bhumidhari* rights is that the former does not carry with it the right of transferability while the latter does. Even this is significant only when one wants to make a transfer and since *bhumidhari* can be acquired even later when the need arises there is no urgency felt by a *sirdar* to acquire it beforehand. The other advantage of a reduction in land revenue by 50 per cent is no real advantage as in effect it only means a 5 per cent rate of return on the amount deposited while a cultivator can always lend in the village at a much higher rate.

Any future drive in this respect has to be multi-pronged. Not only should there be an effective campaign in favour of acquisition of *bhumidhari* rights but what is more important fresh incentives should be provided to the individual as well as to the village community. It may be worthwhile to link expenditure in local and village projects with the amount of deposits for *bhumidhari* acquisition and to earmark the collections in Zamindari Abolition Fund for local works. Moreover, it has to be borne in mind that the ability of cultivators to pay in cash an amount equal to 10 times their revenue is often extremely limited. The alternative of paying in instalments as provided subsequently may prove more fruitful.

7.6. UNIFORMITY OF TENURES

The Principal Act provided for only three tenures, viz. *bhumidhari*, *sirdari* and *asami* to replace the heterogeneity and multiplicity of tenures that existed under the *zamindari* system. Actually it was intended that all cultivators should have permanent and heritable rights (*sirdari*) and further transferability be enjoyed by as large a number of tenure holders as possible through acquisition of *bhumidhari*. The tenure of an a*sami* is temporary and was provided for covering special cases of sub-tenancy etc., say, during a temporary disability of the principal tenure holder. Sub-letting, however, was generally disallowed.

Most of the agricultural land (66 per cent of the total area of holdings) is held under *sirdari* tenure and *bhumidhari* as already explained has not yet attracted the bulk of the cultivators. Only about one-third of the total area is held under the latter tenure while *asamis* occupy an insignificant position limited to 0.39 per cent of the holdings area. Figures about the State in this respect for the last three years are given below:

TABLE No. 18

AREA OF HOLDINGS IN U.P. BY TENURES

(*in Acres*)

Year	Bhumidhari	Sirdari	Asami	Total
1957-58	1,45,79,204	3,00,46,750	1,74,994	4,48,00,948
	(32.54)	(67.07)	(0.39)	(100.00)
1958-59	1,53,21,911	2,98,96,486	1,80,110	4,53,98,507
	(33.75)	(65.85)	(0.40)	(100.00)
1959-60	1,54,54,977	2,99,14,669	1,79,444	4,55,49,090
	(33.93)	(65.68)	(0.39)	(100.00)
Average of three years	1,51,18,697.3	2,99,52,635.0	1,78,182.7	4,52,49,515.0
	(33.42)	(66.19)	(0.39)	(100.00)

N. B. Figures within brackets give percentages.

7.7. LAND MANAGEMENT BY *Gaon Samajs* AND LAND TO LANDLESS

By June 30, 1959, some 9.5 million acres had been vested in the *Gaon Samajs*. The Zamindari Abolition Act made a provision for the vesting of such land as did not form part of the holdings of an individual tenure holder in the *Gaon Samaj*. Besides this a *Gaon Samaj* was to hold land surrendered by a tenure holder or from which a person might have been ejected by it. Thus, initially only non-cultivated area was vested in the *Gaon Samajs*—whole of it, however, was not unculturable as quite a substantial part of it was classified cultivable waste and at least some could be brought under the plough with due effort. At the same time it is clear that not all the culturable waste was cultivable or could be brought under cultivation through ordinary reclamation work.

Out of the 9.5 million acres vested in the *Gaon Samajs* 3.76 million acres was reserved for planned use and only 3.3 million acres was available for allotment to individual cultivators. But, actually, not more than 8 per cent of the area available for allotment or a total of 2.7 lakh acres has so far been allotted to 1.01 lakh households of whom 63,000 belong to the category of landless agricultural labourers. These latter have been allotted a total area of 1.61 lakh acres. This cannot be regarded as satisfactory as it hardly touches even the fringe of the problem. There are nearly 4 million landless agricultural workers in the State and the allotment of land to them by the *Gaon Samajs* during the last 8 years has not benefited even 2 per cent of them. Obviously, the provision of allotment of land to the landless through the agency of *Gaon Samajs* in the scheme of *zamindari* abolition has been well-intentioned but the objective conditions for its effective implementation are wholly lacking.

7.8. LAND CEILINGS AND REDISTRIBUTION

The Principal Act did not provide directly for any redistribution of land along with *zamindari* abolition. It, however, provided for a limit on future acquisition of land holdings—this being fixed originally at 30 acres and then lowered to $12\frac{1}{2}$ acres in 1958. Large holdings were also discouraged through the imposition of a Large Land Holdings Tax since 1957. The burden of this tax was, however, reduced to a considerable extent through the abolition of the agricultural income tax from the same year.

More recently the U.P. Imposition of Ceilings on Land Holdings Act 1960 has been enacted and while it remains to be fully implemented the Large Land Holdings Tax has already been abolished since 1961. It has been estimated that the former would result in the acquisition of some 1.5 million acres of land that will be available in near future for redistribution. In a subsequent chapter we have analysed the pattern of land distribution in the State which suggests that *zamindari* abolition has made little improvement in this respect and land continues to be distributed among the cultivators as inequitably as before. The picture is not likely to change significantly even after the full implementation of the Ceilings Act which itself will still take some time. Meanwhile, the problem is likely to worsen with the increasing pressure of population on soil and land hunger will become more severe than ever.

7.9. CONSOLIDATION OF HOLDINGS

Consolidation of agricultural holdings has been started on a compulsory basis under a separate Act that came into force in March 1954. During the last seven years up to Sept. 30, 1961, consolidation operations covered 38 districts out of a total of 52 in the State. It does not however mean that agricultural holdings in all the villages, *tehsils* or *parganas* of these former districts have been consolidated or are in the process of consolidation. According to the latest statement consolidation has been completed in 15,000 villages only involving a total area of 5.6 million acres, i.e. about one-ninth of the total area of agricultural holdings in the State. In another 12,000 villages consolidation operations are in various stages of implementation. During 1960-61 consolidation was accomplished in about 1.7 million acres and if it be assumed that consolidation of holdings will be completed at a slightly higher rate in future, say over 2 million acres per year, it will still take another 20 years to consolidate all the remaining holdings in the State. In fact the phased State programme for consolidation of agricultural holdings goes up to 1980.

Consolidation results in bringing the fields of a cultivator in a compact block or area. Thus the 14.88 million plots so far covered by consolidation operations have been consolidated into some 2.6 million *chaks* or blocks. It has been further calculated that 61 per cent of the landholders in the consolidated fields have all their plots in a single *chak*, 23 per cent in two *chaks* and only 16 per cent in 3 or more *chaks*. This, however, does not mean that the number of plots and fields has been reduced to the number of *chaks* and the landholders have removed all field boundaries dividing their holding into plots within a *chak*.

7.10. ESTABLISHMENT OF COOPERATIVE FARMS

The *zamindari* abolition scheme did not attempt directly to replace individual farming by cooperative farming in the State. However, the latter was given an indirect encouragement through a provision in the Principal Act for preferential treatment of cooperative farms in regard to certain facilities and services etc., for various reasons. This part of the scheme has not made much progress. By the end of June 1960 there were in U.P. in all 415 cooperative farming societies of all types, the majority being for joint cultivation. The total number of members of all the societies was reported at 9,562. All of these, however, were not working members as only 5,547 were full-time field operators. The rest were either part-time workers or absentee tenure holders. All these societies had a commanded area of 84,046 acres, of which 59,749 acres was the cultivated area. The data on cooperative farming societies are given in the following table while the differences in the various types of cooperative farming societies have been described in the Appendix under the heading of Concepts, Definitions and Explanations.

TABLE No. 19

COOPERATIVE FARMING IN U.P.

(Figures for the year ending June 30, 1960)

Sl. No.	Type of Society	No. of Societies		No. of Members			
		Total	Under-taking Ancillary Industries	Land-holders	Landless Agricul-tural Workers	Others	Total
1.	Joint Farming	296	115	5,883	784	225	6,892
2.	Better Farming	97	42	1,835	244	20	2,099
3.	Collective Farming	21	11	223	103	204	530
4.	Tenant Farming	1	—	37	4	—	41
	Total	415	168	7,978	1,135	449	9,562

Sl. No.	Type of Society	Coverage Area (in Acres)			
		Commanded	Under Cultivation		
			Total	Irrigated	Unirrigated
1.	Joint Farming	67,696	45,473	30,450	15,023
2.	Better Farming	11,453	11,187	7,584	3,603
3.	Collective Farming	4,147	2,739	1,906	833
4.	Tenant Farming	750	350	—	350
	Total	84,046	59,749	39,940	19,809

Here we note that the majority of the farming societies are for joint cultivation, some of which also carry on some ancilliary industries as well. Amongst the members of the cooperative farming societies, besides the landholders, there are landless labourers as well. But these latter constitute less than 12 per cent of the total membership. Besides some non-agriculturists have also found their way into such societies, particularly, in the collective farming societies.

On the whole there has been little progress towards cooperative farming in the State. The total area cultivated by the joint farming societies up to June 1960 (45,000 acres) is only about 0.1 per cent of the total cultivated area of the State. A vigorous drive will have to be undertaken for any progress in this direction. In particular the provision in the Principal Act with regard to preferential treatment of cooperative farms needs to be fully explained, implemented and even extended in its scope; otherwise this part of the legislation will continue to be a dead letter as it has remained so far.

The Principal Act also provided for the compulsory conversion of uneconomic holdings into cooperative farms under certain conditions. This portion of the Act remains wholly unutilised so far and no case could be found by us where the Government might have had occasion to use it. Let the State Government examine this part of legislation more closely so that it may be implemented and, if necessary, even amended along the same lines as the law relating to consolidation of holdings.

7.11. INCREASE IN STATE REVENUE AND IN ITS FINANCIAL LIABILITIES

Strictly from an accounts viewpoint the net gain or loss to the State Government on account of *zamindari* abolition may be measured in terms of the consequential direct or indirect changes in its annual receipts and disbursements. The gross land revenue demand in the year immediately preceding *zamindari* abolition amounted to Rs. 7.16 crores (the average for the quinquennium being Rs. 7.06 crores) out of which Rs. 6.65 crores were actually collected in the year. In 1956-57 it had increased to Rs. 21.73 crores, Rs. 21.49 crores in respect of the area over which *zamindari* has been abolished and   Rs. 24.79 lakhs over the rest. After deducting the nominal and irrecoverable dues the net land revenue demand amounted to Rs. 20.28 crores out of which Rs. 17.22 crores were actually collected—Rs. 17 crores from the area where *zamindari* no longer exists and Rs. 22 lakhs from the rest.

The annual gross land revenue demand has thus increased as a consequence of *zamindari* abolition by Rs. 14.57 crores (Rs. 21.73 crores minus Rs. 7.16 crores). But actual receipts increased by Rs. 10.57 crores (Rs. 17.22 crores minus Rs. 6.65 crores) only. As against this there was a certain fall in other receipts or additional expenditure and disbursements which could be ascribed to the abolition of the *zamindari* system. The sum total of these two items has been estimated at Rs. 10.13 crores as follows:

ESTIMATED ANNUAL LOSS IN REVENUE AND INCREASE IN EXPENDITURE AND DISBURSEMENT ON ACCOUNT OF ZAMINDARI ABOLITION

A. Loss in Revenue

1. Agricultural Income Tax	Rs. 0.76 crores (Perpetual)	
2. Judicial and non-judicial stamps	„ 0.50 „	„
Total	Rs. 1.26 „	

B. Additional Disbursements

1. Additional expenses for land revenue collection — Rs. 1.26 crores
2. Annual Instalment of Principal and Interest on Z. A. C. Bonds — Rs. 2.16 crores (for 40 years)
3. Annual Instalment of Principal on R. G. Bonds — Rs. 2.60 crores (for 25 years)
4. Compensation to Landholders of *adhivasis* Rs. 1.30 crores (Annual average)
5. Annuities to Religious and Charitable *Waqfs* etc., — Rs. 0.35 crores (Perpetual)
6. Reimbursement of Local rates to District Boards — Rs. 1.20 crores (Perpetual)

Total — Rs. 8.87 crores
Grand Total — Rs. 10.13 crores

Source: Records available in the office of the U. P. Board of Revenue

Comparing it with the actual increase in land revenue collection to the tune of Rs. 10.57 crores in the year of accounting it can be concluded that *zamindari* abolition has not affected the State Government resources either way except that there has been a nominal increase of Rs. 0.47 crores in its net receipts. If on the other hand the increase in the gross land revenue demand that represents the total increase in claims, is taken into account the obvious conclusion is that *zamindari* abolition has been financially paying to the State Government since it has tended to increase its net claims by Rs. 4.44 crores (Rs. 14.57 crores minus Rs. 10.13 crores) annually.

This is, however, a rather superficial view of the matter since several disbursements made earlier are not included in the above calculations. Firstly, these estimates do not include the cash payments to intermediaries as compensation or rehabilitation grants or in lieu of the *adhivasi* land. These payments were heavy in the earlier years and it will be wrong to charge them in the account of the single year in which these were made. Secondly, these estimates do not include the additional cost incurred in earlier years on the additional staff required for the assessment of compensation to the ex-zamindars. It has been estimated at Rs. 0.63 crores per year and is likely to continue for another 3 years. The total cost in this respect may roughly be estimated at Rs. 10 crores. Thirdly, no credit has been taken in the above estimates for the change in resource position that might have been due to the receipt of Rs. 40 crores in the Zamindari Abolition Fund.

The impact of *zamindari* abolition on the public exchequer may be better studied through a calculation of interest on the total cost incurred on the scheme and changes in annual receipts and disbursements excluding payment of interest. For calculation of the annual interest charges a rate of 4 per cent would give a fair estimate as this is the rate at which the State Government has been raising long-term loans during this period. We are thus ignoring the lower rate of 2.5 per cent at which the Z.A.C. bonds have been issued and 0.0 rate at which R.G. bonds have been issued. This is justified on the ground that the real burden of raising the financial resources for payment of compensation etc. is represented by the current long-term rate at which the State could have raised such resources from the market rather than by the penal rates at which these resources might have actually been raised. The total increase in the financial liabilities or cost to the State Government for *zamindari* abolition is estimated as follows:

A. Gross:

1. Total Compensation for *Zamindari* Abolition   Rs. 70.00   crores
             (Estimated)
2. Total Rehabilitation Grant (Estimated)   Rs. 56.50   ,,
3. Total Payment for Land under *Adhivasis*   Rs. 12.00   ,,
4. Capitalised Value of Annuities (4 per cent)   Rs. 8.75   ,,

5. Total Administrative Expenditure for Assessment
   of Compensation etc.   Rs.   10.00   crores

                                    Gross Total Rs. 157.25   ,,

B. Less Receipts under Zamindari Abolition Fund   Rs.   40.60   ,,

C. Net Financial Cost   Rs. 116.65   ,,

D. Annual Cost
   (i) Interest @ 4% on Rs. 116.65 crores   Rs.   4.67   ,,
   (ii) Amortisation Fund @ 4% of Principal   Rs.   4.67   ,,

                                         Total   Rs.   9.34   ,,
   (iii) Loss in other revenues as estimated earlier Rs.   1.26 ,,

                                         Total   Rs.   10.60   ,,

E. Annual Additional Revenue
   (i) Gross Land Revenue Demand after *Zamindari*
       Abolition.   Rs.   21.73   ,,
       Less Land Revenue Demand before *Zamindari*
       Abolition.   Rs.   7.16   ,,

   (ii) Gross increase in Revenue Demand   Rs.   14.57   ,,

       (a) Less direct additional expenditure for
           land revenue collection   Rs.   1.26   ,,
       (b) Less reimbursements of local rates to
           District Boards   Rs.   1.20   ,,

                                         Total   Rs.   2.46   ,,

   (iii) Gross increase in Land Revenue Demand
        after necessary charges   Rs.   12.11   ,,
        Less loss in land revenue on account of 40
        years' stay of revenue revision @ 25% of
        demand in 1950-51   Rs.   1.79   ,,

   (iv) Net increase in Gross Land Revenue Demand Rs.   10.32   ,,

The above calculations show that the cost of *zamindari* abolition to the public exchequer has been Rs. 157 crores for about 45.5 million acres. This works out at about Rs. 34.50 per acre out of which payment to the intermediaries averaged Rs. 32.3 per acre. The annual cost of the scheme taking into account interest payment, contribution to an amortisation fund and loss in revenues of agricultural income tax and stamp works out at Rs. 10.60 crores.

Judged by the net increase in gross land revenue demand the State Government revenues have registered an increase of Rs. 10.30 crores. In making this calculation we have deducted an amount of Rs. 1.79 crores by which in our estimation the land revenue demand would have ordinarily increased had the revision of revenue settlements been not stayed for a period of 40 years under the Zamindari Abolition Act.

It is thus obvious that financially the State Government has not gained anything as a result of *zamindari* abolition. There is actually a small deficit of Rs. 0.30 crores per year. But the deficit is substantial if actual collections rather than gross demand are taken into account. There is a difference of nearly Rs. 4 crores in demand and collections and obviously this goes to make *zamindari* abolition an uneconomic measure in a narrow strictly financial sense of the term. In any case this tends to shift the burden of *zamindari* abolition on the other tax-payers who are mainly non-agriculturists.

Hence, steps should be taken to increase the amount of the Zamindari Abolition Fund so as to wipe out the total financial liability in the shortest possible period. Secondly, the wide gap between gross revenue demand and collections (nearly 20 per cent of the gross demand) be speedily reduced, particularly as it tends to impose an inequitable burden on the non-agricultural sector of the State's economy.

SECTION III

Chapter VIII

PATTERN OF LAND HOLDINGS AFTER ZAMINDARI ABOLITION

8.1. Area Held Under New Tenures

After *zamindari* abolition land is being held under three tenures, viz. *bhumidhari, sirdari* and *asami*. In the State as a whole one-third of the total area under holdings is held under *bhumidhari* tenures, a little less than two-thirds under *sirdari* and less than 1% by *asamis*. The relevant figures for the State and for the sample villages are given below:

TABLE NO. 20

CLASSIFICATION OF HOLDINGS AFTER ZAMINDARI ABOLITION

Type of Tenure	All Villages in U.P. (area in acres)	Percentage	Sample Villages (area in acres)	Percentage
1. *Bhumidhari*	1,51,18,697	33.28	22,599.42	36.95
2. *Sirdari*	2,99,52,635	65.92	37,954.03	62.05
3. *Asami*	3,62,961	0.80	611.44	1.00
Total	4,54,34,293	100.00	61,164.89	100.00

N.B. 1. The area figures both for the State as well as sample villages are the averages for three years, viz. 1957-58 to 1959-60.
    2. Figures for the State are computed from Rental and Holding Register of the Board of Revenue.

Within this broad distribution there are marked variations by administrative divisions and districts although not so much by natural regions. According to the Board of Revenue data for 1959-60, whereas 60.5% of the total area under holdings in Meerut division is under *bhumidhari*, less than 20% is under it in the divisions of Rohilkhand and Lucknow.

Classifying the districts by the percentage of area under *bhumidhari*, it is found that at the lowest rung is Rampur with only 8.5% of the total area under holdings as *bhumidhari* and at the top is Meerut with 71.08% of its area under it. In 8 out of 47 districts in which *zamindari* has been abolished *bhumidhari* tenure covers less than 20% of the total area under holdings, in 15 it ranges from 20% to 30%, in 9 from 30% to 40%, in another 9 from 40% to 50% and in the remaining 6 it varies from 50% to 71%. The districts in any of these classes do not fall into any regional pattern nor do they conform to any pattern regarding land utilisation or that of cropping. Thus districts with the highest percentage of area under *bhumidhari* include Meerut, Muzaffarnagar, Saharanpur and Dehradun in the west and Jaunpur and Varanasi in the east. Likewise districts with the least proportion of *bhumidhari* holdings include Rampur and Bareilly in the west, Hardoi and Sitapur in the central region and Bahraich in the east plain.

The proportion of the total area under *bhumidhari* holdings does not conform, as stated earlier, to either land use or pattern of cropping. The correlations with respect to such variables and the percentage of the area under *bhumidhari* in various districts were not found to be statistically significant. Various variables that we took into account in this respect were the proportion of the irrigated area, the intensity of farming as judged by the percentage of double cropped area and the extent of commercial farming, etc.

The variation in the extent of *bhumidhari* holding is equally marked in the sample villages. It varies from 90.70% in one village to 1.28% in another. But when these villages are grouped by natural regions these variations disappear. Such analysis discloses that *bhumidhari* extends to nearly 39% of the total area under holdings in the western region, 35% in the central, 38% in Bundelkhand and 37% in the eastern region. Likewise *sirdari* covers 60% to 62% of the total area under holdings in each region.

Out of 9,267 households with cultivated holdings, only 9,217 were found to be having a tenurial land right over their holdings. Classifying all households with land rights in the sample villages by their principal tenure (i.e. the tenure under which 50% or more of their holding is held) it is found that a little more than one-fifth of all such households (21.34%) are *bhumidhars*, a little more than three-fourths (77.86%) are *sirdars* and less than 1% (0.8%) are *asamis*. There are, however, certain marked variations by regions. In the western region and in Bundelkhand 27% of them are *bhumidhars* as compared to 17.9% in the eastern region and

12.4% in the central. The proportion of *sirdari* households is as high as 87% in the central region and only 71.7% in the western. *Asamis* every-where constitute less than 1.5% of the total households with land rights. These differences are, however, more marked by occupation and castes. Among the farmers 40% to 47% are *bhumidhars* and the remaining 53% to 60% are *sirdars*. As against this, only 7% of the households with land rights among agricultural labourers were classified as *bhumidhars*, while 76% were *sirdars* and 16% *asamis*. Nearly four-fifths of the tillers and others with land rights hold their holdings principally as *sirdars* and less than one-fifth as *bhumidhars*. Finally, one-third of the upper caste Hindu households with land rights hold their holding mainly as *bhumidhars* as compared to 16% of the intermediate caste Hindus and 11.5% of the scheduled caste households. The households of non-Hindus, mainly Muslims, with land rights have been classed as *bhumidhars* to the extent of a little more than 20%.

These data are significant in revealing that as we descend along the occupational ladder or the caste hierarchy the percentage of households having *bhumidhari* as their principal tenure declines. Since *bhumidhari* was acquired partly by conversion and partly by payment or purchase it is obvious that the less prosperous or the more indigent could not acquire *bhumidhari* interest to the same extent as farmers and the upper caste Hindus whose holdings at an average were larger, and who seem to have benefited relatively more in the process of conversion and had also a larger capacity to acquire it by payment than others.

8.2. METHOD OF ACQUISITION OF *Bhumidhari*

As stated earlier, *bhumidhari* rights have been acquired mainly in two ways: (1) by conversion of the unlet *sir* and *khudkasht* as well as groves of the former zamindars into *bhumidhari* and (ii) by acquisition through payment of a certain multiple of the rental to the Government. In so far as *bhumidhari* rights are transferable certain households may acquire and others may lose their *bhumidhari* rights through purchase and sale also. This last method affects only the households and has nothing to do with the total area under *bhumidhari* in the village or the State as a whole. According to the latest records available, out of the total area under *bhumidhari* 45% was acquired through conversion and 55% by payment of the multiple of rental. Just as there are marked differences from one administrative division to another with regard to the total area of holdings under *bhumidhari*, similarly the percentage of the *bhumidhari* area acquired by conversion varies from 28% of the total in Varanasi to 63% in Gorakhpur. In relation to the total area under agricultural holdings the percentage converted into *bhumidhari* varies from about 9% in Rohilkhand, Faizabad and Lucknow divisions to more than 30% in Meerut. In certain divisions the proportion of *bhumidhari* area acquired by payment of the multiple of rental to the total *bhumidhari* area varies from 37% in Gorakhpur to 72% in Varanasi.

Districtwise figures for area converted into *bhumidhari* and acquired by payment were not available from the revenue records. We have therefore estimated these areas on the basis of unlet *sir* and *khudkasht* and the groves at the time of *zamindari* abolition. It has been found that there are wide variations from district to district both in respect to the area converted in *bhumidhari* and acquired by payment.

(a) *Bhumidhari by Conversion*

The area converted into *bhumidhari* being limited to certain categories of land depended on historical factors, particularly the extent to which zamindars were cultivating their own holdings immediately before *zamindari* abolition. It is this which explains the wide variation district by district in the proportion of the total area of holdings converted into *bhumidhari*. In three districts the proportion of such area has been less than 5% of the total area under agricultural holdings, in 12 it varies from 5% to 10%, in 16 from 10% to 15%, in 5 from 15% to 20%, in 9 from 20% to 30% and in the remaining two it is more than 30%. Cultivators in all districts thus did not benefit equally, although the rule regarding conversion was the same for all. At one extreme are the districts of Rampur and Bahraich where only about 2% of the total agricultural area has been converted into *bhumidhari* and at the other is Meerut where more than 40% of the total has been so converted.

(b) *Bhumidhari by Payment*

An option was given to all tenants to acquire *bhumidhari* rights by payment of ten times their rental. This right has not been excercised equally in all districts and this is really intriguing, particularly as it was envisaged that nearly all former tenants shall excercise this right and eventually the State will have a single tenure, viz. *bhumidhari*. As against this expectation only 5% to 10% of the total area under holdings has been acquired by payment as *bhumidhari* in 6 districts; 10% to 15% in 12 districts; 15% to 20% in 13 districts; 20% to 30% in 10 districts;

and it is only in 6 districts that 30% or more has been so acquired. But even in these last there remains a considerable proportion of the total area under *sirdari* tenures.

An analysis of the factors determining acquisition by payment would be very helpful in throwing light on extension of *bhumidhari* tenure in future. In fact a doubt was entertained when the scheme for acquisition of *bhumidhari* rights was in the offing—that due to the non-availability of cash with the peasantry it will not be possible for many of them to acquire *bhumidhari* rights. But the collection of more than Rs. 30 crores as payment for acquisition of *bhumidhari* within a couple of years of the initiation of the scheme tended to discredit any hypothesis that *bhumidhari* acquisition will be inhibited on account of the poverty of the cultivators or lack of ready money.

We have not been able to relate acquisition by payment in various districts to any of the significant economic variables on which the capacity of the peasantry to pay generally depends. For this purpose we worked out correlations between the percentage of the total area under holdings acquired as *bhumidhari* by payment of the required multiple of rental and the percentage of the irrigated area, double cropping and commercial farming. The coefficient of correlation was nearly always found to be either statistically weak or insignificant as shown below:

COEFFICIENT OF CORRELATION

1. Percentage of the *bhumidhari* area acquired by payment to total area under holdings (*a*) and the percentage of the irrigated area to total cropped area. $r = +0.57$

2. (*a*) and percentage of double cropped area. $r = +0.17$

3. (*a*) and percentage of area under sugarcane, cotton and tobacco. $r = -0.13$

4. (*a*) and percentage of area under wheat. $r = -0.18$

The above evidence is inconclusive to prove the hypothesis that lack of cash has been the main limiting factor in acquiring *bhumidhari* rights on a larger scale. Had the lack of ready cash been the sole limiting factor there would have been a strong correlation between factors or variables on which higher agricultural income and cash receipts in agriculture depend and the proportion of area acquired as *bhumidhari* by payment.

A similar conclusion is forced on us by data relating to the sample households. All sample households were classified by us by the size of their total holdings and by the extent and method of acquiring *bhumidhari* rights. According to these data 50.49% of all the sample households have some *bhumidhari* area and it is significant to note that the larger the size of the holding, the greater is the proportion of households with *bhumidhari* rights. Thus, among landholders with 40 acres or more all households have *bhumidhari* while in the size group of less than 3 acres only about one-third have *bhumidhari*. But analysing the data collected, we find that the higher percentage of households with *bhumidhari* in larger holdings is not due to acquisition by payment but is accounted for by conversion. In the largest size group of 40 acres or more only 25% of the *bhumidhars* acquired their rights by payment while in the smallest size group 40% did so. This evidence is conclusive in proving that the households with larger holdings are *bhumidhars* to a greater extent than those with smaller holdings mainly on account of a larger percentage among them having been benefited by conversion rather than because more of them deposited cash money for acquiring *bhumidhari* rights.

A similar analysis has been made with regard to the area held by sample households. Our data discloses that about 45% of the total area held by the sample households is under *bhumidhari* tenure. It also reveals that the larger the size of holding the larger generally is the proportion of the area held as *bhumidhari*. But again what is more revealing is the fact that this larger percentage is obtained by conversion rather than by payment or acquisition. Less than 5% of the area held by households having less than 3 acres each has been obtained as *bhumidhari* through conversion while 40% to 50% of the total area was converted into *bhumidhari* in the case of the landholders having 20 acres or more. It is interesting to note that the larger the size of a holding excepting very large size holdings of 40 acres or more, the smaller is the proportion of the total area acquired as *bhumidhari* by payment of the prescribed multiple of rental or by purchase. Obviously, the large size holders had a larger capacity to pay ready cash than the small holders and yet they did not utilise this capacity for acquisition of larger *bhumidhari* rights.

We also tried to examine the hypothesis that acquisition of *bhumidhari* rights by payment of the prescribed multiple of rental or purchase may be due to a sort of a demonstration effect of the practice of peasant proprietorship. The argument runs like this that in areas or villages where even under the *zamindari* system cultivation was carried on on a substantial scale by owners, advantage was taken by those who had no such rights before to become owners or *bhumidhars* after *zamindari* abolition. But where such practice was limited there did not exist any such ground for emulation. In 21 out of 81 sample villages more than 30% of the area under holdings was converted into *bhumidhari* but it is only in three of these villages that a further 30% or more has been acquired as *bhumidhari* by payment. In as many as 8 of these villages less than 10% of the total area has been acquired as *bhumidhari* by payment. At the other extreme 17 villages were counted where *bhumidhari* has been acquired by payment in 30% or more of the area. It is only in three villages out of these that the proportion of *bhumidhari* by conversion was equally high. In nearly half or 8 out of these 17 villages *bhumidhari* by conversion accounted for less than 10%. In fact there is no correlation between these two proportions and our data do not support any hypothesis that acquisition of *bhumidhari* by payment has been an emulative step on the part of the agricultural households.

To sum up, our evidence has been inconclusive in isolating any economic factor accounting for the acquisition of *bhumidhari* rights by payment. It appears that the political and sociological factors were perhaps more important than the economic ones in the acquisition of *bhumidhari* rights. At the same time our data do not suggest directly that inadequacy of cash was a limiting factor in the acquisition of *bhumidhari* rights although there is considerable indirect evidence to prove this contention.

Firstly, the Reserve Bank of India's Rural Credit Survey Reports seem to indicate that in spite of increased agricultural output and better agricultural prices the cultivators generally do not have adequate cash savings. Secondly, our questionnaire for the intensive survey of the sample households contained an enquiry as to what limits further acquisition of *bhumidhari* rights. This reveals that only 35.5% out of 361 sample households having some *bhumidhari* rights held their entire holdings under *bhumidhari* tenure. The remaining 64.5% had such interest only on a part of their holdings. When these latter were asked as to why they did not acquire *bhumidhari* rights on their entire holdings as many as 78% of them replied that they had no money. Their responses are tabulated in Table No. 21.

A majority of the sample households having a holding (404, i.e. 52.81% of the total) had no *bhumidhari* tenure. They were asked to give their reasons for not acquiring *bhumidhari* rights over their holdings. There was no response from 53 out of these while out of the remaining 351, 130 or 37.04% replied that they were still thinking to acquire *bhumi-*

TABLE No. 21

DISTRIBUTION OF HOUSEHOLDS WITH *Bhumidhari* ON A PART OF THEIR
HOLDING ACCORDING TO REASONS FOR NOT ACQUIRING *Bhumidhari*
RIGHT ON THE ENTIRE HOLDING

Reasons for not acquiring *bhumidhari* rights on the entire holding.	No. of Households	% to Total
1. No money	181	77.68
2. No real gain	30	12.87
3. No change in status	10	4.29
4. Legal handicap	11	4.73
5. Others	1	0.43
Total	233	100.00

dhari rights while the remaining 221 or 62.96% of the non-*bhumidhari* tenure holders entering a response pointed out that they were either not in a position to acquire *bhumidhari* or they thought that it was not worthwhile. The largest number, i.e. nearly three-fourths, however, was of those who pointed out the lack of ready cash as the chief reason for not acquiring *bhumidhari*. The responses of these 221 households are tabulated below:

TABLE No. 22

DISTRIBUTION OF RESPONSES OF SAMPLE HOUSEHOLDS WITHOUT *Bhumidhari*
RIGHTS ACCORDING TO REASONS FOR NON-ACQUISITION OF SUCH RIGHTS

Reasons	No. of Households	% to total
1. No money	163	73.76
2. No real gain	44	19.91
3. Legal handicap	8	3.62
4. No change in status	4	1.81
5. Others	2	0.90
Total	221	100.00

To sum up, out of 765 sample households only 128, i.e. 16.7% had *bhumidhari* over their entire holding. Another 130 or 17.0% reported that they were still thinking or planning to acquire *bhumidhari* rights. The remaining 507 or 66.30% had either *bhumidhari* rights on a part of their holding or no such right at all. Out of these 53 did not give any response for not acquiring *bhumidhari* rights, but as many as 344 or nearly 76% of those responding stated lack of sufficient cash or money as the main reason for not acquiring *bhumidhari* right. A minority of 19 in all, not exceeding 4% of those who could still acquire *bhumidhari* rights, found legal difficulties in their way of acquisition of such rights. The remaining 91 constituting about 20% of such households stated that they were not interested in the acquisition of *bhumidhari* rights because there was no economic or social advantage to be obtained by such acquisition.

These responses indicate that the main bottle-neck experienced subjectively by the peasant in the further extension of *bhumidhari* tenure is the lack of ready cash for payment of the acquisition amount. This finding, however, is not consistent with our earlier analysis that does not establish any direct correlation between capacity to pay and acquisition of *bhumidhari*. How far the subjective estimate about the inadequacy of cash or savings is real is difficult to state on the basis of our present enquiry. One thing, however, is clear that many more would acquire *bhumidhari* and *bhumidhari* tenure would be extended over a larger area if the cultivators have enough cash to meet the demand for acquisition money. This is so as *bhumidhari* is a superior tenure in the estimation of the cultivating households.

The main advantages in acquiring *bhumidhari* tenure over *sirdari* land are the reduction in land revenue by 50% and the right to transfer. The latter becomes significant only when one thinks of a transfer and in so far as a tenure holder seldom thinks of transferring his holding in the immediate future it may not be valued much. As far as the reduction in revenue is concerned it means a return of 5% on the amount paid to the Government for acquisition. From the viewpoint of the peasant it is often a very low rate of return as he can always lend in the village at a much higher rate. To the Government, it means borrowing at a rate about 25% higher than the rate at which it can borow at present in the market. Strictly, in a narrow financial sense, therefore, further extension of *bhumidhari* may be advantageous neither for the Government nor for the peasant. But as a means of resource mobilisation from the agricultural sector its potential is definitely high.

In fact the difference between the whole and half of the revenue is too small a fraction of the gross produce to provide any incentive to a cultivator to pay 10 times the rental for acquisition of *bhumidhari*. Further, this difference tends to decline with every increase in production and prices.

8.3. INTERMIXING OF *Bhumidhari* AND *Sirdari* TENURES

On the basis of the main tenure over 50% or more of their holding, 21% of the tenure holding households in the sample villages have been classified as *bhumidhars*, 78% as *sirdars* and less than 10% as *asamis*. But all those classified as *bhumidhars* do not hold their entire holding as *bhumidhari*. It has been found that only half of them have *bhumidhari* rights over their entire holding and the other half over a part of it only. Similarly 26.36% of the *sirdars* have a part of their holding under *bhumidhari* tenures and 25.68% of the *asamis* also hold some *bhumidhari* tenure. In all 41.84% of the agricultural households with land rights have *bhumidhari* rights over a part or whole of their holdings.

The upper caste Hindu households constitute 26.63% of the total tenure holding households in the sample villages. Among them 56.37 per cent have *bhumidhari* rights over a part or whole of their holding. At the other extreme are the scheduled caste households among whom only a few have a right in land and among these latter only 31% have *bhumidhari* rights and not more than 4% over their entire holding. In between are the intermediate caste Hindus and the Muslims among whom 38% and 35% have *bhumidhari* rights respectively. *Bhumidhari* tenure appears to be correlated with caste hierarchy. As we ascend the caste ladder larger and larger percentages of the households enjoy *bhumidhari* tenure and as we descend superior tenure becomes limited.

Likewise, among the farmers 71 per cent of the households with a tenure have *bhumidhari*—16 per cent over their entire holding and 55 per cent over a part. Among the tillers the respective proportions fall to 40 per cent, 11 per cent and 29 per cent. These proportions fall further to 25 per cent, 4 per cent and 21 per cent respectively in regard to households of agricultural labourers with land rights. Households with land rights but whose main source of livelihood falls outside agriculture are in the most favourable position with 78 per cent among them having *bhumidhari*—11 per cent over their entire holding and 68 per cent over parts.

These differences emphasise that the superior tenure, viz. *bhumidhari* is not shared equally by all classes and castes in the village community and more favoured ones are obviously those with better economic opportunities and higher rank in the social scale. This was also the case before *zamindari* abolition and to the extent that former home-farm lands were converted into *bhumidhari* without payment the earlier inequality in the sharing of land rights has been continued by the very process of land reforms. To the extent *bhumidhari* has been acquired by payment of the prescribed multiple of the rent these were obviously the households and groups with a larger paying capacity than others who have taken advantage of the opportunity.

We have analysed further the data with regard to the size of *bhumidhari* holding per household having any *bhumidhari* interest among the sample households. This indicates that the average size of *bhumidhari* holding of a *bhumidhar* by principal tenure works out at 8.6 acres— 7.0 acres in the western districts, 5.7 acres in the central, 14.8 acres in Bundelkhand and 7.8 acres in the east. The *bhumidhari* holdings of households whose principal tenure is *sirdari* are on an average much smaller, i.e. only 2.5 acres—3.4 acres in the western districts, 2.7 acres in the central, 3.6 acres in Bundelkhand and 1.6 acres in the east. The average size of *bhumidhari* holding of *asamis* is only 0.77 acre. In general, unlike the *zamindari* rights, *bhumidhari* extends over a small area per household. But as discussed later, within this limit the *bhumidhari* tenure is not equitably distributed. Further, the average size of the *bhumidhari* holding of the upper caste Hindu households is more than thrice that of the scheduled caste households and twice that of the intermediate caste Hindu households. Similarly, whereas the average size of the *bhumidhari* holding of farmers is 14.4 acres, that of the tillers is about one-third at 5.4 acres, and that of the agricultural labourers only 0.64 acre. The non-agriculturists who hold *bhumidhari* rights have an average holding of 3.7 acres per household.

A further break-up of *bhumidhari* area of the sample households reveals that 83% of the *bhumidhari* land of a household is in the village of residence and 17% outside it. About one-fifth of the households with *bhumidhari* rights have less than 3 acres each but they hold only about 3% of the total *bhumidhari* area. On the other hand about 12% of households with *bhumidhari* rights hold 20 acres or more each but collectively they hold 45% of the total *bhumidhari* area. The bulk (68% of the total) hold between 3 to 20 acres and have among themselves a little more than half of the total *bhumidhari* area.

Among the sample households with *bhumidhari* rights 69% are tillers, 16% farmers, 7.5% agricultural labourers and the rest non-agriculturists. They hold 59%, 36%, 1% and 4% of the total *bhumidhari* area respectively.

8.4. AVERAGE SIZE OF HOLDINGS

The average size of holdings under all tenures of the sample households has been worked out by the principal tenure of a household and analysed separately by regions, occupations and castes. These figures indicate that the average size of a holding is a little more than 7.0 acres in the State as a whole—7.5 acres in the western districts, 5.2 acres in the central, 12.8 in Bundelkhand and 5.8 acres in the eastern districts. The average holdings of the farmers are the largest, being 17.6 acres and the smallest are those of agricultural labourers at 2.4 acres. The non-agriculturists have an average holding of 4.0 acres and the tillers of 6.8 acres. Again, the average holding of the upper caste Hindu households is the largest at 11.4 acres and that of the scheduled castes the smallest at 3.9 acres. The average holding of the intermediate castes works out at 5.8 acres and of Muslims at 6.6 acres. In each group the average size of a holding of *bhumidhars* is larger than that of the *sirdars* while the average size of holding of the *asamis* is the smallest. These latter, in fact, have tiny holdings and hence can seldom make the two ends meet by working on their holding alone. On the whole the average size of holding of *bhumidhars* works out at 10.5 acres, that of *sirdars* 6.1 acres and that of *asamis* only 2.7 acres.

8.5. DISTRIBUTION AND CONCENTRATION OF AREA HELD

The distribution of all households with the land rights in the sample villages according to size group of holdings and the area held by them indicates that 33 per cent of the households hold less than 3 acres each and share among themselves only about 7% of the total area under holdings. At the other end are some 7.25 per cent of the households each having a holding of 20 acres or more, who hold among themselves nearly 34 per cent of the total area under holdings. Those holding 40 acres or more constitute only about 2 per cent of the total households. But this small minority holds a little more than 14 per cent of the total area (See Table No. 17 in the Statistical Appendix.)

That agricultural land is still inequitably distributed among the tenure holders is a marked feature of all parts of the State. It is, however, much more inequitably distributed in the eastern than in the western districts. In the former some 6 per cent of the households at the top hold nearly one-third of the total area; while nearly 48 per cent of them having less than 3 acres each hold only 11 per cent of the land. In the western districts, on the other hand, the uppermost 8 per cent of the households have less than 30 per cent of the total area and those with a holding of less than 3 acres account for less than 24 per cent of the households. Bundelkhand and the central region fall in between these patterns.

A ceiling of 40 acres as adopted recently is not likely to release, on the basis of the data of our sample villages, more than 10 to 14 per cent of the total area under holdings—8 per cent in the western districts, 5.7 per cent in the central, 26.4 per cent in Bundelkhand and 18.22 per cent in the eastern districts. Since no account has been taken in this calculation of the differences in the quality of land and a rise in ceiling due to the number of persons above 5 in a household as provided in the ceiling legislation, the surplus area actually available in any case will not be much outside Bundelkhand.

Further, the above calculations are based on a break-up of the sample households into various regions without correcting the errors arising out of the differences in the proportions of *bhumidhars*, *sirdars* and *asamis* in the sample and the universe. To deal with this, distribution of all households with land rights in sample villages has been worked out on the basis of the data of the sample households. This, for obvious reasons, gives a more correct estimate of the distribution of the area comprised in holdings by size groups, although due to limited size of the sample it could not be worked out regionwise. These estimates reveal that only 1.3% of the households with land rights have 40 acres or more. They, however, hold among themselves 10.4% of the total area. About 10% of the total households with land rights have 15 acres or more but they have nearly two-fifths of the total area comprised in all holdings. At the other extreme about 32% of the total households with land rights have less than 3 acres each and their total holdings account for no more than 7% of the total area. Distribution of land is more inequitable among *bhumidhars* than among *sirdars*. It is obvious that any future land reform measures will have to take these inequalities into account. (See Tables 18 and 19 in the Statistical Appendix.)

The diagrams Nos. 3-6 at the end of this chapter show the land concentration curves and bring out the inequality in the distribution of the area held by households.

8.6. RENT AND REVENUE AFTER *Zamindari* ABOLITION

For the quinquennium 1946 to 1951 the land revenue demand was calculated at about Rs. 7 crores and the rental demand at Rs. 18.50 crores. After *zamindari* abolition, *bhumidhars* and *sirdars* pay land revenue direct to the State and the *asamis* pay rent to their principal tenure holders. The annual revenue demand works out at Rs. 20.15 crores for the year 1954-55 to 1956-57 and at Rs. 20.90 crores for the years 1957-58 to 1959-60. The incidence of land revenue and rent per acre for the different tenure holders works out as follows:

TABLE NO. 23

INCIDENCE OF LAND REVENUE AND RENT PER ACRE FOR DIFFERENT
TENURE HOLDERS

Year	Revenue per acre in Rs.			Recorded Rent per acre in Rs.
	Bhumidhari land	*Sirdari* land	All land	*Asamis*
1954-55	2.44	5.33	4.36	3.73
1955-56	2.50	5.63	4.63	3.81
1956-57	2.51	5.64	4.64	4.07
1957-58	2.53	5.67	4.64	3.81
1958-59	2.47	5.69	4.60	3.69
1959-60	2.53	5.77	4.67	3.68

N.B. Figures compiled from the *Revenue Administration Reports.*

The above figures make it obvious that land revenue since *zamindari* abolition has been increasing not merely because of the increase in the area assessed to land revenue but also on account of an upward trend in the revenue rates per acre. Since there has been no revision of land revenue settlement the revenue per acre could not be increased either on *bhumidhari* land or on the *sirdari* area. The little increase in the average rates, therefore, is due to the increase in the rates on the marginal land or the areas newly assessed. Another thing that is obvious from the above data is that the land revenue per acre paid by *sirdars* is on an average 128% higher than that paid by the *bhumidhars*. The *sirdars* thus in practice continue to pay as land revenue to the Government what formerly they paid as rent to the zamindars. Therefore, *zamindari* abolition, as far as the rental burden is concerned, has brought little relief to them. The *asamis*, who occupy less than 0.4% of the total area under holdings, pay rent at a lower rate than that paid by the *sirdars*. This does not reflect any advantage to them in respect of rent but seems to be mainly an index of the inferior quality of land occupied by them.

There are still considerable differences in the land revenue per acre in the various districts and divisions. These are practically the same as existed before *zamindari* abolition since no revision of land revenue settlement has taken place since then. These do not necessarily reflect differences in the productivity of land but have often been occasioned by the different dates at which settlements have been made in different districts. A revision of settlement is perhaps necessary to remove these inequalities. The relevant data with regard to land revenue per acre before and after *zamindari* abolition are given below:

TABLE NO. 24

LAND REVENUE PER ACRE BEFORE AND AFTER ZAMINDARI ABOLITION

Division	1946-47		Revenue per acre 1959-60 in Rs.	Present Revenue per acre as % of that in 1946-47	Present Revenue per acre as % of rent per acre in 1946-47
	Rent per acre in Rs.	Revenue per acre in Rs.			
1. Meerut	5.77	2.45	5.04	205.7	87.34
2. Agra	5.33	2.09	4.95	236.8	92.87
3. Rohilkhand	5.32	1.80	5.19	288.3	97.55
4. Allahabad	5.16	2.10	4.69	223.3	90.89
5. Jhansi	2.60	1.06	2.41	227.4	92.69
6. Varanasi	3.69	1.44	4.20	291.7	113.82
7. Gorakhpur	3.44	1.74	3.87	222.4	112.50
8. Lucknow	6.23	2.00	5.61	280.5	90.04
9. Faizabad	5.54	2.03	5.67	279.3	102.34
All	4.88	1.87	4.67	249.7	95.69

N.B. Figures calculated from the data taken from the respective *Revenue Administration Reports.*

The data in the above table make it clear that before *zamindari* abolition rent and revenue per acre differed between one division and another and it will be too bold to assume that all this could be accounted for only by differences in soil productivity of the various parts of the State.

Land revenue per acre even after *zamindari* abolition continued to differ from division to division. This has been due to the postponement of land revenue settlement for a period of forty years. At the same time land revenue per acre has more than doubled in all divisions and at least in four divisions it has practically trebled. This disparate increase may be accounted for by differences in the proportion between *bhumidhari* and *sirdari* area in various divisions as well as by the differences in the increase in the total area under holdings which in all the divisions taken together has increased from 36.38 million acres to 45.31 million acres, i.e. by 24.5%. Further the new area brought under holdings appears to have been assessed at rates that have tended to raise the overall average. Thus, in Varanasi and Rohilkhand divisions where the current land revenue per acre has registered the sharpest increase as compared to the land revenue per acre before *zamindari* abolition, the area under holdings has increased by 31% and 29% respectively. But this does not explain all cases as in Jhansi where land revenue per acre is still the least and has registered one of the least increases the area under holdings has gone up by nearly 49%.

The current land revenue per acre for the State as a whole is about 95% to 96% of the former rental demand per acre. In no division it is less than 87% of the pre-*zamindari* abolition rent per acre. But in three divisions, viz. Varanasi, Gorakhpur and Faizabad it exceeds the rent per acre under the *zamindari* system.

These disproportionate increases in land revenue per acre, the wide disparity in its incidence in different divisions of the State and the differences in the land revenue paid by *bhumidhars* and *sirdars* can seldom be correlated to differences in soil fertility or its productivity. All this calls for a revision of land revenue assessment mainly with a view to distribute its burden equitably among cultivators.

DIAGRAM No. 3

CONCENTRATION CURVES SHOWING AREA
HELD BY ALL HOUSEHOLDS BY REGIONS
AFTER ZAMINDARI ABOLITION

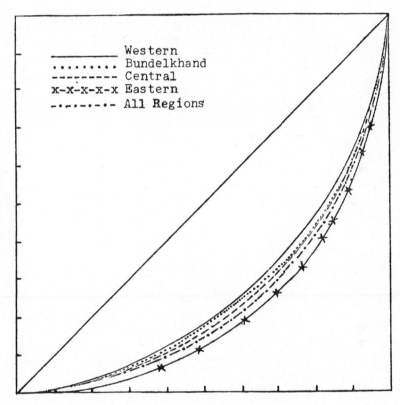

Cumulative percentages of Households

DIAGRAM NO. 4

CONCENTRATION CURVES SHOWING DISTRIBUTION OF AREA
HELD BY ALL HOUSEHOLDS WITH LAND RIGHTS
AFTER ZAMINDARI ABOLITION

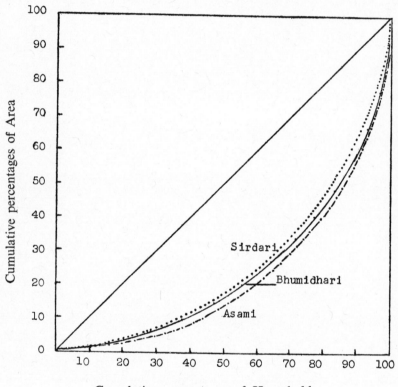

Cumulative percentages of Households

DIAGRAM No. 5

CONCENTRATION CURVES FOR *Bhumidhari* AREA
HELD BY SAMPLE HOUSEHOLDS BY REGIONS

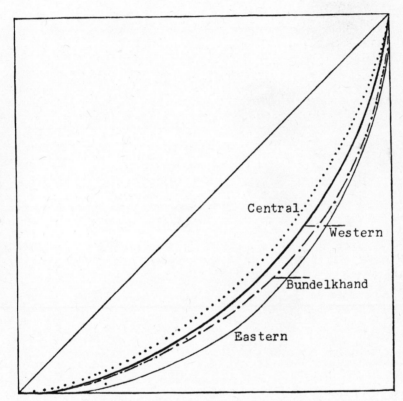

Cumulative percentages of Area

Cumulative percentages of Households

DIAGRAM No. 6

CONCENTRATION CURVES SHOWING DISTRIBUTION
OF *Bhumidhari* AND *Sirdari* AREAS
AMONG SAMPLE HOUSEHOLDS

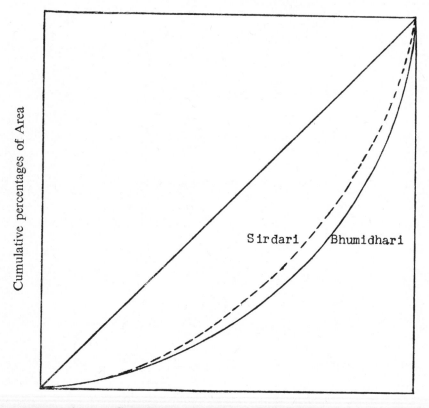

Cumulative percentages of Households

CHAPTER IX

CULTIVATED HOLDINGS AFTER ZAMINDARI ABOLITION

9.1. Total Area Held and Total Area Cultivated

In a previous chapter we have given estimates about the size and distribution of land holdings of the area held by the rural households under various tenures as *bhumidhars*, *sirdars* or *asamis*. In the following table are given figures about the total area held and the total area cultivated by the sample households:

TABLE No. 25

Distribution of Sample Households by Principal
Tenures and the Area Held and Cultivated by Them

Principal Tenure	No. of Households	Area Held (acres)	Area in Cultivated Holding (acres)	Excess of Cultivated Area over Area Held (acres)	% of the Excess to Cultivated Area
1. *Bhumidhars*	235	2,469.81	2,463.97	−5.84	−0.24
2. *Sirdars*	406	2,459.50	2,492.69	+33.19	+1.33
3. *Asamis*	74	198.98	398.89 ⎫		
4. Non-Tenure Holders	50	—	172.45 ⎬ +372.36	+65.17
Total	765	5,128.29	5,528.00	399.71	7.81

The area cultivated by the sample households exceeds the area held by them by 7.8%.[33] It is significant to note that not only is there no such

[33] More or less a similar result was reported by the N.S.S.—8th Round, July 1954 to March 1955. In this a distinction was made between the area operated and the area owned. For U.P. the sample revealed a 5.29% to 7.01% excess of operated area over area owned. The N.S.S. Report on land holdings remarked that this might be due to several reasons, e.g. some owners of the land operated by rural households were residing in urban areas or in Pakistan, the effect of non-household ownership etc. The Report, however, did not discuss these points in detail nor did it examine any other explanation for the excess. Ownership holding was taken to constitute a holding

excess in the case of *bhumidhars* but it is negative by a small margin. In the case of the *sirdars* also it is not substantial and is limited to 1.3% only. But it is as high as 65.17% in case of the remaining cultivating households which include *asamis* as well as others who are found to be cultivating land without having any recorded tenurial rights over the area cultivated by them. For *asamis* alone the excess is 50.12% of the total area cultivated by them. It is further found that while there is only a minor difference in the area held and cultivated by the sample households of *bhumidhars* and *sirdars* taken together there are many individual cases even among them where there are substantial differences.

Several explanations suggest themselves for this excess of the cultivated area over the area held, the most apparent being that the area cultivated by such a household may be held by a household outside our sample. This is, however, not tenable since in the area held by a household we have included all land held by him under any tenure whatsoever, i.e. permanent or otherwise. The excess in fact refers to the area cultivated by a household without any apparent legal right over it. This may be due to the occupation of land without consent of the principal tenure holder. But this can also be due to the wrong entries in the revenue records or to what is a more prevalent practice, i.e. sub-letting or share-cropping of land without it being shown as such in the village papers. Nearly all the non-tenure holder cultivators and *asamis* are agricultural labourers who have under their cultivation petty holdings. Very often they have no legal right recorded as such to the holding that they cultivate. Obviously this is an evasion of law against sub-letting. But this class of people is apparently made to agree to suffer this handicap since they cannot get otherwise the little land that they cultivate. On the whole our findings indicate that nearly 7% to 8% of the total cultivated area (the excess of cultivated area over area held) is still surreptitiously sub-let mostly to the agricultural labourers on the condition that no such entry of sub-letting will be made in the revenue records. Out of the 50 sample households who were found to be cultivating a holding without any tenurial right to it 48 or 96% were reported to be agricultural labourers.

with the right of permanent heritable possessions with or without the right to transfer such titles. It was distinguished from actual physical possession of land. For U.P. it thus included all *bhumidhari* and *sirdari* holdings only and land in the possession of a person with no ownership right on that plot and holding it from the principal holder was counted in the holding of the permanent tenure holder. An operational holding on the other hand was defined as all land that was "directed or managed by one or more persons, alone or with the assistance of others, without regard to titles, size or location." (p. 8)

The plight of the agricultural labourers can be seen from the fact that out of some 14,000 rural households in the sample villages nearly 2,300 (79 share-croppers +2,207 casual and regular farm workers), i.e. 16.43% were those of agricultural labourers. Out of them only 445, i.e. less than one-fifth (19.35%) had some land to cultivate. Again, out of 149 sample cultivating households of agricultural labourers as many as 48 (32.22%) were found to be without any legal right to their holdings. Applying this ratio to all households of agricultural labourers in the sample villages it is calculated that only 13.13% of such households had a recorded right over their holding although as many as 19.35% had a cultivated holding.

9.2. Cultivating Interests of Various Groups

The average area cultivated by a *bhumidhar, sirdar, asami* or non-tenure holder in each region, occupation and caste has been taken to be the same as revealed by the sample of 765 households selected for intensive study. These averages have been multiplied by the number of all cultivating households in the sample villages in the corresponding category to arrive at the overall estimates of cultivated area and its distribution. The average size of a holding in any particular category is thus based on the actual number of cultivating households enumerated in the sample villages in that category and the cultivated area estimated as above.

In accordance with the principal land tenure of a household over its holding, it is found that in the sample villages as a whole 21% of the cultivating households are *bhumidhars*, 77% *sirdars*, less than 1% *asamis* and about 0.5% those who have no recorded land rights over their holdings. The *bhumidhars* cultivate 32% of the total cultivated area and the *sirdars* about 67%. Less than 1% of the total is cultivated by the *asamis* and the non-tenure holders.

The average size of a cultivated holding varies from 3.45 acres to 10.48 acres. It is the largest in the case of the *bhumidhars* at 10.48 acres followed by *sirdars* and *asamis* at 6.13 and 5.39 acres respectively. The non-tenure holders have the smallest size of average holding, i.e. 3.45 acres. The average for all cultivating households in the State has been worked out at a cultivated holding of 7.08 acres.

The average size of a cultivated holding for all cultivating households is the largest in Bundelkhand at 10.93 acres followed by the western region at 7.97 acres, the eastern region at 5.49 acres and the central region at 5.19 acres. The average holding in Bundelkhand is almost twice as large as in the central and the eastern districts and nearly 33% larger than in the western districts. But there is also a difference in the quality and general fertility of soil and if that is taken into account the cultivating households in Bundelkhand may not be found to be comparatively better off than elsewhere in this respect. At the same time it is obvious that there is a heavy pressure of population on soil in the central and eastern districts. On the other hand agriculturists in the western districts have on an average larger and better quality holdings than those in the eastern districts.

Most of the households engaged in cultivation cultivate their fields by their own labour. They constitute 84% of the total cultivating households in the sample villages while those cultivating mainly through hired labour, viz. farmers account for only 6% of the total. Out of the remaining 10% nearly half are agricultural labourers and the other half are primarily engaged in non-agricultural occupations. The farmers, however, cultivate nearly two and a half times as much area as available to them on the basis of their proportion in the total cultivating households while the agricultural labourers have less than 2% of the total area under their cultivation. Thus even now 15% of the total cultivated area is cultivated through permanent hired labourers while another 2.5% is under the cultivation of the non-agriculturists. This of course excludes the area cultivated by share-croppers or sub-let.

For obvious reasons the average size of holding of the farmers (16.69 acres) is more than two and a half times as large as that of the peasants who cultivate with their own labour (6.59 acres). The average size of holding of agricultural labourers is the smallest at only 2.38 acres which is even smaller than that of the non-agriculturist at 3.52 acres.

The Hindus constitute the bulk of the cultivating households and the non-Hindus who are mainly Muslims are less than 9%. The latter have a pattern of holding which is very much similar to that of the intermediate caste Hindus. Combining these two groups together it is found that in the sample villages the upper caste Hindus account for 28.5% of all cultivating households, the scheduled caste for 13.8% and the rest for 57.7%. But the first have under their cultivation 43% of the total cultivated area, the scheduled caste 8% and others 48%. In consequence, the average holdings of the upper caste Hindus are the largest at 10.78 acres and those of the scheduled caste the smallest at 4.27 acres. The average holding of the others i.e. intermediate caste Hindus and the the Muslims works out at 5.97 acres.

To sum up, the average size of a cultivated holding is small at about 7.0 acres and within this limit there are certain groups whose holdings are large with the result that the less privileged groups particularly the scheduled caste Hindus and the agricultural labourers have petty holdings that seldom suffice even for their miserably low standard of living. A redistribution of land, if undertaken seriously, while correcting some of the individual inequalities, will go a long way in doing justice and in equalising opportunity for entire social groups. (See Table No. 20, Statistical Appendix for summary data.)

9.3. AVERAGE SIZE AND DISTRIBUTION OF CULTIVATED HOLDING

Data in respect of the sample households reveal that the average size of holdings varies from region to region, occupation to occupation and caste to caste. Further, in each region, occupation or caste group the holdings of the *bhumidhars* are the largest and those of non-tenure holders the smallest. *Sirdars* have usually larger holdings than those of *asamis* but smaller than those of the *bhumidhars*.

TABLE NO. 26

AVERAGE SIZE OF CULTIVATED HOLDINGS OF SAMPLE HOUSEHOLDS
AFTER ZAMINDARI ABOLITION
(*Figures in acres*)

Variables	Bhumidhars	Sirdars	Asamis	Non-Tenure Holders
A. Region				
i. Western	8.99	7.60	7.63	5.39
ii. Central	6.62	5.09	3.78	3.74
iii. Bundelkhand	19.08	7.96	7.50	—
iv. Eastern	9.68	4.65	1.75	1.65
B. Occupation				
i. Farmers	22.14	11.83	—	—
ii. Peasants	8.44	6.12	2.80	—
iii. Agri. Labourers	0.79	1.59	5.81	3.53
iv. Miscellaneous	5.88	3.03	1.14	1.41
C. Caste				
i. Upper caste Hindus	14.80	9.08	8.09	12.00
ii. Scheduled	8.16	3.83	4.15	1.58
iii. Others	7.91	5.57	5.80	5.61
Total	10.48	6.13	5.39	3.45

Our data further reveal that the cultivated area is not only unequally distributed as between various social groups and economic classes but within each category there is a marked inequality in land distribution between different households. (See Tables No. 21 and 22 in Statistical Appendix and Diagram No. 7.) Thus, while *bhumidhars* have the largest size of holdings, 37% among them cultivate less than 5 acres each and have less than 10% of the area cultivated by all the *bhumidhars* taken together. Less than one-fifth among them (17.87%) cultivate more than half (54.12%) of the total area under their cultivation. More or less the same is true about *sirdars* among whom the proportion of households having less than 5 acres to cultivate is even larger at 56.16% and they cultivate only 22% of the total area cultivated by the *sirdars*. On the other hand 8% of the households of *sirdars* cultivate 31% of their total cultivated area. The *asamis* and non-tenure holders are in no better position and even among them, while the average size of holding is small, a few cultivate more than one-fourth of the total area cultivated by this group. The summary data are given in the following table:

TABLE No. 27

ESTIMATES OF PERCENTAGE DISTRIBUTION OF ALL CULTIVATING
HOUSEHOLDS IN SAMPLE VILLAGES AND OF THE AREA
CULTIVATED BY THEM AFTER ZAMINDARI ABOLITION
BY SIZE OF CULTIVATED HOLDINGS AND
BY PRINCIPAL TENURES OF HOUSEHOLDS

Tenure	Bhumidhars		Sirdars		Asamis	
Size of Holdings	House-holds	Cultivated Area	House-holds	Cultivated Area	House-holds	Cultivated Area
Less than 5 acres	36.60	9.33	56.16	22.28	56.75	25.86
5 to 15 acres	45.53	36.55	35.71	46.81	36.49	50.45
15 acres & above	17.87	54.12	8.13	30.91	6.76	23.69
Total	100.00	100.00	100.00	100.00	100.00	100.00

Tenure	Non-Tenure Holders		All	
Size of Holdings	Households	Cultivated Area	Households	Cultivated Area
Less than 5 acres	82.00	42.81	51.89	18.25
5 to 15 acres	14.00	27.75	37.39	43.55
15 acres & above	4.00	29.44	10.72	38.20
Total	100.00	100.00	100.00	100.00

DIAGRAM NO. 7
CONCENTRATION CURVES FOR CULTIVATED HOLDINGS
OF ALL HOUSEHOLDS IN THE SAMPLE VILLAGES
ACCORDING TO THEIR TENURIAL STATUS
AFTER ZAMINDARI ABOLITION

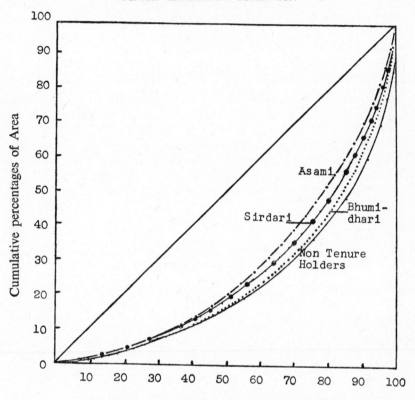

Cumulative percentages of Households

At the same time it is obvious that the distribution of cultivated holdings has become less inequitable after *zamindari* abolition than it was before it. This may be due to the fact that as the larger estates were broken up the smaller cultivators gained. This effect was, however, very limited since large-scale cultivation by the zamindars was very limited and the redistribution of their cultivated holdings has not taken place to any substantial extent. Diagrams No. 8, 9 and 10 portray the situation in this respect while relevant figures are given in Tables No. 23 and 24 in the Statistical Appendix.

DIAGRAM NO. 8

CONCENTRATION CURVES FOR CULTIVATED HOLDINGS
BEFORE AND AFTER ZAMINDARI ABOLITION
(ALL HOUSEHOLDS)

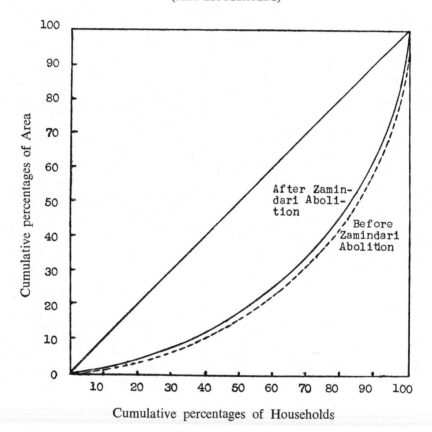

DIAGRAM NO. 9

REGION-WISE CONCENTRATION CURVES FOR CULTIVATED
HOLDINGS OF SAMPLE HOUSEHOLDS BEFORE
ZAMINDARI ABOLITION

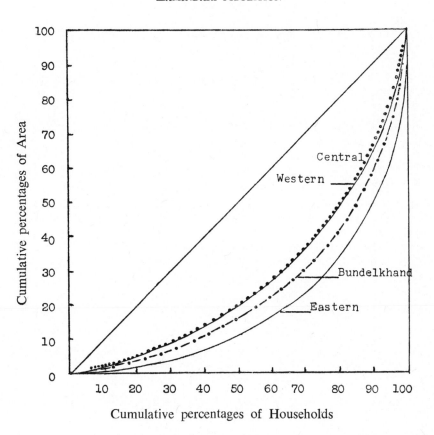

Cumulative percentages of Households

DIAGRAM No. 10

REGION-WISE CONCENTRATION CURVES FOR CULTIVATED
HOLDINGS OF SAMPLE HOUSEHOLDS AFTER
ZAMINDARI ABOLITION

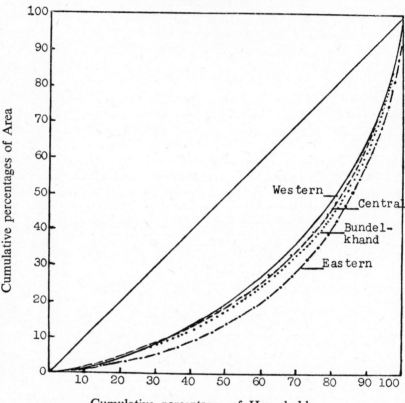

Cumulative percentages of Households

9.4. TYPE OR METHOD OF CULTIVATION

All cultivating households and the area cultivated by them have
been classified into three types according to whether they cultivate their
holding with their own labour and that of their family members, or
mainly through hired labour or through share-croppers. This last excludes those share-cropping arrangements under which a person sub-lets
his holding on a crop-sharing basis and transfers the holding for culti-

vation to a share-cropper. It has been found that as the size of holding increases the proportion of labour-cultivated area also increases. Secondly, *bhumidhars* in each size group cultivate their holdings to a larger extent through outside labour than the *sirdars* and the latter more than the *asamis* and the non-tenure holders. Finally, there are marked regional differences as in the western and the central districts personal culti-vation is carried on to a larger extent than that in the Bundelkhand and eastern districts.

To illustrate, personal cultivation by *bhumidhars* is limited to 58% of their total cultivated area whereas it is as high as 83% in the case of *sirdars* and more than 99% in the case of others. The differences cannot simply be explained by the larger size of holdings of the *bhumidhars* than those of the *sirdars* and others. In fact in each size group we find the same pattern. The area cultivated by *bhumidhars* in the size group of less than 3 acres is under their personal cultivation to the extent of 84% while the proportion in the same size group rises to 91% in case of *sirdars* and 100% in case of others. Similar differences are found in all size groups up to 30 acres. It is only after 30 acres that the proportion of the area cultivated through outside labour is more in the case of *sirdars* than that of the *bhumidhars*. Holdings above 40 acres are culti-vated by all mainly through hired labour. (See Table 25 in Statistical Appendix.)

Taking all cultivators together, it is found that while holdings of less than 5 acres are cultivated to a very small extent through outside labour their proportion increases sharply with an increase in the area of the holdings above 10 acres. More than 90% of the holdings below 10 acres are cultivated personally with little assistance from outside labour but the proportion of such cultivation is reduced to less than 76% in holdings of 15 acres to 30 acres, to 59% in holdings of 30 to 40 acres and is nil in holdings of 40 acres and above.

In all, 75% of the total cultivated area is cultivated by the cultivating households mainly through their own labour, 21% mainly through hired labour and about 4% through share-croppers.

The regional differences are obvious from the fact that in the size group of 3 to 10 acres, 95% are cultivated personally in the western districts, 88% in the central districts, 91% in Bundelkhand and only 82% in the eastern districts. In the next size group of 10 to 20 acres these differences between the western and the eastern districts are even more marked. In the former case 87% of the area is personally cultivated while it is only 40% in the latter. Cultivation mainly through hired labour in this size group is limited to less than 10% in the western districts while it is as high as nearly 60% in the eastern districts. In the next size group of 20 to 40 acres 85% of the area is cultivated personally in the western districts and 92% in Bundelkhand but it is only 32% in the central districts and nil in the eastern districts. All cultivation in the eastern districts in holdings above 20 acres is carried on mainly through outside labour whereas this situation is reached in the western districts and in Bundelkhand only after a limit of 40 acres. Nearly 53% of the area in holdings of 20 acres or more in the central districts is also labour-cultivated and another 15% share-cropped. There is thus ample evidence to indicate that not only are the larger holdings cultivated to a greater extent through hired labour but the point at which such cultivation begins is much lower in the central and in particular in the eastern districts than in the western districts or Bundelkhand. (See Table No. 26 in Statistical Appendix).

On the basis of sample data the cultivating households have been classified into four groups, viz. small, medium, large and very large. The first have a holding of less than 5 acres and account for 52% of the total but have under their cultivation only 18% of the total cultivated area. To the extent of 90% of their holdings they cultivate through their own labour, the labour-cultivated area being less than 3% and the share-cropped area is more than 7% of the total cultivated holding.

The cultivating households having medium holdings of 5 to 15 acres constitute less than two-fifths (37.39% of the total cultivating households). They have under their cultivation a little more than two-fifths (43.55%) of the total cultivated area. A little more than 87% of the area under their cultivation is personally cultivated, 11% through hired labour and about 2% through share-croppers.

The large cultivators are those whose holdings are of 15 to 40 acres. These account for a little less than 10% of the total households although they have under their cultivation nearly 30% of the total cultivated area. Their holdings are cultivated to the extent of only 72% through their own labour or that of their family members. A little more than 23% of the area under their cultivation is cultivated mainly through hired labour and another 4% through share-croppers.

Finally, there are the rich cultivators with very large holdings of 40 acres or more who do not cultivate any portion of their holding through their own labour. In their case cent per cent of their holdings are cultivated through hired labour. (See Table No. 27 in Statistical Appendix).

9.5. COMPARISON WITH ZAMINDARI PERIOD

In the following section a comparison about the average size and distribution of cultivated holdings has been made between the post-*zamindari* abolition and the pre-*zamindari* abolition period. The estimates refer to the years 1950-51 and 1959-60 and are based on the intensive sample household enquiry. Apart from *zamindari* abolition there has been another significant factor, viz. the increase in rural population that has had its own impact in this field. According to the preliminary estimates of the census of 1961 the rural population of the State has increased by 17.74% during the last 10 years.

The average size of cultivated holdings of the sample households was found to be about 7 acres in 1959-60 as compared to more than 7.5 acres in 1950-51. This represents a decrease of nearly 7.0% in the average size of cultivated holdings which is obviously smaller than the rate of increase of population. This difference can be explained largely by the increase in the area under cultivation which is reported to be of the order of 11.48 per cent for the State as a whole during 1950-51 and 1959-60. Deducting this from the rate of growth of population (17.74%— 11.48%) it is obvious that the average size of a cultivated holding, assuming little change in the occupational structure of the rural population and the average size of their household, was likely to decline by more than 6 per cent in the State as a whole. Our sample survey reveals a decline of more or less the same order in the average size of the cultivated holdings.

There are, however, considerable differences by tenures in the average decline in the size of holdings during this period. These may have been due to the impact of *zamindari* abolition as the land reforms tended to protect certain types of cultivators more than others. We may therefore state that these differential declines in the average size of cultivated holdings alone rather than the general decline can be attributed to measures of land reforms. (For figures see Table No. 28 in the Statistical Appendix).

According to the data of sample households the average size of the cultivated holdings of *bhumidhars* has registered a decline of more than 15% as compared to that of 5.5% in case of *sirdars*. Similarly, the average size of the cultivated holdings of the farmers has declined by nearly 24% as compared to a fall of less than 1% in that of the peasants. At the same time the average size of the cultivated holdings of agricultural labourers has been reduced to practically half. It appears that the process of *zamindari* abolition and subsequent land legislation has resulted in a definite break-up of large-size farming and it is this which accounts for the considerable decrease in the average size of cultivated holdings of the *bhumidhars* and farmers. This is true in spite of the adoption of large-scale farming to a certain extent by the former zamindars on the eve of *zamindari* abolition.

It also appears that farming through hired labour has been at a discount and some of the area formerly so cultivated is now cultivated by households who cultivate it mainly through their own labour.

The extent of the break-up of large-scale farming and cultivation of land so released by households cultivating their holdings through their own labour has differed in various regions and has affected the various caste groups differently. At the one extreme is the eastern region where before *zamindari* abolition many cultivating households did not touch the plough and carried on their cultivation through hired labour or share-croppers. The decline in the average size of holdings in the eastern districts has been more than 23%.

Comparing the average size of cultivated holdings by caste groups it is found that the holdings of the scheduled caste households have registered the least decline and those of the upper caste Hindus the maximum. This can again be explained by the same factors, viz. the break-up of the larger holdings and the discount on cultivation through hired labour. The former is very clear from our estimates of the distribution of all cultivating households and the area comprised in the cultivated holdings by size groups before and after *zamindari* abolition. Our data reveal that the very large-size cultivating households, i.e. those having a cultivated holding of 40 acres or more have declined both in absolute numbers as well as in their proportion to the total number of cultivating households. What is even more significant is that the total area under their holdings has declined by about 35% while the aggregate holdings of those within the size group of a cultivated holding of less than 15 acres has registered an increase of 9% to 10%. Obviously there has been a change in the distribution of cultivated holdings which has benefited the small and medium cultivating households. The summary data in this respect are given in Tables No. 29 & 30 in the Statistical Appendix. Along with the break-up of large-sized cultivated holdings there has been a decline in the labour-cultivated holdings and a corresponding increase in holdings cultivated either personally or through share-croppers. The total area under labour-cultivated holdings has declined by nearly 13% and the labour-cultivated holdings now account for some 21% of the total area in the holdings of all the cultivating house-

holds in the sample villages as compared to nearly 25% in the year immediately preceding *zamindari* abolition. The area under personally cultivated holdings has increased by nearly 7% and accounts for more than
75% of the total in contrast to less than 72% before *zamindari* abolition.
(See Table No. 31 in the Statistical Appendix).

9.6. EMPLOYMENT OF PERMANENT OUTSIDE LABOUR

Agricultural labourers are hired on a permanent and seasonal
basis as well as on daily and casual basis. During the peak season of
sowing and harvesting even ordinary cultivators, who cultivate their
holdings mainly with their own labour and that of their family members,
need help of outside labour. On these occasions the cultivators either
employ casual agricultural labourers on wages payable in cash or kind
or invite neighbouring cultivators to work with them on a mutual
exchange basis. This type of casual employment constitutes the main
employment for agricultural workers.

Apart from such employment another source of employment for
agricultural labourers is cultivation by farmers with the help of permanent farm servants. All farmers, however, do not always employ
agricultural labourers on their fields on a yearly or permanent basis.
Many among them cultivate their holdings by employing casual or
daily labour. Still others cultivate with the assistance of share-croppers.
Again, farmers are not the only employers of permanent farm servants.
In certain cases peasants also employ outside agricultural labour on a
yearly basis, particularly when their holdings are too large to be cultivated with the help of family labour alone. In such cases family labour
has to be supplemented by outside labour more or less on a permanent
or continuous basis.

Out of 765 sample households in our sample 62 employed permanent
farm servants before *zamindari* abolition and 58 at present. Not only
has the total number of households employing permanent outside labour
declined in this period but what is even more significant the total number
of farm servants so employed has declined from 139 to 94. The distribution of sample households employing permanent farm servants in
cultivating their holdings is given in Table No. 32 in the Statistical
Appendix.

Zamindari abolition appears to have a direct bearing on the increasing insecurity of employment of agricultural labourers. It has
meant the disappearance of large estates that employed permanent

farm-servants, a breaking-up of the large farms employing such labour in anticipation of the ceiling on agricultural holdings, and adoption of personal cultivation by at least some who formerly depended on hired labour under an apprehension that otherwise they might lose their land. Other factors too have been in operation, e.g. the decline in the size of holdings. Our data reveal that the average number of permanent farm servants per household giving such employment has declined from 2.24 before *zamindari* abolition to 1.62 at present. Among the farmers the proportion of permanent farm servants to the total number of their households was 68% before *zamindari* abolition and it is a little less than 58% at present. On an average 8 permanent farm servants were employed per 100 cultivating households before *zamindari* abolition. This number is now reported to be only 7.6.

CHAPTER X

SUB-LETTING AND SHARE-CROPPING

10.1. SUB-LETTING BEFORE ZAMINDARI ABOLITION

Under the *zamindari* system, as pointed out earlier, sub-letting was resorted to a considerable extent both by zamindars in respect of their home-farm land and by tenants. Besides, some land was occupied without the consent of the principal tenure-holder and the position of such occupants was insecure as that of the sub-tenants. Another category of sub-tenants was that of tenants of rent-free grantees. In all the sample villages taken together the area occupied by all these types of sub-tenants aggregated to 4,450 acres or 8.04% of the total area under holdings in the years immediately preceding *zamindari* abolition. The extent of sub-tenancy varied from 5.8% of the area under holdings in the central region to 6.0% in the western districts, 9.22% in Bundelkhand and 11.5% in the eastern districts. The extent of sub-tenancy of various types varied from region to region as is clear from the following figures:

TABLE No. 28

PERCENTAGE DISTRIBUTION OF THE AREA UNDER VARIOUS TYPES
OF SUB-TENANTS BY REGIONS IN THE SAMPLE VILLAGES
BEFORE ZAMINDARI ABOLITION
(*Average for the years* 1948-49 *to* 1950-51)

Type of sub-Tenancy	Western	Central	Bundelkhand	Eastern	All
1. *Sir* and *Khud-kasht* Tenants	17.55	14.09	54.06	40.02	36.13
2. Sub-tenants	37.90	31.97	23.40	15.51	25.91
3. Occupiers without consent	35.44	50.91	16.49	43.04	32.78
4. Tenants of Rent-free Grantees	9.11	3.03	6.05	1.43	5.18
Total	100.00	100.00	100.00	100.00	100.00

N.B. All the four types above were sub-tenants in the sense of having no secure rights and in all these cases these principal tenure-holder is other than the cultivator. Type 2 referred to the tenants of holdings sub-let by tenants.

10.2. SUB-LETTING AFTER ZAMINDARI ABOLITION

Zamindari abolition has resulted in the creation of permanent tenures for most tenants and at the same time the current land legislation has very much restricted the right to sub-let. Even then nearly 2% of the total area under holdings in the sample villages was found to be under the occupation of different types of sub-tenants. The total area under sub-tenants declined from 4,450 acres before *zamindari* abolition to 1,130 acres and is now no more than a quarter of its previous size. The decline has, however, not been uniform—it being greater where the incidence of sub-tenancy was high under the *zamindari* system and lower where it was low. The relevant information is summarised in the following table:

TABLE No. 29

PERCENTAGE OF THE AREA UNDER SUB-TENANCY TO THE TOTAL AREA
UNDER HOLDINGS IN THE SAMPLE VILLAGES

Region	Before *Zamindari* Abolition	After *Zamindari* Abolition
1. Western	6.05	2.10
2. Central	5.84	2.37
3. Bundelkhand	9.22	1.11
4. Eastern	11.53	2.22
Total	8.04	1.87

Out of a total area of 1,130 acres under sub-tenancy (recorded in Part II of Khatauni) only 233 acres or 20.6% of the total is held by *asamis* of handicapped tenure holders and *sirdars* who are eligible to sub-let. Another 10.24% was held by *adhivasis*. But as much as 69% was held by *asamis* without consent. This latter indicates the wide extent of land hunger and is an index of disputes over land. The region-wise figures of the sample villages are given in Table 33 of the Statistical Appendix.

10.3. INCIDENCE OF SUB-TENANCY IN THE AREA HELD BY THE SAMPLE HOUSEHOLDS

The sample households were asked to give information about the area cultivated by them as sub-tenants before and after *zamindari* abolition. For this purpose the area cultivated by them as share-croppers was not to be included in it and thus they were to report only the area held by them as *shikmi* before *zamindari* abolition and as *asami* after *zamindari* abolition. Such area was to be reported irrespective of the entry in the village records. The relevant information is summarised in the following table:

TABLE NO. 30

SUB-TENANCY CULTIVATION BY THE SAMPLE HOUSEHOLDS BEFORE AND AFTER ZAMINDARI ABOLITION

Region	Before Zamindari Abolition			After Zamindari Abolition		
	Cultivated Holdings Area (acres)	Area held as *Shikmi* (acres)	% of 3 to 2	Cultivated Holdings Area (acres)	Area held as *Asami* (acres)	% of 6 to 5
1	2	3	4	5	6	7
1. Western	2,530.31	167.41	6.61	2,449.03	77.64	3.18
2. Central	818.85	9.14	1.12	853.78	8.14	0.95
3. Bundel-khand	1,074.78	69.50	6.49	1,070.90	6.72	0.63
4. Eastern	1,507.12	48.45	3.22	1,154.29	9.01	0.79
Total	5,931.06	294.50	4.96	5,528.00	101.51	1.83

The above figures indicate that the incidence of sub-tenancy cultivation was as high as 4.96% before *zamindari* abolition. This has now been reduced to 1.83% denoting a decline of more than 65% in the incidence of sub-tenancy. This may generally measure the extent to which the incidence of sub-tenancy has declined since the abolition of *zamindari*.

A limitation of the above measure is that this does not include the area cultivated as share-croppers or held without consent. For the sample villages as a whole we found, as indicated earlier, that nearly 70% of the area under sub-tenancy is held by *asamis* without consent. Information collected from the sample households did not reveal any area held by them without consent. This was so for the obvious reason that none would like to report holding any area without consent of the principal tenure holder. We had, however, information about the area cultivated by the sample households as share-croppers. Actually, such area is cultivated by the latter as sub-tenants. But as the Act does not recognise such cultivation as sub-tenancy cultivation it was reported under the cultivation of the principal tenure holders. This should, however, be added to the area cultivated as *asamis* to find out the correct incidence of sub-tenancy.

The sample households reported that 534.55 acres were cultivated by them as share-croppers before *zamindari* abolition and 479.17 acres after it. Adding this to the area held by sample households as *shikmis* and *asamis* we find that the total area under sub-tenancy was 829.05 acres before *zamindari* abolition and 580.68 acres after it. This works out at 13.98% of the total area cultivated by the sample households before *zamindari* abolition and 10.50% at present. The decline in the incidence of sub-tenancy has thus been only 29.95% rather than more than 66% as revealed by figures of *shikmi* and *asami* cultivation only.

10.4. Tenancy of Share-cropping

The fact is that *zamindari* abolition has had little effect on share-cropping and the Act has left a back door open for sub-tenancy cultivation through this practice. We had asked the sample households two distinct questions, viz. (*a*) how much area do they get cultivated through share-croppers; and (*b*) how much area do they themselves cultivate as share-croppers. There is a wide difference between the two figures as the sampe households reported that before *zamindari* abolition they cultivated through share-croppers only 223.35 acres although they themselves cultivated as share-croppers 534.55 acres. Similarly, the respective figures for the period after *zamindari* abolition, that is the year of enquiry, were 172.05 acres and 479.17 acres. The percentage decline in the area cultivated as share-croppers is thus 10.36 only. The proportion of the area cultivated as share-croppers to the total area comprised in the cultivated holdings of the sample households amounted to 9.01% before *zamindari* abolition and stands at 8.67% at present. Accordingly, the decline in the incidence of share-cropping has been only 3.77%. This tenacity of the proportion of share-cropping is a serious weakness of the existing land system.

It is rather interesting to note that land is cultivated under the share-cropping system not simply by the *asamis* or the petty-size holders but by many others. As many as 22.6% of the total sample households were found to have taken land from others on a share-cropping basis and these included even those cultivating on an average a holding of 10 acres or more. It appears that since the right to sub-let has been greatly restricted households resort to sub-letting through share-cropping and such arrangement is acceptable even to medium and large-size cultivators because it is only through this method that they can add a little more to their existing holdings. The system is, however, pernicious as it allows sub-letting indirectly in a manner that results in the exploitation of the actual tiller of the soil more than possible under direct sub-letting. The wide-spread extent of this practice can be seen from the following table:

TABLE No. 31

DISTRIBUTION OF SAMPLE HOUSEHOLDS AND THE AREA TAKEN BY
SHARE-CROPPERS AFTER ZAMINDARI ABOLITION BY
SIZE OF HOLDINGS AND TENURES

Size of Holdings	Households			Area		
	Total	Taking land as share-croppers	% of 3 to 2	Total holding (acres)	Holding taken as share-croppers (acres)	% of 6 to 5
1	2	3	4	5	6	7
Less than 3 acres	239	74	30.96	381.26	66.98	17.57
3 to 10 acres	362	81	22.38	1,957.94	237.13	12.11
10 to 20 acress	109	12	11.01	1,389.07	74.80	5.38
20 to 40 acres	44	6	13.64	1,142.14	100.26	8.78
40 acres and above	11	0	0.00	657.59	0.00	0.00
Total	765	173	22.61	5,528.00	479.17	8.67
PRINCIPAL TENURE						
1. *Bhumidhars*	235	8	3.40	2,463.97	11.49	0.47
2. *Sirdars*	406	61	15.02	2,492.69	83.62	3.35
3. Others	124	104	83.87	571.34	384.06	67.22
Total	765	173	22.61	5,528.00	479.17	8.67

Land is taken as share-croppers mainly by small and petty cultivators and particularly by *asamis* and non-tenure holders. Nearly 31% of the cultivators having 3 acres were reported to be cultivating as share-croppers and 18% of their total holding was held as such. The proportion of the cultivators cultivating as share-croppers declines with an increase in the size of holding. Only 3.4% of the *bhumidhars* were found to have taken land as share-croppers and less than 0.5% of their total cultivated holdings were held as such. On the other hand 15% of the *sirdars* and 84% of the *asamis* and non-tenure holders were found to be cultivating some land as share-croppers and the area held by them under this system amounted to 3.4% and 67.2% of the total area of their holdings respectively.

CHAPTER XI

EJECTMENTS AND LAND TRANSFERS

11.1. EJECTMENTS BEFORE ZAMINDARI ABOLITION

According to the data given in the *Revenue Administration Reports* of the State tenants began to be ejected at twice the normal rate in the years 1944 and 1949. This was presumably in anticipation of the *zamindari* abolition scheme—the U.P. Legislative Assembly having adopted a resolution for the abolition of the rights of the intermediaries on August 8,1946. Later the State Government stopped most of the ejectments with the result that in the years immediately preceding *zamindari* abolition the area from which tenants were ejected was very limited. The relevant figures are given in Table No. 34 in the Statistical Appendix.

During the ten years preceding *zamindari* abolition tenants were ejected from more than a million acres of land (1,040,482.71 acres). This represented 2.37% of the total area under holdings.

11.2. EJECTMENTS AFTER ZAMINDARI ABOLITION

According to the data of the sample villages for the years 1951-52 to 1959-60 there have been in all 462 cases of ejectment covering an area of 800.36 acres. Nearly half of these cases (228) and nearly 70% (556.96 acres) of the area was accounted for by the sample villages of Bundelkhand. On the whole the area over which ejectments have taken place amounts to nearly 1.5% of the total holdings area in sample villages. This is rather a high figure, particularly in view of the fact that the rate of ejectment varied between 0.03% to 0.15% of the holdings area in the four years immediately preceding *zamindari* abolition in the State as a whole. In so far as ejectments are now confined largely to cases of disputed or unauthorised possession this unchanged rate of ejectment may be taken to be an index of a transitory phase.

11.3. SALES, PURCHASES AND GIFTS AFTER ZAMINDARI ABOLITION

Bhumidhari land can be transferred through sale or gift. Table 35 in the Statistical Appendix gives figures for all transfers of land whether through sale or gift, in the sample villages for a period of nine years since *zamindari* abolition.

During the nine years after *zamindari* abolition a little less than 4% of the total area of the cultivated holdings has been transferred through sale at an average price of Rs. 324.86 per acre. Transfers through gifts have been rather insignificant. A larger proportion of area has been sold and purchased in the sample villages of the western districts than else-where. Actually, sales and purchases of land involved nominal areas in the first three years after *zamindari* abolition and it was in 1956-57 that the peak was reached. The area sold and purchased during the last three years has again been not much. On the whole, it may be stated that although transferability is enjoyed under the *bhumidhari* tenure the extent to which land is actually sold and purchased in any single year is often less than a fraction of one per cent. As against this we find that the sample households sold a total of 79.90 acres and purchased a total of 122.86 acres of land during this period. The discrepancy between the area sold and purchased by the sample households may be due to the fact that sales and purchases are not confined within the sample household and some part of the land purchased by the sample households has obviously been sold by households outside our sample. The total area held by the sample households aggregated to 5,128.29 acres in 1959-60. The total area sold by the sample households in nine years thus amounted to 1.56% of their holdings.

Relatively speaking, a larger proportion of their holdings area has been sold by the poor and small holders having less than 5 acres each than by the medium or the large-size tenure holders. Further, land has been sold by all classes of tenure holders mainly for meeting social and domestic expenditure which accounts for sale of nearly 66% of the total area sold. Another 11% of the area sold is for litigation and a further 10% for repayment of old debts. For about 13% of the area sold it was stated that the tenure holders found their holdings unmanageable. The relevant figures are given in Table No. 36 and 37 in the Statistical Appendix.

11.4. Land Purchases by Sample Households

A total area of 122.6 acres has been reported to have been purchased by the sample households during a period of nine years since *zamindari* abolition. This amounts to 2.4% of the total area held by them in 1959-60.

A little more than half of this total area was purchased by the medium-size cultivators (landholders of 5-15 acres) and a little less than one-third by the small and petty cultivators holding less than 5 acres each. The large-size holders, particularly those with a holding of 40 acres or more, purchased little land. It is also found that land was purchased mainly by those whose holdings were mainly under the *bhumidhari* tenure. Further, it has been revealed that land has largely been purchased for cultivation or farming rather than for residential purposes. The relevant figures are given in Table No. 38 and 39 in the Statistical Appendix.

11.5. PRICE PER ACRE OF LAND

The average price per acre of land sold in the sample villages has varied widely from region to region, village to village, year to year and even from plot to plot. We give below the average prices per acre received by the sample households for the area sold by them:

TABLE NO. 32

AVERAGE PRICE PER ACRE OF LAND SOLD IN
THE SAMPLE VILLAGES

(Amount in Rs)

Year	Western	Central	Bundelkhand	Eastern	Total
1951-52	—	—	—	985.92	985.92
1952-53	—	—	—	1,313.35	1,313.35
1953-54	1,875.00	—	115.27	1,814.10	1,217.83
1954-55	557.14	696.93	146.13	703.20	520.53
1955-56	467.36	497.81	101.83	1,189.70	520.77
1956-57	102.65	530.14	128.67	10,43.33	154.55
1957-58	436.16	522.91	188.08	797.72	468.52
1958-59	294.10	299.75	340.60	1,024.84	386.61
1959-60	387.68	310.94	72.86	319.79	337.53

The average prices per acre have varied to such an extent that it is difficult to speak of any trend in the market price of agricultural land Nothing can be inferred from the above figures except that each plot seems to have its own price that depends on the amount at which the bargain is struck between the buyer and the seller at the time of the actual transaction.

11.6. CULTIVATORS' OPINION WITH REGARD TO TRANSFERABILITY OF LAND RIGHTS

Enquires were made from the sample households whether all tenure holders should be given the right to transfer their holdings.. As many as 503 out of 765 households i.e. 65.75% were in favour of giving such rights to all tenure holders while the remaining 262 or 34.24% were opposed to this proposal. More than half of those in favour of the right of transferability being given to all (54.47%) supported the idea as in their opinion it would enable a landholder to transfer his land at the time of real necessity. Another 27.63% felt that this would release some land for the landless labourers; 15.71% favoured it for obtaining credit and the remaining 2.19% thought that transferability is desirable as it would result in the reduction of the size of large holdings. As against this those who opposed it did so because they feared that it would make credit too cheap, result in further sub-division of holdings, and might render several of the present holders landless.

CHAPTER XII

IMPACT ON LAND USE, FARM EQUIPMENT, ETC.

12.1. LAND USE

It is difficult to assess the impact of *zamindari* abolition on land use since during the same period certain other forces, particularly increased irrigation, community development, land reclamation programme, etc. have also been at work. Besides these the increasing pressure of population must have been exercising its own weight in extending the limits of cultivation and in changing the pattern of cropping. We, however, record the changes that have taken place during this period although these cannot be ascribed directly to *zamindari* abolition. The percentage distribution of land by its use in the whole State and in the sample villages is given in Table No. 40 of the Statistical Appendix.

The data relate to the averages for the three years before *zamindari* abolition and for three years after it ending with 1959-60. Certain marked changes have taken place during the last eight or nine years. Firstly, the area under cultivation including current fallow has increased by more than 8%. Secondly, the area under old fallow and culturable waste has decreased—the former by 41% to 60% and the latter by about one-fifth. Thirdly, the area of land under "graveyards and otherwise barren" has decreased by about 20%. Finally, the area under groves has declined by about one-eighth. It is obvious that the sub-marginal land has been brought under cultivation and there is evidence to indicate that the abolition of *zamindari* system has at least indirectly contributed in this process. It is significant to note that while cultivation has been extended to old fallows and culturable waste land, some of the orchards have also been cut and ploughed. The former zamindars were allowed to hold their groves as their *bhumidhari* area and they found it paying to sell the wood at high prices and convert later their groves into cultivated field.

A region-wise break-up of the distribution of land in sample villages shows that the trend has been more or less the same in all regions. There are, however, certain regional differences of degree only which are accounted for by differences in the pressure of population on land. To illustrate, the cultivated area including current fallow increased by 14%

in Bundelkhand and by less than 5% in the eastern region. This is due to the fact that in the latter 79% of the total area was already under cultivation before *zamindari* abolition while it was so to the extent of only 51% in the former. It is for the same reason that the culturable waste and grove and the otherwise barren land have been reduced to a larger extent in the eastern districts than in Bundelkhand.

The intensity of land use varies in the sample villages from region to region. In all the sample villages taken together 21% of the net cultivated area is double-cropped. But it varies from 4.2% in the sample villages of Bundelkhand to 23.9% in those of the central region, 28.5% in the western region and 31.6% in the eastern region. Likewise, nearly 30% of the total cropped area is irrigated in all the sample villages taken together. But it is as low as 7.1% in Bundelkhand and as high as 41% in the western region. The corresponding figures for the central and eastern regions are 29.94% and 35.78% respectively.

12.2. INTENSITY OF CULTIVATION

Intensity of cultivation may be calculated by the percentage of the total cropped area to the net cultivated area, i.e. by the proportion of the double-cropped area to the net cultivated area. For the State as a whole it has been found that the index of intensity of cultivation has increased from an average of 124.83 for the years 1948-49 to 1950-51 to an average of 127.05 for the years 1957-58 to 1959-60 as indicated in the following table:

TABLE No. 33

INTENSITY OF CULTIVATION IN U.P. BEFORE AND
AFTER ZAMINDARI ABOLITION

Particulars	Average area in lakh acres	
	Before Z.A. (1948-49 to 1950-51)	After Z.A. (1957-58 to 1959-60)
Net Cultivated Area	379.10	404.82
Double-Cropped Area	94.12(24.83)	109.52(27.05)
Total Cropped Area	473.22	514.34
Index of Intensity of Cropping	124.83	127.05

Source: *Season & Crops Reports of U.P.*
N.B. Figures within brackets indicate the % of double-cropped area to net cultivated area.

The present index of intensity of cultivation in the sample villages is 128.52 in the western districts, 123.92 in the central, 104.21 in Bundelkhand and 131.61 in the eastern districts.

12.3. Changes in Crop Pattern

Changes in the crop-pattern for the State as a whole have been worked out on the basis of averages for three years before *zamindari* abolition and for three years ending with the year 1959-60. There has been a general increase in all crops and in the total cropped area with the exception of barley and pulses. The area under wheat has increased by 16% and that under paddy by 12%. The area under millets has increased by less than 1% while that under barley declined by 8% and that under pulses by 2.5%. But the largest increase under foodgrains has been in the cultivation of maize whose area has increased by about 34%. The area under the six principal food crops taken together has increased by about 7% only and their proportion to the total cropped area has fallen from 72.65% before *zamindari* abolition to 71.56% after *zamindari* abolition.

In contrast there have been substantial increases in the cultivation of commercial crops—the area under sugarcane has increased by 31%, under oilseeds by 36%, potatoes by 37% and fibres by nearly 40%. There is little doubt about the increasing commercialisation of farming. But this has been due probably more to changes in the agricultural price structure and other factors than due to *zamindari* abolition.

The crop pattern, however, differs from region to region. In the sample villages of the western districts 21% of the total cropped area is under wheat which occupies only 1% in Bundelkhand, 10% in the central and 12% in the sample villages of the eastern districts. Paddy, on the other hand, occupies 30% of the total cropped area of the sample villages of the eastern districts but only 1.4% of that in Bundelkhand, 7.6% in the central and 6.7% in the western districts. The inferior food crops—millets and *bejhar*—occupy 75% of the cropped area of the sample villages of Bundelkhand, 34% of that in the western districts, 36% of that in the central and 8% of that in the eastern districts. The commercial crops consisting of sugarcane, potatoes, oilseeds and fibres occupy less than 3% of the total cropped area of Bundelkhand, but more than 10% of that in the western districts, nearly 8% of that in the central districts and about 4.5% in the eastern districts.

12.4. EXPENDITURE ON FARM EQUIPMENT AND IMPROVEMENTS

Zamindari abolition was expected to create conditions for improved and better farming. Improvements may lie in using new and improved varieties of seeds, compost making, the use of chemical fertilisers, adoption of scientific farm practices and better crop rotations on the one hand and in the accumulation and use of more and better farm equipment including improved breeds of cattle on the other. An attempt was, therefore, made to collect information on these aspects. Improvements were classified into three categories: (1) Permanent improvements in land including construction of a well—masonry or non-masonry, a tube-well, construction of an irrigation or drainage-channel and raising of permanent fencing; (2) Purchase of new farm equipment consisting of livestock as well as dead-stock such as a persian wheel, improved implements like tractors, iron ploughs, cane-crushers and chaff-cutters, etc. and improved breeds of bullocks; (3) Adoption of improved farm practices including use of improved varieties of seeds, fertilisers and new crop rotations, etc.

The first two classes of improvements are in the nature of capital formation on the farm and it is these which have been analysed in this section. These consist of permanent improvements in land as well as purchase of new farm equipment. They are calculated at the cost price as reported by the respondents concerned, who reported the actual expenditure incurred by them in monetary terms and did not make any allowance for the cost of their own labour or the materials used by them in construction. Hence, the value of new capital formation is not its total value as it excludes these latter nor is it the historical cost of such improvements as no allowance has been made for depreciation, nor still its market value. It simply represents the money expenditures incurred by the cultivators on these items. Table No. 41 in the Statistical Appendix summarises the relevant data in this regard.

In a period of eight years since *zamindari* abolition the sample households spent an average of Rs. 282 per household on purchasing new farm equipment, particularly bullocks and on permanent improvements in land. But it is only about half of the total sample households who have reported to have incurred such expenditure. If we take into account only such households as incurred such expenditure, the expenditure per household amounts to Rs. 561.

The expenditure per household as well as the proportion of households making improvements varies from region to region. In the sample villages of the western districts 61% of the sample households were reported to have made improvements and purchased new stock as compared to 37% in the central region, 51% in Bundelkhand and 44% in the eastern districts. Such expenditure per household was the highest in Bundelkhand at Rs. 442 and the lowest in the central districts at Rs. 183. The corresponding figures for the western and eastern regions are Rs. 350 and Rs. 200 respectively.

There are similar differences in the principal tenure of a cultivator. Among the *bhumidhars* 63% were reported to have made improvements in contrast to 47% among *sirdars* and 44% among others. This expenditure averaged Rs. 446 per household of *bhumidhars*, Rs. 228 of *sirdars* and Rs. 150 of 'others'. Underlying these differences, however, are in essence the differences in the size of holdings. The larger the size of a holding the larger is such expenditure per household. Thus cultivators with a holding of less than 3 acres each have incurred an expenditure of Rs. 80 per household, those with a holding of 3 to 10 acres Rs. 229 per household, those with a holding of 10 to 15 acres Rs. 553 and those with a holding of 20 acres or more Rs. 970 or so. Apparently the value of improvements per household made by the large-size holders is more than 12 times that made by petty cultivators of holdings of 3 acres or less.

But it does not mean that such expenditure on a per acre basis has been more on the large-size holdings than on the small-size holdings. On the contrary, it works out at Rs. 50 per acre for the smallest size of holdings and only Rs. 16 per acre for holdings of 40 acres or more. Relevant figures are given in the following table:

TABLE No. 34

EXPENDITURE ON NEW FARM EQUIPMENT AND PERMANENT IMPROVEMENTS IN LAND MADE BY THE SAMPLE HOUSEHOLDS FROM 1952-53 to 1959-60.

Size of Holdings	Total No. of Households	Area Cultivated (acres)	Total Expenditure (Rs.)	Expenditure per House- hold (Rs.)	Expenditure per Acre of Land Cultivated
Less than 3 acres	239	381.26	19,230	80	50
3 to 10 acres	362	1,957.94	83,055	229	42
10 to 20 acres	109	1,389.07	60,222	553	43
20 to 40 acres	44	1,142.14	42,808	973	37
40 acres and more	11	657.59	10,623	966	16
Total	765	5,528.00	215,938	282	39

Nearly three-fourths (76.35%) of the total expenditure has been on the purchase of improved breeds of bullocks. Another one-sixth has been on the improvement of irrigation facilities including construction of *pucca* and *kutcha* wells or irrigation channels and installation of persian wheels. Another 5% of the total has been on the purchase of chaff-cutters. Figures about the expenditure on various items by the sample households are given in Table No. 42 of the Statistical Appendix.

It is, however, difficult to say that all such expenditure has been met out of current agricultural incomes. On the other hand there is some evidence to indicate that at least part of it has been financed through sale of assets or even fresh borrowings. We have not, however, collected any direct evidence on this point, though there is some indirect evidence to this effect. Firstly, some of the sample households have disposed of a part of their property and livestock during this period and secondly, a part of the compensation and rehabilitation grant has been utilised towards farm improvements and purchase of implements or livestock. The sample households reported a total receipt of Rs. 4,920 from sale of assets: Rs. 2,200 from sale of houses, Rs. 1,845 from sale of bullocks and other cattle, Rs. 475 from carts, Rs. 150 from jewellery and Rs. 250 from miscellaneous other assets. Such receipts, however, amount to about 2 per cent of the total expenditure on improvements.

12.5. Utilisation of Compensation and Rehabilitation Grant

The sample households reported a total receipt of Rs. 54,373 as compensation and rehabilitation grant up to 1959-60. Its utilisation on various items was given as follows:

TABLE No. 35

Utilisation of Compensation & Rehabilitation Grant by the Sample Households up to 1959-60

Items	Amount in Rs.	% to Total
1. Permanent Improvements	5,985	11.01
2. Purchase of Bullocks & Milch Cattle	3,370	6.20
3. Purchase of Agricultural Implements	200	0.37
4. House Construction	1,000	1.84
5. Repayment of Debts	596	1.10
6. Marriages	14,365	26.42
7. Daily Maintenance	9,947	18.29
8. Miscellaneous	10,660	19.60
9. Cash or Unutilised	8,250	15.17
Total	54,373	100.00

About 18% of the total grant received by the sample households was utilised by them for making either permanent improvements in their holdings such as construction of wells or for purchase of livestock and implements. Another 15% was reported to be still available with them as unutilised or cash. But the bulk of it, i.e. 26.4% of the total was utilised for performing social ceremonies, particularly marriages, and another 18% was used for daily maintenance. On the whole the payment of compensation and rehabilitation grant in cash or in the form of bonds that the cultivators could easily dispose of at low prices did not help much in capital formation in agriculture.

APPENDICES

APPENDIX I

A NOTE ON SAMPLE VILLAGES

LOCATION

As stated earlier there are 81 sample villages. These are spread over 27 parganas in an equal number of *tehsils* in 25 districts of the nine administrative divisions as shown below:

TABLE No. 1

DISTRIBUTION OF SAMPLE VILLAGES ACCORDING TO DIVISIONS

Name of Division	Number of			
	Districts	Tehsils	Parganas	Villages
1. Meerut	3	3	3	9
2. Agra	3	3	3	9
3. Rohilkhand	3	3	3	9
4. Allahabad	3	3	3	9
5. Jhansi	3	3	3	9
6. Varanasi	3	3	3	9
7. Gorakhpur	3	3	3	9
8. Lucknow	1	3	3	9
9. Faizabad	3	3	3	9
Total	25	27	27	81

All the villages under study are situated in the interior of the districts.

AREA OF VILLAGES

The total area of a sample village varies from 156 to 2,908 acres in the western region, 61 to 1,154 acres in central, 169 to 1,115 acres in eastern and from 1,257 to 6,716 acres in the Bundelkhand region. The distribution of villages according to total village area is given in the following table:

TABLE No. 2

DISTRIBUTION OF SAMPLE VILLAGES ACCORDING TO AREA

Total Village Area	Number of Villages in Regions				
	Western	Central	Eastern	Bundelkhand	Total
Less than 200 acres	1	2	3	—	6
	(3.70)	(11.11)	(11.11)		(7.41)
200 to 500 ,,	8	9	13	—	30
	(29.63)	(50.00)	(48.15)		(37.04)
500 to 1000 ,,	7	4	8	—	19
	(25.93)	(22.22)	(29.63)		(23.45)
1000 acres & more	11	3	3	9	26
	(40.74)	(16.67)	(11.11)	(100.00)	(32.10)
Total	27	18	27	9	81
	(100.00)	(100.00)	(100.00)	(100.00)	(100.00)

The average area per village works out at 1,045.54 acres in western, 616.06 acres in central, 491.33 acres in eastern and 3,131.31 acres in Bundelkhand region as against 997.12 acres for all sample villages.

CULTIVATED AREA

The proportion of net cultivated area to total village area varies from 30.12% to 95.40%. The distribution of villages according to range of such proportion is given in Table No. 3.

These figures indicate that in the eastern districts no village has less than 60% of its total area under cultivation. But it may be noted that more than 74% of the villages in the eastern districts have more than 80% of the village area under cultivation. The average cultivated area per village works out at 365.55 acres in western, 403.94 acres in central, 382.11 acres in eastern and 1,664.0 acres in Bundelkhand region as against 633.65 acres for all villages. The distribution of villages according to actual area under cultivation is given in Table No. 4.

TABLE No. 3

DISTRIBUTION OF SAMPLE VILLAGES ACCORDING TO PROPORTION OF
CULTIVATED AREA TO TOTAL VILLAGE AREA

% of Cultivated Area to Total Village Area	Number of Villages in Regions				
	Western	Central	Eastern	Bundelkhand	Total
Less than 40%	1 (3.70)	—	—	2 (22.22)	3 (3.70)
40 to 60%	2 (7.41)	1 (5.56)	—	—	3 (3.70)
60 to 70%	3 (11.11)	6 (33.33)	5 (18.52)	3 (33.33)	17 (20.99)
70 to 80%	1 (3.70)	6 (33.33)	4 (14.81)	4 (44.45)	15 (18.52)
80% or more	20 (74.08)	5 (27.78)	18 (66.67)	—	43 (53.09)
Total	27 (100.00)	18 (100.00)	27 (100.00)	9 (100.00)	81 (100 00)

TABLE No. 4

DISTRIBUTION OF SAMPLE VILLAGES ACCORDING TO THE NET CULTIVATED AREA

Net Cultivated Area	Number of Sample Villages in Regions				
	Western	Central	Eastern	Bundelkhand	Total
Less than 200 acres	1 (3.70)	5 (27.78)	9 (33.33)	—	15 (18.52)
200 to 500 acres	9 (33.34)	8 (44.44)	8 (29.63)	—	25 (30.86)
500 to 1000 acres	11 (40.74)	5 (27.78)	10 (37.04)	2 (22.22)	28 (34.57)
1000 acres & more	6 (22.22)	—	—	7 (77.78)	13 (16.05)
Total	27 (100)	18 (100)	27 (100)	9 (100)	81 (100)

IRRIGATION

As many as 74 out of 81 of the sample villages, i.e. 91.36% have irrigation facilities. The various sources of irrigation include canals, tube-

TABLE No. 5

DISTRIBUTION OF SAMPLE VILLAGES ACCORDING TO IRRIGATION FACILITIES

Regions	Number of Villages reporting Irrigation from				Number of Villages according to number of sources of irrigation				Number of Villages		Total Number of Villages
	Canal	Tube-well	Well	Other Sources	1	2	3	4	With Irrigation	Without Irrigation	
1	2	3	4	5	6	7	8	9	10	11	12
Western	10 (37.04)	8 (29.63)	16 (59.26)	10 (37.04)	8 (34.78)	9 (39.13)	6 (26.09)	—	23 (85.19)	4 (14.81)	27 (100.00)
Central	12 (66.67)	2 (11.11)	13 (72.22)	9 (50.00)	7 (38.89)	4 (22.22)	7 (38.89)	—	18 (100.00)	—	18 (100.00)
Eastern	—	5 (18.52)	22 (81.48)	22 (81.48)	7 (26.92)	15 (59.69)	4 (15.39)	—	26 (96.30)	1 (3.70)	27 (100.00)
Bundelkhand	5 (55.56)	—	2 (22.22)	2 (22.22)	5 (71.43)	2 (28.57)	—	—	7 (77.78)	2 (22.22)	9 (100.00)
Total	27 (33.33)	15 (18 52)	53 (65.43)	43 (53.09)	27 (36.49)	30 (40.54)	17 (22.97)	—	74 (91.36)	7 (8.64)	81 (100.00)

Note:
1. Figures within brackets in Cols. 10 and 11 are percentage proportions to total figures in Col. 12.
2. Figures within brackets in Cols. 6, 7, 8, 9 are percentage proportions to total number of irrigated villages as in Col. 10.
3. Figures within brackets in Cols. 2, 3, 4, 5 are percentage proportions to total number of villages in the region as in Col. 12. The sum total of these figures for a region is not equal to that given in Col. 12 because the whole figures are overlapping for villages have more than one source of irrigation.

wells, ordinary wells and other means. Of all the villages, 36.49% are reported to have only one source of irrigation, 40.54% had two sources of irrigation, and 22.97% villages obtained irrigation water from three sources. Canal irrigation was reported by one-third of the villages; 65.43% villages have ordinary wells and 18.52% villages had tube-wells. With the exception of 4 or 14.81% villages in the western, 1 or 3.7% in eastern and 2 or 22.22% in the Bundelkhand regions which had no irrigation at all, all the remaining villages are provided with irrigation facilities as shown in Table No. 5.

Thus, it will be seen from this table that more than three-fifths (65.43%) of the villages have well irrigation. Canals provide irrigation water in one-third of the villages. Tube-wells are available only in 18.52% of the villages. In brief, it can be said that irrigation facilities are available practically in all the sample villages. The following table shows the extent to which irrigation is actually available in the sample villages:

TABLE No. 6

DISTRIBUTION OF SAMPLE VILLAGES ACCORDING TO EXTENT OF IRRIGATION

% of Irrigated Area to Gross Cropped Area	Number of Villages in Regions				
	Western	Central	Bundelkhand	Eastern	Total
Nil	4	—	2	1	7
	(14.82)		(22.22)	(3.71)	(8.64)
Less than 10%	4	3	4	1	12
	(14.82)	(16.67)	(44.44)	(3.71)	(14.82)
10—20%	1	1	2	2	6
	(3 70)	(5.56)	(22.22)	(7.40)	(7.41)
20—30%	—	4	—	6	10
	(0.00)	(22.22)	(00.00)	(22.22)	(12.34)
30—40%	3	5	1	7	16
	(11.11)	(27.78)	(11.11)	(25.92)	(19.75)
40—50%	5	4	—	3	12
	(18.51)	(22.22)	(00.00)	(11.11)	(14.82)
50—60%	3	1	—	3	7
	(11.11)	(5.55)	(00.00)	(11.11)	(8.64)
60—70%	4	—	—	—	4
	(14.82)	(00.00)	(00.00)		(4.94)
70% & above	3	—	—	4	7
	(11.11)	(00.00)	(00.00)	(14.82)	(8 64)
Total	27	18	9	27	81
	(100.00)	(100.00)	(100.00)	(100.00)	(100.00)

DOUBLE CROPPING

Provision of irrigation facilities generally tends to promote intensity of cropping. The following table shows the extent to which double cropping is practised in the sample villages:

TABLE No. 7

DISTRIBUTION OF VILLAGES ACCORDING TO EXTENT OF DOUBLE CROPPING

% of Double Cropped Area to Total Net Cultivated Area	Number of Villages in acres				
	Western	Central	Bundelkhand	Eastern	Total
Nil	1 (3.70)	—	1 (11.11)	3 (11.11)	5 (6.18)
Less than 10%	4 (14.82)	2 (11.11)	7 (77.78)	3 (11.11)	16 (19.75)
10—20%	4 (14.82)	3 (16.67)	1 (11.11)	5 (18.52)	13 (16.05)
20—30%	4 (14.82)	.6 (33.33)	—	3 (11.11)	13 (16.05)
30—40%	7 (25.91)	2 (11.11)	—	5 (18.52)	14 (17.28)
40—50%	2 (7.41)	3 (16.67)	—	4 (14.82)	9 (11.11)
50—60%	2 (7.41)	1 (5.55)	—	1 (3.70)	4 (4.94)
60—70%	2 (7.41)	—	—	1 (3.70)	3 (3.70)
70% & above	1 (3.70)	1 (5.56)	—	2 (7.41)	4 (4.94)
Total	27 (100.00)	18 (100.00)	9 (100.00)	27 (100.00)	81 (100.00)

The actual double cropped area per village works out at 198.15 acres in western, 96.61 acres in central, 120.78 acres in eastern and 70.00 acres in the Bundelkhand division as against 127.86 acres for all villages.

POPULATION

The population of sample villages varies from 96 in western region to 3,303 in the central region. The average population for all villages is calculated to be 1,001. The villages are most populous in the western districts where the average population per village works out at 1,076 as against 1,058 in Bundelkhand, 1,044 in central and 889 in the eastern region. Besides, more than one-fifth of the villages in this region have each a population of more than 2,000 persons as against only 11% in the central, 7% in eastern and no village of this order in the Bundelkhand division. The frequency distribution of villages according to range of population in the various regions is given in the following table while the village-wise figures of population have been given in Table No. 1 in the Statistical Appendix.

TABLE No. 8

REGION-WISE DISTRIBUTION OF SAMPLE VILLAGES ACCORDING TO RANGE
OF POPULATION

Population	Number of Villages in Regions				
	Western	Central	Eastern	Bundelkhand	Total
Less than 100 persons	1 (3.70)	—	—	—	1 (1.23)
100 to 200 „	1 (3.70)	—	3 (11.11)	—	4 (4.94)
200 to 500 „	7 (25.93)	6 (33.33)	6 (22.22)	1 (11.11)	20 (24.69)
500 to 1000 .,	5 (18.52)	7 (38.89)	9 (33.33)	4 (44.44)	25 (30.86)
1000 to 2000 „	7 (25.93)	3 (16.67)	7 (25.93)	4 (44.44)	21 (25.93)
2000 & more „	6 (22.22)	2 (11.11)	2 (7.41)	—	10 (12.35)
Total	27 (100.00)	18 (100.00)	27 (100.00)	9 (100.00)	81 (100.00)

OCCUPATIONAL PATTERN

With the exception of two villages in the western region where only 30 to 50% of the heads of households reported that agriculture was their main occupation, in the remaining villages 60 per cent or more households reported agriculture as their main occupation as shown in the following table:

TABLE No. 9

DISTRIBUTION OF SAMPLE VILLAGES ACCORDING TO PROPORTION OF HEADS OF HOUSEHOLDS REPORTING AGRICULTURE AS THEIR MAIN OCCUPATION

% of Heads of Households reporting Agriculture as their Main Occupation	Western	Central	Eastern	Bundel- khand	Total
30 to 40%	1 (3.70)	—	—	—	1 (1.24)
40 to 50%	1 (3.70)	—	—	—	1 (1.24)
50 to 60%	—	—	—	—	—
60 to 70%	3 (11.11)	3 (16.67)	—	5 (18.52)	11 (13.57)
70 to 80%	4 (14.81)	1 (5.55)	2 (22.22)	—	7 (8.64)
80% & more	18 (66.67)	14 (77.78)	7 (77.78)	22 (81.48)	61 (75.31)
Total	27 (100.00)	18 (100.00)	9 (100.00)	27 (100.00)	81 (100.00)

It is thus obvious that in three-fourth of the villages more than 80% of the heads of households are engaged in agriculture as their main occupation. Further, the proportion of villages where 80% or more heads of households have agriculture as their main occupation is the largest (81.48%) in Bundelkhand and is least (66.67%) in the western region.

CONCEPTS, DEFINITIONS AND EXPLANATIONS

VARIABLES

The statistical material has been analysed according to three variables, viz. region, occupation and caste as these are considered to be important factors in the context of the present study.

REGIONS

U. P. is a big State which includes as many as 54 districts well known for diverse agricultural situations, social and economic conditions, occupational pattern and standard of living. Therefore, in order that such differences may be easily pointed out we have divided the State into 4 regions, viz., western, central, eastern and Bundelkhand. Geographically, according to 1951 census there are five natural divisions, viz. Himalayan, East Plain, Central Plain, West Plain and Hills and Plateau. For administrative purposes the State is divided into 10 Revenue divisions. The comparative layout of districts according to these three methods is given below:

TABLE No. 10

CLASSIFICATION OF DISTRICTS INTO DIFFERENT DIVISIONS

Natural Divisions	Revenue Divisions	Our Regional Divisions
(i) *Himalayan*	(i) *Kumaun*	(i) *Western region*
1. Garhwal	1. Garhwal	1. Dehra Dun
2. Tehri Garhwal	2. Tehri Garhwal	2. Shaharanpur
3. Naini Tal	3. Naini Tal	3. Muzzaffarnagar
4. Almora	4. Almora	4. Meerut
5. Dehra Dun		5. Bulandshahr.
	(ii) *Meerut*	6. Aligarh
	1. Dehra Dun	7. Mathura
(ii) *East Plain*	2. Saharanpur	8. Agra
1. Gorakhpur	3. Muzzaffarnagar	9. Mainpuri
2. Deoria	4. Meerut	10. Etah.

TABLE No. 10—(*contd*).

Natural Divisions	Revenue Divisions	Our Regional Divisions
3. Basti	5. Bulandshahr	11. Bareilly
4. Gonda		12. Bijnor
5. Bahraich	(iii) *Agra*	13. Pilibhit
6. Banaras	1. Aligarh	14. Rampur
7. Jaunpur	2. Mathura	15. Badaun
8. Ghazipur	3. Agra	16. Moradabad
9. Ballia	4. Mainpuri	17. Shahjahanpur
10. Azamgarh	5. Etah	18. Kheri
(iii) *Central Plain*	(iv) *Rohilkhand*	(ii) *Central*
1. Kanpur	1. Bareilly	1. Kanpur
2. Fatehpur	2. Bijnor	2. Fatehpur
3. Allahabad	3. Pilibhit	3. Allahabad
4. Lucknow	4. Rampur	4. Etawah
5. Unnao	5. Budaun	5. Farrukhabad
6. Rae-Bareli	6. Moradabad	6. Lucknow
7. Sitapur	7. Shahjahanpur	7. Unnao
8. Hardoi		8. Rae-Bareli
9. Faizabad	(v) *Allahabad*	9. Sitapur
10. Sultanpur	1 Kanpur	10 Hardoi
11. Pratapgarh	2. Fatehpur	11. Bara Banki
12. Bara Banki	3. Allahabad	
	4. Etawah	(iii) *Eastern*
(iv) *West Plain*	5. Farrukhabad	1. Varanasi
1. Saharanpur		2. Jaunpur
2. Bareilly	(vi) *Jhansi*	3. Ghazipur
3. Bijnor	1. Jhansi	4. Ballia
4. Pilibhit	2. Jalaun	5. Mirzapur
5. Rampur	3. Hamirpur	6. Gorakhpur
6. Kheri	4. Banda.	7. Deoria
7. Muzzaffarnagaɪ		8. Basti
8. Meerut	(vii) *Varanasi*	9. Azamgarh
9. Bulandshahr	1. Varanasi	10. Gonda
10. Aligarh	2. Jaunpur	11. Bahraich
11. Mathura	3. Ghazipur	12. Faizabad
12. Agra	4. Ballia	13. Sultanpur
13. Mainpuri	5. Mirzapur	14. Pratapgarh
14. Etah		
15. Budaun	(viii) *Gorakhpur*	(iv) *Bundelkhand*
16. Moradabad	1. Gorakhpur	1 Jhansi
17. Shahjahanpur	2. Deoria	2. Jalaun

TABLE No. 10.—(contd).

Natural Divisions	Revenue Divisions	Our Regional Divisions
18. Etawah	3. Basti	3. Hamirpur
19. Farrukhabad	4. Azamgarh	4. Banda
(v) *Hills & Plateau*	(ix) *Lucknow*	
1. Jhansi	1. Lucknow	
2. Jalaun	2. Unnao	
3. Hamirpur	3. Rae-Bareli	
4. Banda	4. Sitapur	
5. Mirzapur	5. Hardoi	
	6. Kheri	
	(x) *Faizabad*	
	1. Gonda	
	2. Bahraich	
	3. Faizabad	
	4. Sultanpur	
	5. Pratapgarh	
	6. Bara Banki.	

Thus it will be seen that our western region includes all the districts included in the three administrative divisions, viz. Meerut, Agra and Rohilkhand. Besides, Kheri district has been added to this region as this district is treated as a part of the West Plain also according to natural division's scheme. Etawah and Farrukhabad included in the West Plain present conditions more akin to those in the districts included in the central region and therefore we have put them in this latter region. Dehra Dun is a part of the Himalayan division according to natural division's scheme, but we have included it in the western region because it is a part of the Meerut division where *zamindari* system has been abolished. We have excluded from study the Kumaun division which consists of the hill districts or the districts of the Himalayan division where *zamindari* system has not yet been abolished. Our central region consists of districts of Allahabad and Lucknow divisions except Kheri district. Bara-Banki district has been put in this region for it is also included in the Central Plain. Our eastern region includes Varanasi, Gorakhpur and Faizabad divisions. We have included Faizabad, Sultanpur and Pratapgarh, which are otherwise included in the Central Plain, in the eastern region for these districts are economically as backward as is the eastern part of the State. Our Bundelkhand region corresponds to the Jhansi division or the Plateau division.

HOUSEHOLDS AND THEIR MEMBERS

The basic sample unit for investigation is the household which means a primary group living together and partaking from the same kitchen. In other words, it is a commensal family. If two or more brothers or any other relations make separate arrangements, due to convenience for their cooking but are living jointly for every purpose and partake from a common pool of income through joint-family cultivaton or business, they are to be treated as a single household although there may not be one kitchen for all of them. They can, however, be regarded as partaking from the same kitchen since they draw from a common stock of food.

The members of a household include those who are ordinarily resident and living in the village. It will thus exclude married daughters, whose "*Gauna*" has taken place and who live either with their in-laws or husbands even though they may be present in the family at the time of enquiry. On the other hand, it will include daughter-in-laws, wives and mothers who normally live in the family but are temporarily absent from the village at the time of enquiry or have gone to live with their parents for a short period as is customary. Sons and daughters who live elsewhere for studying have to be included among the members but not those who have left their village home for work in another village or town and are residing there. Resident members are those who are ordinarily resident in the village and carry on their main occupation there; others, if members of the family, are non-resident.

By head of a household is meant the chief bread-winner of the family.

OCCUPATION AND INDUSTRY

All households have been classified into various industries and occupations according to the source from which the head of a household draws his main livelihood. The various occupations of heads of households have been classified according to the sector of economic activity where the person is engaged. In this respect we have followed the industrial classification as given by the Indian Statistical Institute. According to this scheme, each gainfully occupied person is classified by the sector of economic activity and the sectors are classified according to goods and services produced. Thus, an individual has been classified according to the commodity, or service produced by the sector of economic activity, e.g. a clerk employed in a factory will be classified in the 'Manufacturing Industry' but another clerk working in an educational institution will be classed in the 'Services'. If a person is engaged normally in more than one industry his class will be the industry from which the major proportion of his total earnings is derived. Thus, to suit the local requirements the following divisions of main industries have been made.

1. *Agriculture*

1.1 Cultivator: is one who is engaged in cultivation either of his own or any other land with his own labour or through hired labour. A cultivator may thus be (i) cultivator (owner) or (ii) cultivator (tenant). Again, he may be either a farmer, peasant or a share-cropper.

1.2 Farmer: is one who cultivates his own land mainly with hired labour. It will also include those who have given their land to sub-tenants or share-croppers.

1.3 Peasant: is one who cultivates his own land mainly without hired labour.

1.4 Share-Cropper: has generally no land of his own to cultivate but takes up the cultivation of others' land on a crop-sharing basis which forms the major part of the land cultivated by him.

1.5 Agricultural Labourers: are casual and permanent hired workers employed in farm operations.

1.6 Others: will include grass cutters, wood cutters, fuel collectors, plantation labour, *malis*, fishermen, hunters, rearers of animals and birds, cattle grazers.

2. *Village Industries and Crafts:* will include cottage workers and artisans as carpenters, smiths, tailors, potters, bakers, butchers confectioners, weavers, dyers, and printers, shoemakers, tanners, bangle makers, metal workers.

3. *Trade and Commerce* will include shopkeepers, traders, money-lenders etc.

4. *Service and Professions*

4.1 Menials and Servants: such as washermen, *bhistis*, domestic servants, sweepers, *chaukidars* etc.

4.2 Others: such as *lekhpals*, teachers, V̇.L.Ws *panchayat* secretaries, supervisors, priest, *mullas*.

5. *Miscellaneous:* will include these who could not be included in any one of the above groups.

CASTES

The various households under survey reported in all 53 castes and two communities which we have broadly classified in four groups, viz. (i) Upper Caste Hindus, (ii) Scheduled Caste Hindus and (iii) other Hindus and (iv) Non-Hindus. In the classification of the various Hindu Castes we have followed the social stratification suggested by Mukerjee and Colleagues in the Inter Caste Tensions in respect of social hierarchy or caste gradation in U.P.'s rural society based on social distance and segregation and economic disparity. Thus these four groups include the following:

I. *Upper Caste Hindus:*

1. Brahman
2. Thakur
3. Vaishya
4. Kayastha

II. *Other Hindus:*

1. Ahir
2. Aarakh
3. Bhumihar
4. Bhar
5. Bhat
6. Barhai
7. Bhujua or bhooj
8. Chai
9. Dhimar
10. Dhunia
11. Gujar
12. Gadaria
13. Jat
14. Kahar
15. Kewat
16. Kurmi
17. Kumhar
18. Kori
19. Koeri
20. Kachhi
21. Lohar
22. Lodh
23. Luniya
24. Mali
25. Murao
26. Nai
27. Shimpi
28. Tamoli
29. Teli

III. *Scheduled Caste Hindus:*

1. Bason
2. Bedia
3. Bhangi
4. Chamar
5. Dhanuk
6. Dhobi
7. Jatava
8. Khatik
9. Kol
10. Khangar
11. Pasi

IV. *Non-Hindus:*

1. Dhuniya
2. Faqir
3. Julha
4. Khan
5. Pathan
6. Nai
7. Shaikh
8. Teli

TENURIAL STATUS

There was a large variety of tenures before *zamindari* abolition but the present law recognises only three types of tenure holders, viz. *bhumidhars*, *sirdars* and *asamis*. It was of no use to adopt the tenurial pattern which does not exist today and, therefore, we have classified the various sample households according the present tenures. In case a person held land under more than one tenure his status was decided according to the tenure under which a major part of his holding was held. Thus, a household is classified as *bhumidhar's* if most of its land is *bhumidhari* land, it is *sirdar's* household if most of land is held under *sirdari* tenure. Households other than those of *bhumidhars* and *sirdars* are those of *asamis* and share-croppers.

TYPE OF HOLDING

Area of land 'recorded' in the name of a person is called the 'Area Held' by that person. But generally it is observed that a person or a household may actually cultivate more or less than the area thus held and therefore we have used another term, viz. 'Land Cultivated' which means the total area of land which is actually cultivated by a household irrespective of its title over land.

FORM OF CULTIVATION

Again, if the head of a household cultivates his land wholly or largely personally or with the help of the members of his family, such holdings are called personally cultivated holdings. In case land is cultivated wholly or largely with the help of permanent hired labourers, the holdings have been classified as labour-cultivated holdings. Permanent farm servants in this context are those workers who are employed on a yearly basis and are paid in cash, kind or both. The holdings which are wholly or largely cultivated with the help of share-croppers or *asamis* are termed as share-cropped holdings.

PERIOD

This survey was in the nature of a 'before and after' enquiry designed to indicate the change brought about by the abolition of *zamindari* system. Therefore, we have tried to compare the existing situation with that which obtained prior to *zamindari* abolition. The *zamindari* system was abolished with effect from July 1, 1952. Since conditions vary from year to year, we have, therefore, taken into account a period of three years so that seasonal or yearly variations may be averaged out. Thus the period before *zamindari* abolition covers three years, viz. 1948-49, 1949-50 and 1950-51 and that after *zamindari* abolition includes the years 1957-58, 1958-59 and 1959-60.

DIFFERENT FORMS OF CO-OPERATIVE FARMING SOCIETIES

A co-operative farming society may take one of the following four forms:

(*i*) *Co-operative Better Farming Society*: The society is designed to introduce improved methods of farming. The members agree to follow a plan of cultivation laid down by it. In furtherance of its object it may undertake joint purchase of seed or manure, or pooling, cleaning, grading, and selling the produce, or joint ploughing or joint harvesting, or joint arrangements for watch and ward, or joint use of machinery. Each member is, however, independent except for the specific purposes for which he joins the society, He pays for the services which he receives, and at the end of the year he may receive a patronage dividend.

(*ii*) *Co-operative Joint Farming Society*: This type of society suggests pooling of land on the part of small owners whose separate holdings are not large enough to permit economic farming. Members work on the pooled land in accordance with the direction of an elected committee and the manager appointed by it. They work jointly and each member receives wages for his daily labour. The ownership of each member in his holding continues and is recognised by the payment of a dividend in proportion to the value of his land. The produce which is raised collectively, is also disposed of collectively, and the proceeds after meeting all the expenses of cultivation including payment for the use of land, wages and cost of management and providing for a reserve fund are shared by members in proportion to the wages earned by each. The ordinary functions of this form of society are the planning of a crop programme, the joint purchase of farm requirements and joint sale of farm produce, raising of funds on the security of land, crops and other moveable and immoveable assets of the society for land improvement, purchase of machinery and payment of operational expenses, land improvement and all other activities calculated to promote the development of agriculture. A subsidiary agreement is generally made between the society and each member that if any improvement is made on his plot of land he will repay its cost when he ceases to belong to the society.

(*iii*) *Co-operative Tenant Farming Society*: This type of society owns land in freehold or leasehold, but its holding is divided into smaller holdings each of which is leased to an individual tenant cultivator who is a member of the society. The whole area is cultivated in accordance with a plan laid down by the society, but the manner in which the plan is executed is left to the discretion of each individual tenant. The society undertakes to supply credit, seed, manure and costly agricultural implements and even to arrange for the marketing of the tenant members' produce, but it is open to each tenant member whether or not to avail of these facilities. Each tenant pays a fixed rent for his holding, but the produce of the holding is his own and entirely at his disposal. This type of society replaces the superior landlord and the profits, after meeting all expenses and providing for a reserve fund, are distributed among the tenant members in proportion to the rent paid by each.

(*iv*) *Co-operative Collective Farming Society*: This type of society also holds land in freehold or leasehold and owns all other means of production. It undertakes joint cultivation for which all its members pool their labour resources and each receives in return prescribed wages. Large-scale cultivation facilitates mechanisation of agricultural production, and this is the society's most important gain. The profits are worked out at the end of the year after deducting wages, cost of management and allotment to reserves, and divided in proportion to the wages earned by each member.*

* Extracts from the *Govt. of India Report of the Co-operative Planning Committee*, pp. 29-32.

LAND REVENUE SYSTEM OF UTTAR PRADESH*

In this province, the settlement is made with the *taluqdar* in the case of *taluqdari mahals* and with the proprietors in the case of other *mahals*. The unit of assessment is a *mahal* and if there are more than one proprietor in a *mahal*, the settlement is made either with the *lambardar* or with all the proprietors. All the proprietors are jointly and severally responsible to the Government for the payment of land revenue. If the proprietor refuses to accept the assessment declared by the Settlement Officer, he can be excluded from the settlement for a term not exceeding fifteen years and the Collector can either form the *mahal* or hold it under direct management.

In the case of a *mahal* where there are more than one proprietor, who bear to each other the relation of superior and inferior landholder, the settlement is made with the party possessing the superior right.

The settlement operations consist mainly in fixing the rents of the *mahals* or the estates concerned. The villages are grouped into assessment circles possessing similarity of soil and physical character. The rent rate for each class of soil is then determined. The rent is fixed after taking into consideration the following factors:

(a) The level of rents paid by tenants who held or were admitted to land at different times and in particular the level of rents agreed to by tenants who were admitted to holdings in or between the years 1309 *Fasli* and 1313 *Fasli*;

(b) The prices of agricultural produce prevailing at such times;

(c) Changes in the crops grown and in the amount of the produce;

(d) The valuation of the produce with a view to seeing that the valuation of the holdings of hereditary tenants at the proposed rates does not exceed one-fifth of such value; and

(e) The expenses of cultivation and the cost to the cultivator of maintaining himself and his family.

* Reproduced from the *Report of the Taxation Enquiry Commission* 1953-54. Vol. III, pp. 272-74.

The basis of assessment of land revenue are the 'net assets' which are worked out by deducting the allowance for proprietary cultivation (15 to 30 per cent), for improvements (10 per cent) and for shortage in recoveries (1 to 6 per cent) from the assets of a *mahal*.

The revenue assessed on a *mahal* has to be ordinarily 40 per cent, but in no case can exceed 45 per cent of the net assets.

If the number of the proprietors in a *mahal* is large and their circumstances are poor, the revenue assessed does not exceed 38 per cent of the net assets, provided it does not mean a reduction in the existing demand. Further, where the number and circumstances of the proprietors or the existence of heavy charges on account of *malikana* justify a lower assessment, the revenue may be assessed at any rate between 25 and 35 per cent. At any revision of assessment, the land revenue of a *mahal* cannot be enhanced by more than one-third of the previous assessment. If, however, even with this increase by one-third, the revised assessment of a *mahal* amounts to less than 30 per cent of its net assets, the assessment is fixed ordinarily at 30 per cent of the net assets. Since the abolition of intermediaries, the entire net assets of a village are now treated as land revenue.

The term of settlement is generally 40 years though it may be shorter in the case of a *mahal* when there is extensive deterioration in land or where there is considerable concealment of assets. A part of the State was under permanent settlement after the pattern of Bengal till recently.

The present land reforms have abolished all intermediaries; and hence the recorded rents, which form the principal starting point of the settlement so far, cannot form the basis for future settlements. The Zamindari Abolition Act provides for this and the basis of assessment in future will be the estimated average surplus produce of the holding after deducting the ordinary expenses of cultivation. The percentage of the surplus produce to be taken as land revenue is to be determined by the Pradesh Legislature on each occasion. The village as unit of assessment and joint responsibility of the cultivators for payment of land revenue will, however, continue as hitherto.

The Act has fixed the present land revenue at the rates of rent payable by different classes of tenants and has further provided that there would be no change in their rates for the next 40 years. A revision of settlement can, however, be taken up even within that period if there is a substantial decline in prices of agricultural produce and depression is likely to continue for some time.

LEGISLATIVE MEASURES

LIST OF LAND LEGISLATION BY SPECIAL AREAS WHERE ZAMINDARI WAS ABOLISHED AND LAND REFORMS WERE INTRODUCED LATER THAN IN THE REST OF THE STATE IN JULY 1952.

I. Land Reforms in Pargana Kaswar Raja in the Banaras District

  i. Application of U.P. Act I of 1951—Sept. 30, 1952.
  ii. The U. P. Land Tenures (Pargana Kaswar Raja) (Removal of Difficulties) Order 1952—Oct. 30, 1952.
  iii. Application of U.P. Act XX of 1954—Oct. 30, 1954.
  iv. Application of U.P. Act XVIII of 1956—July 1, 1958.
  v. Application of U.P. Act XXXVII of 1958—June 30, 1959.

II. Land Reforms in the former Banaras State

  i. Application of U.P. Act I of 1951 as amended by Act XVI of 1953—June 30, 1953.
  ii. Application of U.P. Act I as amended by Act XVI of 1953 to the Government Estates without Intermediaries—July 1, 1954.
  iii. Application of U.P. Act XX of 1954—Oct. 30, 1954.
  iv. Application of U.P. Act XX of 1954 to the Government Estates without Intermediaries—Nov. 22, 1954.
  v. Application of U.P. Act XVIII of 1956—July 1, 1958.
  vi. Application of U.P. Act XVIII of 1956 to the Government Estates without Intermediaries—July 1, 1958.
  vii. Application of U.P. Act XXXVII of 1958—June 30, 1959.
  viii. Application of U. P. Act XXXVII of 1958 to the Government Estates without Intermediaries—June 30, 1959.

*III. Land Reforms in the Enclaves of former Indian States absorbed in
Uttar Pradesh*

    i. Application of U.P. Act. I of 1951 as amended by U.P. Act XVI
of 1953.

    ii. Application of U.P. Act I of 1951 as amended by U.P. Act XVI
of 1953 to the Govt. Estates without Intermediaries—July 1, 1954.

    iii. Application of U.P. Act XX of 1954—Dec. 29, 1954.

    iv. Application of U.P. Act 1954 to the Govt. Estates without Inter-
mediaries—Dec. 29, 1954.

    v. Application of U.P. Act XVIII of 1956—July 1, 1958.

    vi. Application of U.P. Act XVIII of 1956 to the Government Estates
without Intermediaries—July 1, 1958.

    vii. Application of U.P. Act XXXVII of 1958—June 30, 1959.

    viii. Application of U.P. Act XXXVII of 1958 to Government Estates
without Intermediaries—June 30, 1959.

IV. Land Reforms in the former Rampur State

    i. Rampur Stay of Ejectment Suits and Proceedings Ordinance
1951—Aug. 9, 1951.

    ii. Rampur Stay of Ejectment Suits and Proceedings Act 1951—
Oct. 1, 1951.

    iii. Rampur Thekedari and Pattedari Abolition Act 1953—April
24, 1954.

    iv. Application of U.P. Act 1 of 1951—June 30, 1954.

    v. Application of U.P. Act 1 of 1951 to the Government Estates
without Intermediaries—Jan. 26, 1956.

    vi. Application of U.P. Act 1 of 1951 to Thekedari and Pattedari
Government Estates without Intermediaries—Jan. 26, 1959.

    vii. Application of U.P. Act XX of 1954—July 1, 1956.

    viii. Application of U.P. Act XX of 1954 to the Government Estates
without Intermediaries—Jan. 26, 1959.

    ix. Application of U.P. Act XVIII of 1956—April 18, 1959.

    x. Application of U.P. Act XVIII of 1956 to the Government Estates
without Intermediaries—June 30, 1959.

    xi. Application of U.P. Act XXXVII of 1956 to the Thekedari
and Pattedari Government Estates without Intermediaries—
Jan. 26, 1959.

xii. Application of U.P. Act XXXVII of 1958—June 30, 1959.

xiii. Application of U.P. Act XXXVII of 1958 to the Government Estates without Intermediaries—June 30, 1959.

V. Land Reforms in scattered Government Estates

i. The U.P. Government Land (Eviction and Rent Recovery)

ii. Application of U.P. Act I of 1951—March 31, 1955.

iii. Application of the U.P. Act XX of 1954—June 30, 1955.

iv. Application of U.P. Act XVIII of 1956—July 1, 1958.

v. Application of U.P. Act XXXVII of 1958—June 30, 1959.

VI. Land Reforms in the portion of the Mirzapur District south of the Kaimur Range

i. U. P. Stay of Suits and Proceedings (Mirzapur) Act 1952—Oct. 4, 1952.

ii. Application of U.P. Act 1 of 1951 as amended by U.P. Act XVI of 1953—June 30, 1953.

iii. Application of U.P. Act I of 1951 as amended by U.P. Act XVI of 1953 to the Government Estates without Intermediaries—July 1, 1954.

iv. Application of U.P. Act XX of 1954—Dec. 29, 1954.

v. Application of U.P. Act XXXVIII of 1958 to the Government Estates without Intermediaries—June 30, 1959.

VII. Land Reforms in Pargana Jaunsar-Bewar in the Dehradun District

i. The Khat Haripur Bias (Jaunsar-Bewar Parganas) Tenants' Protection Regulations 1940—Oct. 1, 1941.

ii. The Jaunsar-Bewar Pargana (Sayanas) Regulations 1948—May 28, 1949.

iii. The Jaunsar-Bewar Pargana (excluding Khat Haripur Bias) Tenants' Protection Regulations 1949—May 7, 1949.

iv. The Jaunsar-Bewar Security of Tenure and Land Reforms Act 1952—Feb. 15, 1953.

v. The Jaunsar-Bewar Zamindari Abolition and Land Reforms Act 1956.

VIII. Land Reforms in Kumaun Division including the former Tehri-Garhwal

i. Kumaun Agricultural Land (Mix Provision) Act 1954— Oct. 21, 1954.

IX. Land Reforms in Urban Areas

i. The U.P. Urban Area Zamindari Abolition and Land Reforms Act 1956—March 12, 1957.

X. Land Reforms in Government Estates where there was Thekedari System

i. The U.P. Government Estate Thekedari Abolition Act 1958— June 20, 1959.
ii. Application of U.P. Act I of 1951—June 30, 1959.
iii. Application of U.P. Act XX of 1954—June 30, 1959.
iv. Application of U.P. Act XVIII of 1956—Jan. 30, 1959.
v. Application of U. P. Act XXXVII of 1958—June 30, 1959.

N.B. The dates against each indicate the date of publication in the Gazette.

IMPORTANT LEGISLATIVE AMENDMENTS IN THE PRINCIPAL ACT

EXTRACTS FROM STATEMENT OF OBJECTS AND REASONS FOR THE VARIOUS AMENDMENTS TO THE UTTAR PRADESH ZAMINDARI ABOLITION AND LAND REFORMS ACT 1950.

1st Amendment (Bill dated Dec. 1, 1952)—Act Published June 16, 1953.

The U.P. Zamindari Abolition and Land Reforms Act, 1950 came into force on January 26, 1951 and the vesting order under section 4 thereof was issued on July 21, 1952. A further study of this Act and experience of its working particularly during the course of preparation of compensation statements revealed certain deficiencies. For the removal thereof this Bill is being introduced.

The more important provisions of this Bill are:

(1) it is proposed that private wells, even if they are not situated in a holding, grove or village *abadi*, should remain vested in the owners of the wells themselves.

(2) the position of tenants of *sir* land of intermediaries who did not pay local rates has been clarified as also of those who hold *sir* land from intermediaries some of whom might be paying Rs. 250 or more as land revenue per year and other less than this amount.

(3) a grove holder is proposed to be declared a *bhumidhar* outright.

(4) annuities are to be paid to *waqfs*, Trusts and Endowments for religious and charitable purposes even if the land revenue payable by them exceeded Rs. 10,000 a year. Annuities will be payable from the date of vesting and interim compensation to such *waqfs*, Trusts, etc. will be adjusted against annuities and not against compensation.

(5) constitution of *gaon samaj* and formation of Land Management Committee had been simplified.

(6) provision for management of the land outside the boundaries of a local body but included within a revenue village has been made.

(7) provisions for the acquisition of *bhumidhari* rights have been further simplified.

(8) a landless agricultural labourer has been promoted to the second place in the order of priority in section 198.

(9) it has been provided that a person against whom there are any dues realisable as arrears of land revenue may be arrested and detained.

(10) the procedure to be adopted in cases in Revenue Courts in which question of title is raised has been modified.

2nd Amendment (Bill dated May 10, 1954)—Act Published Oct. 10, 1954.

"The application of provisions in the Zamindari Abolition Act has created certain difficulties in the implementation of the provisions of the Evacuee Property Law. The Zamindari Abolition Act requires certain changes in order to remove these difficulties. An experience of about two years working to the Land Revenue Section of the Zamindari Abolition and Land Reforms Act has revealed some scope for the improvement of the Land Reforms Schemes contained therein, particularly in the matter of *adhivasis* and in connection with the uncultivated holdings area. It has also come to light that certain provisions of U.P. Land Revenue Act, 1901, and the U.P. Land Reforms (Supplementary) Act, 1952, required slight amendments in order that they may fall into line with the scheme of the U.P. Zamindari Abolition and Land Reforms Act, 1950. It is for the above mentioned purposes that this Bill is being introduced."

3rd Amendment (Bill dated Feb. 12, 1955)—Act Published March 22, 1955.

"As a result of publication of notification dated October 30, 1954 under section 240-A of the Uttar Pradesh Zamindari Abolition and Land Reforms Act, 1950, *adhivasis* have become *sirdars*. As such, if they have to file declaratory suits or suits for dispossession of trespassers, they shall have to go to civil courts. In many cases the question will arise whether any party was or was not an *adhivasi* on a particular date and it is doubtful if it would be possible to refer the issue to a revenue court under sections 332-A and 332-B, of the Uttar Pradesh Zamindari Abolition and Land Reforms Act. As it was the intention of Government that the cases of *adhivasis* should go to revenue courts, the position has been clarified by issuing the Uttar Pradesh Zamindari Abolition and Land Reforms (Amendment) Ordinance, 1955.

To replace the Ordinance this Bill is being introduced."

4th Amendment (Bill dated Jan. 17, 1956)—Act May 28, 1956.

"A study of the working of the Uttar Pradesh Zamindari Abolition and Land Reforms Act, 1950, has revealed certain defects and deficiencies in the context of the Consolidation of Holdings Scheme and the administration of evacuee agricultural lands; besides, difficulties have also been experienced in the realisation of *Gaon Samaj* dues. The tenure-holders, who are mostly persons of small means, will find it more convenient and inexpensive to litigate in Revenue Courts. With a view to removing these and a few other minor difficulties this Bill is being introduced."

5th Amendment (Bill dated Dec. 17, 1956)—Act Jan. 1957.

"The Bill is intended to repeal the Uttar Pradesh Zamindari Abolition and Land Reforms (Amendment) Act, 1955, and to make certain minor amendments in the Uttar Pradesh Zamindari Abolition and Land Reforms Act, 1950, and the Indian Tolls Act, 1904 and the Uttar Pradesh General Clauses Act, 1904. The Uttar Pradesh Zamindari Abolition and Land Reforms (Amendment) Act, 1955, is being replealed as it has served its purposes.

The amendments in the Uttar Pradesh Zamindari Abolition and Land Reforms Act, 1950, are to correct the errors or other clerical omission detected therein. The amendments in the other two Acts are of a minor nature."

6th Amendment (Bill dated July 19, 1957)—Act Aug. 29, 1957.

"Schedule V of the Uttar Pradesh Zamindari Abolition and Land Reforms Act, 1950, dealing with evacuee lands was last amended by the Land Reforms (Amendment) Act, No. XVIII of 1956, to enable *adhivasis* under section 20(a) to acquire *bhumidhari* rights after making certain deposits. To facilitate final disposal of evacuee properties, it is now sought to provide the Custodian and the Government of India with powers to transfer *sirdari* interests vested in him and to give opportunity to certain occupiers to acquire superior rights similarly."

7th Amendment (Bill dated March 31, 1958)—Act April 15, 1958.

"The word 'estate', as defined in the existing clause (8) of section 3 of the Zamindari Abolition and Land Reforms Act, means the area included under one entry in any of the registers prepared and maintained under section 32 of Land Revenue Act. In the writ petition filed by Rajas of Bihaigarh and Agori-Barhar, district Mirzapur, the High Court made observations pointing out some inaccuracy in this definition. The maintenance of annual registers is done under section 33 of the Land Revenue Act and not under 32. To remove this inaccuracy and to further clarify the position with regard to the entries made in registers prepared or maintained under any previous enactment repealed by the Land Revenue Act and in any registers prepared or maintained under the Laws or Orders of any Indian State, whose territories have merged with the State of Uttar Pradesh before the date of vesting it is necessary that an amendment, as sought in this Bill, should be made."

8th Amendment (Bill dated Sept. 11, 1958)—Act Nov. 7, 1958.

"Last two years' experience of the working of the Zamindari Abolition and Land Reforms Act, 1950 as amended by the Amending Act No. XVIII of 1956, has revealed certain shortcomings. For example, powers conferred upon *Gaon Samajs* for enforcement of the various measures of land reforms by means of regular suits have been found to be quite cumbersome. There were also difficulties in the conduct of *Gaon Samaj* litigation. There has been a general public demand that the suits and proceedings relating to *bhumidhari* should be decided by the Revenue Courts so as to provide speedy justice at cheaper cost. It has been found necessary that the ex-intermediaries should be made to move applications for the assessment and payment of their rehabilitation grant within a reasonable time to avoid unnecessary delay and expenditure. The need to devise some expeditious method for the disposal of mutation cases is also imperative. The requirement of joint family in section 154 is being so interpreted as to enable one earning unit to hold as many times to thirty acres of land as there are adult males in the family. A change in the definition of the family necessarily calls for a reduction in the ceiling for future acquisition. With a view to remove the aforesaid difficulties and a few other minor defects, this bill is being introduced."

STATISTICAL TABLES

TABLE NO. 1

PARTICULARS OF SAMPLE VILLAGES

Sl. No.	Name of the Village	Pargana	Tehsil	District	Division	Total Population	Total Village Area (in acres)
WESTERN REGION							
1.	Balal Kheri	Nakur	Nakur	Saharanpur	Meerut	239	229.00
2.	Kotra	Nakur	Nakur	Saharanpur	Meerut	484	629.00
3.	Khera Afghan	Nakur	Nakur	Saharanpur	Meerut	2702	776.00
4.	Daryapur	Hastinapur	Mawana	Meerut	Meerut	609	468.00
5.	Saidipur Seth	Hastinapur	Mawana	Meerut	Meerut	325	486.00
6.	Jalalpur Zora	Hastinapur	Mawana	Meerut	Meerut	419	2908.00
7.	Umrara	Dibai	Anupshahar	Bulandshahar	Meerut	2000	838.00
8.	Bajhera	Dibai	Anupshahar	Bulandshahar	Meerut	1210	716.00
9.	Kharak Wari	Dibai	Anupshahar	Bulandshahar	Meerut	1682	612.00
10.	Gorola	Tappal	Khair	Aligarh	Agra	1595	1170.50
11.	Bairam-Ganj	Tappal	Khair	Aligarh	Agra	346	276.25
12.	Bajauta	Tappal	Khair	Aligarh	Agra	2201	2445.80
13.	Bhadaura	Fatehabad	Fatehabad	Agra	Agra	254	664.80
14.	Nicha Khera	Fatehabad	Fatehabad	Agra	Agra	1112	1432.10
15.	Uncha	Fatehabad	Fatehabad	Agra	Agra	1323	1261.50
16.	Sakara	Bhogaon	Bhogaon	Mainpuri	Agra	2623	2412.00
17.	Kusmara	Bhogaon	Bhogaon	Mainpuri	Agra	2646	1317.00
18.	Bhainsrauli	Bhogaon	Bhogaon	Mainpuri	Agra	2012	1765.00

TABLE NO. 1—*Contd.*

Sl. No.	Name of the Village	Pargana	Tehsil	District	Division	Total Population	Total Village Area (in acres)
19.	Mahendra Nagar	Afzalgarh	Nagina	Bijnor	Rohilkhand	186	318.00
20.	Salabat Nagar	Afzalgarh	Nagina	Bijnor	Rohilkhand	527	1476.00
21.	Madhowala	Afzalgarh	Nagina	Bijnor	Rohilkhand	509	495.00
22.	Kaman	Salimpur	Dataganj	Badaun	Rohilkhand	1308	2079.87
23.	Sainjani	Salimpur	Dataganj	Badaun	Rohilkhand	1062	1993.62
24.	Karanpur Pukhta	Salimpur	Dataganj	Badaun	Rohilkhand	579	312.31
25.	Tahkhurd-Kalan	Khutar	Pawayan	Shahjahanpur	Rohilkhand	741	640.00
26.	Ram Pur Nadhota	Khutar	Pawayan	Shahjahanpur	Rohilkhand	96	156.00
27.	Lal Pur	Khutar	Pawayan	Shahjahanpur	Rohilkhand	279	352.00
	CENTRAL REGION						
28.	Salempur Bangar	Kannauj	Kannauj	Farukhabad	Allahabad	486	61.00
29.	Mitrasen Pur	Kannauj	Kannauj	Farukhabad	Allahabad	438	173.00
30.	Malika Pur	Kannauj	Kannauj	Farukhabad	Allahabad	560	881.00
31.	Alam Pur	Bhognipur	Bhognipur	Kanpur	Allahabad	370	488.00
32.	Vaina	Bhognipur	Bhognipur	Kanpur	Allahabad	1390	1154.00
33.	Amraodha	Bhognipur	Bhognipur	Kanpur	Allahabad	3303	438.00
34.	Itia Ibrahim Pur	Kewai	Handia	Allahabad	Allahabad	804	498.00
35.	Kasaudhan	Kewai	Handia	Allahabad	Allahabad	1795	1007.00
36.	Kishora	Kewai	Handia	Allahabad	Allahabad	489	371.00
37.	Bhatauli	Bangarmau	Safipur	Unnao	Lucknow	816	469.00
38.	Garha	Bangarmau	Safipur	Unnao	Lucknow	495	467.00
39.	Bhatiya Pur	Bangarmau	Safipur	Unnao	Lucknow	797	222.00

TABLE NO. 1—*Contd.*

Sl. No.	Name of the Village	Pargana	Tehsil	District	Division	Total Population	Total Village Area (in acres)
40.	Jagat-Khera	Magrayar	Purwa	Unnao	Lucknow	493	215.00
41.	Magrayar	Magrayar	Purwa	Unnao	Lucknow	2943	2204.00
42.	Danda Mau	Magrayar	Purwa	Unnao	Lucknow	531	279.00
43.	Palti Khera	Sareni	Dalmau	Raebareli	Lucknow	1354	841.00
44.	Dula Pur	Sareni	Dalmau	Raebareli	Lucknow	772	639.00
45.	Paliabir Singhpur	Sareni	Dalmau	Raebareli	Lucknow	961	682.00
	EASTERN REGION						
46.	Hiraman Pur	Ganswar	Machhlisahar	Jaunpur	Varanasi	484	299.00
47.	Delhu Pur	Ganswar	Machhlisahar	Jaunpur	Varanasi	193	169.00
48.	Korha	Ganswar	Machhlisahar	Jaunpur	Varanasi	1296	764.00
49.	Sarauli	Mohammadabad	Mohammadabad	Ghazipur	Varanasi	330	190.00
50.	Karam Chandpur	Mohammadabad	Mohammadabad	Ghazipur	Varanasi	278	243.00
51.	Kanuwan	Mohammadabad	Mohammadabad	Gahzipur	Varanasi	1693	1032.00
52.	Meondi Kalan	Bhadawan	Rasna	Ballia	Varanasi	1030	724.00
53.	Pindhori	Bhadawan	Rasna	Ballia	Varanasi	800	783.00
54.	Khadargalki	Bhadawan	Rasna	Ballia	Varanasi	244	300.00
55.	Bahidandi	Urwal	Bansgaon	Gorakhpur	Gorakhpur	534	232.00
56.	Barban	Urwal	Bansgaon	Gorakhpur	Gorakhpur	637	269.00
57.	Bahoripur Buzurg	Urwal	Bansgaon	Gorakhpur	Gorakhpur	865	307.00
58.	Nagra Badli	Amorha	Harriaya	Basti	Gorakhpur	965	436.00
59.	Gorya	Amorha	Harriaya	Basti	Gorakhpur	500	276.00
60.	Harhi	Amorha	Harriaya	Basti	Gorakhpur	148	282.00

TABLE NO. 1—*Contd.*

Sl. No.	Name of the Village	Pargana	Tehsil	District	Division	Total Population	Total Village Area (in acres)
61.	Bhainsa Kharga	Ghosi	Ghosi	Azamgarh	Gorakhpur	1049	211.00
62.	Raj Pura	Ghosi	Ghosi	Azamgarh	Gorakhpur	468	171.00
63.	Kuchahara	Ghosi	Ghosi	Azamgarh	Gorakhpur	674	289.00
64.	Bishnu Pur	Balrampur	Balrampur	Gonda	Faizabad	2160	1113.00
65.	Shewa Nagar	Balrampur	Balrampur	Gonda	Faizabad	914	659.00
66.	Belha	Balrampur	Balrampur	Gonda	Faizabad	1918	659.00
67.	Tarwa Tappa Bank	Utrauli	Utrauli	Gonda	Faizabad	2777	1081.00
68.	Mahli	Utrauli	Utrauli	Gonda	Faizabad	1403	845.00
69.	Birda Baniakhari	Utrauli	Utrauli	Gonda	Faizabad	1568	863.00
70.	Balipur Khurdwan	Amethi	Amethi	Sultanpur	Faizabad	304	287.00
71.	Aghar	Amethi	Amethi	Sultanpur	Faizabad	607	573.00
72.	Paharpur	Amethi	Amethi	Sultanpur	Faizabad	171	209.00
BUNDELKHAND REGION							
73.	Kairokhar	Garautha	Garautha	Jhansi	Jhansi	1133	2678.02
74.	Kotra	Garautha	Garautha	Jhansi	Jhansi	569	2055.79
75.	Parsua	Garautha	Garautha	Jhansi	Jhansi	931	4230.36
76.	Bachrauli	Hamirpur	Hamirpur	Hamirpur	Jhansi	1596	3781.90
77.	Bhauli Danda	Hamirpur	Hamirpur	Hamirpur	Jhansi	1829	1645.42
78.	Barwa	Hamirpur	Hamirpur	Hamirpur	Jhansi	497	1257.28
79.	Sesasubbara	Mau	Mau	Banda	Jhansi	861	2478.00
80.	Lauri	Mau	Mau	Banda	Jhansi	1527	6716.00
81.	Semra	Mau	Mau	Banda	Jhansi	580	3330.00

TABLE NO. 2

UNIVERSE AND THE SAMPLE SIZE

Division Particulars	Meerut	Agra	Rohil-khand	Allaha-bad	Jhansi	Vara-nasi	Gorakh-pur	Luck-now	Faiza-bad	Total
1. Total No. of Districts	5	5	7	5	4	5	4	6	6	47
2. No. of Sample Districts	3	3	3	3	3	3	3	2	2	25
3. Total No. of Parganas	65	51	70	53	30	78	50	104	71	572
4. No. of Parganas with Consolidation	29	14	24	21	—	8	10	28	23	157
5. No. of Parganas without Consolidation	36	37	46	32	30	70	40	76	48	415
6. No. of Sample Parganas	3	3	3	3	3	3	3	3	3	27
7. Total No. of Villages in Sample Parganas	393	477	507	811	432	723	1635	352	938	6268
8. No. of Sample Villages	9	9	9	9	9	9	9	9	9	81
9. Percentage of Col. 8 to Col. 7	2.29	1.89	1.78	1.11	2.08	1.24	0.55	2.56	0.96	1.29
10. Total No. of Households with a Holding in Sample Villages	1065	1559	912	1103	1215	506	830	1031	1046	9267
11. No. of Sample Households with a Holding in Original Sample	116	136	54	71	83	45	103	100	67	775
12. Percentage of Col. 11 to Col. 10	10.89	8.72	5.93	6.44	6.43	8.89	12.40	9.69	6.41	8.36
13. Final Sample of Household with Land Right	116	136	53	69	82	44	98	100	67	765
14. Percentage of Col. 13 to Col. 10	10.89	8.72	5.81	6.26	6.75	8.70	11.81	9.70	6.41	8.26

TABLE NO. 3

UNIVERSE AND SIZE OF SAMPLE HOUSEHOLDS

	Total No. of House-holds in Sample Villages	% to the Total	Sample House-holds	% of the Sample to the Universe	Final Sample	% of the Sample to its Universe
A. WITH LAND HOLDINGS						
(1) *Bhumidhars*	1,967	14.01	237	12.04	235	11.94
(2) *Sirdars*	7,175	51.13	414	5.77	406	5.66
(3) Others	124	0.88	124	100.00	124	100.00
Total ..	9,267	65.90	775	8.36	765	8.26
B. WITHOUT ANY LAND						
Having no land at all (including landless agri-cultural labourers and those engaged in other professions and services	4,769	33.92	nil	0.00	0.00	0.00
C. STATUS NOT KNOWN	26	0.18	nil	0.00	0.00	0.00
Total	14,062	100%	775	5.51	765	5.45

TABLE NO. 4

PERCENTAGE DISTRIBUTION OF THE NUMBER OF ZAMINDARS AND AREA OWNED BY THEM ACCORDING TO SIZE AND REGION

	SIZE OF THE LAND HOLDING OWNED BY ZAMINDARS									
	below 5 acres	5 to 10 acres	10 to 25 acres	25 to 50 acres	50 to 100 acres	100 to 200 acres	200 to 500 acres	500 to 1000 acres	1000 acres & above	Total
WESTERN REGION										
Zamindars	45.41	21.43	14.87	9.54	3.94	2.97	1.31	0.44	0.09	100
Cumulative % households	45.41	66.84	81.71	91.25	95.19	98.16	99.47	99.91	100.00	
Area owned	3.90	7.70	10.17	14.30	11.97	17.44	15.74	13.40	5.38	100
Cumulative % of area	3.90	11.60	21.77	36.07	48.04	65.48	81.22	94.52	100.00	
CENTRAL REGION										
Zamindars	73.18	6.51	9.34	6.62	2.50	1.09	0.43	0.33	—	100
Cumulative % of area	73.18	79.69	89.03	95.65	98.15	99.24	99.67	100.00	100.00	
Area owned	6.69	3.94	12.40	19.38	15.35	13.91	9.18	19.15	—	100
Cumulative % of area	6.69	10.63	23.03	42.41	57.76	71.67	80.85	100.00	100.00	
BUNDELKHAND										
Zamindars	43.40	10.33	15.58	13.04	9.22	3.82	3.50	0.95	0.16	100
Cumulative % of zamindar households	43.40	53.73	69.31	82.35	91.57	95.39	98.89	99.84	100.00	
Area owned	1.63	1.43	6.39	11.70	16.44	14.00	26.25	16.47	5.69	100
Cumulative % of area	1.63	3.06	9.45	21.15	37.59	51.59	77.84	94.31	100.00	

TABLE NO. 4—Contd.

		Size of the Land Holding Owned by Zamindars								
	below 5 acres	5 to 10 acres	10 to 25 acres	25 to 50 acres	50 to 100 acres	100 to 200 acres	200 to 200 acres	500 to 500 acres	1000 acres & above	Total
Eastern Region										
Zamindars	85.19	5.16	4.86	2.43	1.15	0.67	9.24	0.24	0.06	100
Cumulative % of area	85.19	90.35	95.21	97.64	98.79	99.46	99.70	99.94	100.00	
Area owned	11.93	5.39	9.91	11.33	10.93	10.23	12.55	19.37	8.34	100
Cumulative % of area	11.93	17.32	27.23	38.56	49.49	59.74	72.29	91.66	100.00	
All										
Zamindars	66.11	10.48	10.00	6.73	3.34	1.82	1.04	0.41	0.07	100
Cumulative % of Zamindar's Households	66.11	79.59	86.59	93.32	96.66	98.48	99.52	99.93	100.00	
Area owned	4.94	4.69	9.22	13.70	13.76	14.56	17.67	16.28	5.18	100
Cumulative % of area	4.94	9.63	18.85	32·55	46.31	60.87	78.54	95·82	100 00	

TABLE NO. 5

Region-wise Percentage Distribution of Zamindars and the Zamindari Area according to the Area Owned in Sample Villages in 1951-52

Area Owned		Western			Central			Bundelkhand		
		% of Zamindars	% of Area Owned	Average Size of Area Owned (in acres)	% of Zamindars	% of Area Owned	Average Size of Area Owned (in acres)	% of Zamindars	% of Area Owned	Average Size of Area Owned (in acres)
Less than 5 acres	..	45.41	3.90	1.99	73.18	6.69	1.12	43.40	1.63	1.47
5 - 25 acres	..	36.30	17.87	11.43	15.85	16.34	12.58	25.91	7.82	11.87
25 - 100 acres	..	13.48	26.27	45.27	9.12	34.73	46.49	22.26	28.14	49.75
100 - 500 acres	..	4.28	33.18	179.81	1.52	23.09	185.41	7.32	40.25	216.60
500 acres or more	..	0.53	18.78	831.34	0.33	19.15	717.50	1.11	22.16	783.60
Total	..	100.00	100.00	23.23	100.00	100.00	12.21	100.00	100.00	39.35

TABLE NO. 5—*Contd.*

Area Owned	EASTERN			ALL		
	% of Zamindars	% of Area Owned	Average Size of Area Owned (in acres)	% of Zamindars	% of Area Owned	Average Size of Area Area Owned (in acres)
Less than 5 acres ..	85.19	11.93	1.09	56.11	4.94	1.30
5 - 25 acres ..	10.02	15.30	11.92	20.48	13.91	11.79
25 - 100 acres ..	3.58	22.26	48.51	10.07	27.46	47.38
100 - 500 acres ..	0.91	22.80	195.37	2.86	32.23	195.97
500 acres or more ..	0.30	27.71	712.03	0.48	21.46	770.76
Total ..	100.00	100.00	7.89	100.00	100.00	17.37

TABLE NO. 6

DISTRIBUTION OF SAMPLE HOUSEHOLDS HAVING ZAMINDARI BY AREA OWNED AND LOCATION OF THEIR ESTATES

Area Owned	No. of Households	Zamindari in the Villages of Residence (in acres)	Zamindari outside the Villages of Residence (in acres)	Total Area
Less than 3 acres	17 (11.73)	22.63 (95.77) (0.58)	1.00 (4.23) (0.03)	23.63 (100.00) (0.35)
3 to 10 acres	49 (33.79)	257.07 (88.59) (6.55)	33.11 (11.41) (1.15)	290.18 (100.00) (4.28)
10 to 20 acres	29 (20.00)	308.24 (86.51) (7.86)	48.08 (13.49) (1.70)	356.32 (100.00) (5.26)
20 to 40 acres	21 (14.48)	367.53 (70.51) (9.38)	153.73 (29.49) (5.38)	521.26 (100.00) (7.69)
40 acres and above	29 (20.00)	2965.98 (53.10) (75.63)	2620.66 (46.90) (91.74)	5586.64 (100.00) (82.42)
Total	145 (100.00)	3921.45 (57.86) (100.00)	2856.58 (42.14) (100.00)	6778.03 (100.00) (100.00)

N.B. Figures within brackets indicate percentages.

TABLE NO. 7

DISTRIBUTION OF SAMPLE HOUSEHOLDS HAVING ZAMINDARI BY AREA OWNED AND BY CASTE AND COMMUNITY

Caste	Upper		Intermediate		Scheduled	
Size of Holding	No. of Households	Area (in acres)	No. of Households	Area (in acres)	No. of Households	Area (in acres)
1. Less than 1 acre	—	—	2 (3.64)	0.92 (71.31) (0.04)	—	—
2. 1 to 3 acres	6 (8.33)	9.28 (41.54) (0.24)	5 (9.09)	8.56 (38.32) (0.40)	2 (66.67)	2.50 (11.19) (39.68)
3. 3 to 5 acres	6 (8.33)	20.05 (37.76) (0.52)	6 (10.91)	21.50 (40.48) (1.00)	1 (33.33)	3.80 (7.16) (60.32)
5. 5 to 10 acres	16 (22.22)	104.59 (44.12) (2.71)	14 (25.45)	104.69 (44.16) (4.86)	—	—
5. 10 to 15 acres	8 (11.11)	96.44 (37.32) (2.50)	14 (25.45)	151.98 (58.81) (7.05)	—	—
6. 15 to 20 acres	3 (4.17)	50.90 (51.99) (1.32)	2 (3.64)	30.00 (30.65) (1.39)	—	—
7. 20 to 30 acres	11 (15.28)	239.93 (62.60) (6.23)	4 (7.27)	94.00 (24.53) (4.36)	—	—
8. 30 to 40 acres	1 (1.39)	35.00 (25.36) (0.91)	2 (3.64)	65.00 (47.10) (3.02)	—	—
9. 40 acres and above	21 (29.17)	3297.26 (59.02) (85.57)	6 (10.91)	1678.38 (38.04) (77.88)	—	—
Total	72 (100.00)	3853.45 (56.85) (100.00)	55 (39.93)	2155.03 (31.80) (100.00)	3 (2.07)	6.30 (0.09) (100.00)

TABLE NO. 7—*Contd.*

Caste	Non-Hindus		Total	
Size of Holdings	No. of Households	Area (in acres)	No. of Households	Area (in acres)
1. Less than 1 acre	1 (6.67)	0.37 (28.69) (0.05)	3 (2.07)	1.29 (100.00)
2. 1 to 3 acres	1 (6.67)	2.00 (8.95) (0.26)	14 (9.66)	22.34 (100.00)
3. 3 to 5 acres	2 (13.35)	7.75 (14.60) (1.01)	15 (10.34)	53.10 (100.00)
5. 5 to 10 acres	4 (26.70)	27.80 (11.72) (3.64)	34 (23.45)	237.08 (100.00)
5. 10 to 15 acres	1 (6.67)	10.00 (3.87) (1.30)	23 (15.86)	253.42 (100.00)
6. 15 to 20 acres	1 (6.67)	17.00 (17.36) (2.23)	6 (4.14)	97.90 (100.00)
7. 20 to 30 acres	2 (13.35)	49.33 (12.87) (6.45)	17 (11.72)	383.26 (100.00)
8. 30 to 40 acres	1 (6.67)	38.00 (27.54) (4.99)	4 (2.76)	138.00 (100.00)
9. 40 acres and above	2 (13.35)	611.00 (10.94) (80.07)	29 (20.00)	5586.64 (100.00)
Total	15 (10.34) (100.00)	763.25 (11.26) (100.00)	145 (100.00)	6778.03 (100.00)

TABLE NO. 8

Incidence of Rent per Acre according to Tenure in U.P. before Zamindari Abolition
(On Cash-Rented Holdings)

Year	1943-44			1945-46		
Tenure	Area of Holdings (in acres)	Recorded Rent Rs.	Incidence per acre Rs.	Area of Holdings (in acres)	Recorded Rent Rs.	Incidence per acre Rs.
AGRA						
Permanent Tenure Holders	1,449	2,781	1.92	1,652	3,276	1.98
Fixed Rate Tenants	7,05,783	28,08,341	3.98	7,06,186	28,06,901	3.97
Exproprietary Tenants	7,36,242	34,91,387	4.74	7,39,582	35,16,831	4.76
Occupancy Tenants (all kinds)	1,21,46,738	5,78,21,511	4.76	1,20,43,716	5,75,39,289	4.78
Hereditary	79,42,199	4,81,16,737	6.06	82,45,475	5,01,74,661	6.09
Non-occupancy Tenants	1,48,546	8,61,879	5.84	1,65,356	9,65,342	5.84
OUDH						
Exproprietary Tenants	65,830	3,35,970	5.10	67,421	3,45,056	5.12
Occupancy Tenants (all kinds)	99,913	3,64,913	3.65	99,229	3,66,327	3.67
Hereditary Tenants (all kinds)	73,83,872	4,71,39,416	6.38	74,81,835	4,77,11,764	3.68
Non-Occupancy Tenants	30,820	2,02,520	6.57	31,361	2,19,854	7.01
Total	2,92,61,392	16,11,51,755	5.51	2,95,81,813	16,36,47,301	5.53

TABLE NO. 8—*Contd.*

Year		1949-50			1951-52		
Tenure		Area of Holdings (in acres)	Recorded Rent Rs.	Incidence per acre Rs.	Area of Holdings (in acres)	Recorded Rent Rs.	Incidence per acre Rs.
AGRA							
Permanent Tenure Holders	..	1,740	3,722	2.14	1,690	3,160	1.87
Fixed Rate Tenants	..	8,16,622	33,55,192	4.11	8,17,304	33,57,914	4.11
Exproprietary Tenants	..	7,51,472	35,69,436	4.75	7,41,738	35,17,647	4.74
Occupancy Tenants (all kinds)	..	1,22,34,158	5,82,19,336	4.76	1,24,10,715	6,06,85,073	4.89
Hereditary	..	96,87,052	5,85,36,223	6.04	1,02,88,098	5,86,77,911	5.70
Non-occupancy Tenants	..	2,77,630	16,43,438	5.92	3,38,534	20,29,346	5.99
OUDH							
Exproprietary Tenants	..	68,997	3,53,625	5.13	68,864	3,53,667	5.14
Occupancy Tenants (all kinds)	..	99,354	3,68,691	3.71	99,679	3,69,997	3.71
Hereditary Tenants (all kinds)	..	78,82,165	4,98,38,090	6.32	82,45,300	5,13,48,684	6.23
Non-occupancy Tenants	..	34,235	3,86,341	11.28	34,965	4,07,294	11.65
Total U.P.	..	3,18,53,425	17,62,74,094	5.53	3,30,46,887	18,07,50,693	5.47

Source: Z.A.C.R. Part II, Rev. Adv. Report.

TABLE NO. 9

Division-wise Rental and Revenue Demand and Per Acre Rent and Revenue in 1946-47

Administrative Division	Area in Acres	Rental Demand Rs.	Revenue Demand Rs.	Per Acre Rent Rs.	Per Acre Revenue Rs.	Per Acre Zamindar Margin Rs.	Margin per Re. of Land Revenue
Meerut ..	36,90,093	2,12,89,799	90,27,782	5.77	2.45	3.32	1.36
Agra ..	38,76,957	2,06,53,234	80,97,327	5.33	2.09	3.24	1.55
Rohilkhand ..	47,23,560	2,57,14,552	84,94,420	5.32	1.80	3.52	1.96
Allahabad ..	38,19,874	1,97,06,400	79,18,145	5.16	2.10	3.06	1.46
Jhansi ..	33,60,947	87,47,030	35,52,161	2.60	1.06	1.54	1.45
Varanasi ..	31,27,221	1,15,43,471	44,98,064	3.69	1.44	2.25	1.56
Gorakhpur ..	44,89,726	1,54,35,824	78,44,648	3.44	1.74	1.70	0.98
Lucknow ..	44,60,073	2,77,76,228	89,31,988	6.23	2.00	4.32	2.16
Faizabad ..	48,30,800	3,67,60,421	98,123,04	5.54	2.03	3.52	1.73
All ..	3,63,79,251	17,76,26,959	6,81,76,839	4.88	1.87	3.01	1.61

Source: Revenue Administration Reports.

TABLE NO. 10

AREA UNDER SUB-TENANTS IN SAMPLE VILLAGES BY REGIONS BEFORE ZAMINDARI ABOLITION

Tenure	Western Area (in acres)	%	Central Area (in acres)	%	Bundelkhand (in acres)	%	Eastern Area (in acres)	%	Total Area (in acres)	%
Tenants of *Sir* and *Khudkasht*	196.95 (17.51)	7.65	75.28 (14.09)	9.20	842.11 (54.06)	16.58	493.12 (40.02)	18.80	1607.46 (36.13)	14.49
Sub-Tenants	426.30 (37.90)	} 5.70	170.82 (31.97)	} 6.72	364.50 (23.40)	} 6.06	191.12 (15.51)	} 10.25	1152.74 (25.91)	} 6.78
Land held without consent	399.02 (35.48)		272.01 (50.91)		256.95 (16.91)		530.45 (43.04)		1458.42 (32.78)	
Tenants of Rent-free Grantees	102.50 (9.11)	66.23	16.17 (3.03)	23.88	94.28 (6.05)	51.64	17.56 (1.43)	42.00	230.50 (5.18)	51.72
Total	1124.77 (100.00)	6.05	534.28 (100.00)	5.84	1157.84 (100.00)	9.22	1232.25 (100.00)	11.53	4449.12 (100.00)	8.04

NOTE: (1) Figures represent average for the year 1948-49, 1949-50 and 1950-51.
(2) Figures within brackets indicate percentages to the total area under sub-tenancy.
(3) Figures in the percentage column indicate percentage of sub-tenancy to the total area under the tenure. The area of sub-tenants and land held without consent has been worked out for this purpose as a percentage to the total area under permanent tenants.

TABLE NO. 11

ESTIMATED POPULATION AND CULTIVATING HOUSEHOLDS IN SAMPLE VILLAGES BY REGIONS BEFORE AND AFTER ZAMINDARI ABOLITION

Region		Population		Percentage increase of 3 over 2	Cultivating Households		Percentage Increase of 5 over 6
		1951	Mid-1960		Mid-1960	Estimated 1951	
1		2	3	4	5	6	7
Western	..	26,594	29,069	9.31	3,535	3,235	9.31
Central	..	16,486	18,797	14.02	2,135	1,873	14.02
Bundelkhand	..	8,777	9,523	7.83	1,215	1,127	7.83
Eastern	..	20,656	24,010	16.24	2,382	2,051	16.24
All	..	72,513	81,399	12.25	9,267	8,285	11.87

NOTE: (1) As recorded in census of 1951.
(2) As reported under the census undertaken during the course of present enquiry.
(3) As found in the course of the present enquiry.
(4) Calculated by reducing the number of households at the time of present enquiry by the same ratio as the increase in population of the sample villages by regions.

TABLE NO. 12

Estimates of Percentage Distribution of All Cultivating Households in the Sample Villages and of the Estimated Area of Cultivated Holdings before Zamindari Abolition by Size of Holdings and by Tenures

Present Principal Tenures / Size Groups	Bhumidhars		Sirdars		Asamis		Non-Tenure Holders		All	
	House-holds	Cultivated Area	House-holds	Cultivated Area	House-holds	Cultivated Area	House-holds	Cultivated Area	House-holds	Cultivated Area
Less than 1 acre	2.20	0.10	4.02	0.36	8.70	0.83	30.30	5.78	3.80	0.29
1 to 3 acres	14.98	2.43	29.40	8.20	30.43	9.45	32.50	15.28	26.35	6.25
3 to 5 acres	18.94	5.81	22.11	12.79	18.84	12.57	15.00	17.24	21.38	10.41
5 to 10 acres	29.07	16.46	24.62	25.95	24.64	29.62	17.50	32.08	25.54	22.75
10 to 15 acres	15.42	14.21	10.80	19.12	11.59	23.53	—	—	11.73	17.42
15 to 20 acres	4.41	5.97	3.77	9.59	1.45	4.50	—	—	3.86	8.29
20 to 30 acres	6.61	12.12	3.02	11.39	2.90	10.75	5.00	29.62	3.79	11.68
30 to 40 acres	3.08	7.97	1.76	9.30	1.45	8.75	—	—	2.03	8.82
40 acres & above	5.29	34.93	0.50	3.30	—	—	—	—	1.52	14.09
Total	100.00	100.00	100.00	100.00	100.00	100.00	100.00	100.00	100.00	100.00

TABLE NO. 13

CUMULATIVE PERCENTAGE DISTRIBUTION OF ALL CULTIVATING HOUSEHOLDS IN THE SAMPLE VILLAGES AND OF THE ESTIMATED AREA OF THEIR CULTIVATED HOLDINGS BEFORE ZAMINDARI ABOLITION BY SIZE OF HOLDINGS AND BY TENURES

Present Principal Tenures / Size Groups	Bhumidhars		Sirdars		Asamis		Non-Tenure Holders		All	
	Households	Cultivated Area	Households	Cultivated Area	Households	Cultivated Area	Households	Cultivated Area	Households	Cultivated Area
Less than 1 acre	2.20	0.10	4.02	0.36	8.70	0.83	30.00	5.78	3.80	0.29
,, 3 acres	17.18	2.53	33.42	8.56	39.13	10.28	62.50	21.06	30.15	6.54
,, 5 acres	36.12	8.34	55.53	21.35	57.97	22.85	77.50	38.30	51.53	16.95
,, 10 acres	65.19	24.80	80.15	47.30	82.67	52.47	95.00	70.38	77.07	39.70
,, 15 acres	80.61	39.01	90.95	66.42	94.20	76.00	—	—	88.80	57.12
,, 20 acres	85.02	44.98	94.72	76.01	95.65	80.50	—	—	92.66	65.51
,, 30 acres	91.63	57.10	97.94	87.40	98.55	91.25	100.00	100.00	96.45	77.09
,, 40 acres	94.71	65.07	99.50	96.70	100.00	100.00	—	—	98.48	85.91
40 acres & more	100.00	100.00	100.00	100.00	—	—	—	—	100.00	100.00

TABLE NO. 14

PERCENTAGE DISTRIBUTION OF AREA IN THE CULTIVATED HOLDINGS OF THE SAMPLE HOUSEHOLDS BEFORE ZAMINDARI ABOLITION BY SIZE GROUP AND BY FORM OF CULTIVATION

Size Group Present Tenure & Region		Less than 3 acres	3-10 acres	10-20 acres	20-40 acres	40 acres & above	Total
TENURE							
A. *BHUMIDHARS*							
(*i*) Personally Cultivated	..	88.44	81.44	77.74	58.99	3.59	49.16
(*ii*) Labour Cultivated	..	6.66	14.11	18.42	35.27	87.21	44.58
(*iii*) Share-Cropped	..	4.90	4.45	3.84	5.74	9.20	6.26
Total	..	100.00	100.00	100.00	100.00	100.00	100.00
B. *SIRDARS*							
(*i*) Personally Cultivated	..	95.26	96.22	84.23	67.64	—	83.61
(*ii*) Labour Cultivated	..	2.26	2.23	12.88	31.33	100.00	14.53
(*iii*) Share-Cropped	..	2.48	1.55	2.89	1.03	—	1.86
Total	..	100.00	100.00	100.00	100.00	100.00	100.00
C. *OTHERS*							
(*i*) Personally Cultivated	..	100.00	100.00	100.00	100.00	100.00	100.00
(*ii*) Labour Cultivated	..	—	—	—	—	—	—
(*iii*) Share Cropped	..	—	—	—	—	—	—
Total	..	100.00	100.00	100.00	100.00	100.00	100.00

TABLE NO. 14—*Contd.*

Size Group Present Tenure & Region		Less than 3 acres	3-10 acres	10-20 acres	20-40 acres	40 acres & above	Total
REGION							
A. WESTERN							
(*i*) Personally Cultivated	..	93.49	93.10	91.10	80.65	15.22	82.37
(*ii*) Labour Cultivated	..	—	3.29	6.61	14.25	78.26	13.63
(*iii*) Share-Cropped	..	6.51	3.61	2.29	5.00	6.52	4.00
Total	..	100.00	100.00	100.00	100.00	100.00	100.00
B. CENTRAL							
(*i*) Personally Cultivated	..	97.26	91.74	92.22	36.00	—	87.12
(*ii*) Labour Cultivated	..	—	6.35	3.76	57.26	—	9.66
(*iii*) Share-Cropped	..	2.74	1.91	4.02	6.74	—	3.22
Total	..	100.00	100.00	100.00	100.00	100.00	100.00
C. BUNDELKHAND							
(*i*) Personally Cultivated	..	100.00	92.56	100.00	92.83	—	62.28
(*ii*) Labour Cultivated	..	—	7.44	—	7.17	94.57	35.86
(*iii*) Share-Cropped	..	—	—	—	—	5.43	1.86
Total	..	100.00	100.00	100.00	100.00	100.00	100.00
D. EASTERN							
(*i*) Personally Cultivated	..	93.32	87.96	44.61	7.09	0.00	40.88
(*ii*) Labour Cultivated	..	6.68	10.99	49.67	92.91	88.17	54.11
(*iii*) Share-Cropped	..	0.00	1.05	5.72	0.00	11.83	5.01
Total	..	100.00	100.00	100.00	100.00	100.00	100.00

TABLE NO. 15

ADMINISTRATIVE DIVISIONS OF THE STATE ARRANGED BY PERCENTAGE OF BHUMIDHARI AREA TO TOTAL AREA UNDER HOLDINGS (1959-60)

Administrative Divisions of the State		Total Area of Holdings (in acres)	Total *Bhumidhari* Area (in acres)	% of *Bhumidhari* Area to Total Area of Holdings
1. Meerut	..	41,49,790	25,11,975	60.53
2. Varanasi	..	41,62,763	21,12,370	50.74
3. Gorakhpur	..	51,79,850	21,32,538	41.17
4. Jhansi	..	51,41,533	20,25,804	39.40
5. Agra	..	43,67,664	15,51,768	35.53
6. Allahabad	..	48,92,592	13,78,146	28.17
7. Faizabad	..	60,10,494	13,95,765	23.22
8. Rohilkhand	..	61,41,952	12,14,451	19.77
9. Lucknow	..	56,96,343	11,07,695	19.45
Total of the State excluding hill districts		4,57,42,981	1,54,30,512	33.73

Source: Rental and Holdings Register, Revenue Department.

TABLE NO. 16

DISTRICTS BY PERCENTAGE OF ESTIMATED AREA CONVERTED INTO BHUMIDHARI TO TOTAL AREA UNDER HOLDINGS

Less than 5%	5% to 10%	10% to 15%	15% to 20%	20% to 30%	30% & above
1. Rampur (2.18)	1. Kheri (5.14)	1. Fatehpur (10.35)	1. Ballia (16.76)	1. Banda (20.22)	1. Saharanpur (33.39)
2. Bahraich (2.29)	2. Sitapur (6.38)	2. Barabanki (10.36)	2. Bulandshahar (18.10)	2. Ghazipur (20.69)	2. Meerut (40.81)
3. Pilibhit (3.84)	3. Bareilly (7.28)	3. Farukhabad (10.68)	3. Hamirpur (18.50)	3. Mathura (20.69)	
	4. Mainpuri (8.51)	4. Agra (10.93)	4. Jhansi (18.61)	4. Deoria (21.96)	
	5. Lucknow (8.89)	5. Rai-Bareili (11.03)	5. Dehradun (19.24)	5. Jalaun (22.29)	
	6. Gonda (9.03)	6. Varanasi (11.17)		6. Azamgarh (24.83)	
	7. Etawah (9.19)	7. Mirzapur (11.86)		7. Gorakhpur (26.91)	
	8. Sultanpur (9.35)	8. Allahabad (11.98)		8. Muzzafarnagar (29.24)	
	9. Etah (9.38)	9. Kanpur (12.29)		9. Basti (29.61)	
	10. Badaun (9.50)	10. Hardoi (12.85)			
	11. Moradabad (9.50)	11. Pratapgarh (13.16)			
	12. Shahjahanpur (9.75)	12. Faizabad (13.17)			
		13. Jaunpur (13.82)			
		14. Bijnor (14.01)			
		15. Unnao (14.83)			
		16. Aligarh (14.99)			

N.B. Figures in brackets denote percentage.

TABLE NO. 17

PERCENTAGE DISTRIBUTION OF ALL HOUSEHOLDS WITH LAND RIGHTS IN SAMPLE VILLAGES AND OF THE AREA
HELD BY THEM AFTER ZAMINDARI ABOLITION BY TENURE AND BY SIZE OF HOLDING

Tenure Size Groups	Bhumidhar		Sirdars		Asamis		Total	
	Households	Area	Households	Area	Households	Area	Households	Area
Less than 1 acre	4.26	0.22	5.42	0.55	33.78	5.13	5.40	0.15
1 to 3 acres	13.19	2.48	30.30	8.86	36.49	23.34	26.69	6.85
3 to 5 acres	19.57	6.77	22.66	13.70	16.22	22.67	21.95	11.50
5 to 10 acres	28.94	18.87	23.40	25.89	9.46	22.22	24.47	23.62
10 to 15 acres	10.17	17.66	9.86	18.87	—	—	11.13	18.42
15 to 20 acres	4.26	6.70	3.69	9.96	4.05	26.64	3.82	8.97
20 to 30 acres	7.65	17.17	2.71	10.60	—	—	3.74	12.38
30 to 40 acres	1.70	5.17	1.47	8.00	—	—	1.51	7.07
40 acres above	4.26	24.96	0.49	3.57	—	—	1.29	10.44
Total	100.00	100.00	100.00	100.00	100.00	100.00	100.00	100.00

TABLE NO. 18

PERCENTAGE DISTRIBUTION OF ALL HOUSEHOLDS WITH LAND RIGHTS IN SAMPLE VILLAGES AND OF THE AREA HELD BY THEM AFTER ZAMINDARI ABOLITION BY SIZE OF HOLDING

Size of Holding	Western		Central		Bundelkhand		Eastern		Total	
	Household	Area	Household	Area	Household	Area	Household	Area	Household	Area
Less than 1 acre	4.45	0.32	6.62	0.68	—	—	17.99	1.51	7.83	0.55
1 to 3 acres	19.52	4.59	38.41	13.51	9.64	1.46	30.69	9.45	25.42	6.32
3 to 5 acres	24.66	12.30	23.18	16.33	14.46	3.97	16.40	10.19	20.86	10.57
5 to 10 acres	28.43	25.60	15.90	20.64	34.94	18.67	17.99	20.86	23.74	22.19
10 to 15 acres	11.30	17.00	9.27	21.04	16.87	14.93	8.99	18.77	10.98	17.54
15 to 20 acres	4.79	10.90	4.64	14.95	3.61	4.24	2.12	5.80	3.92	8.96
20 to 30 acres	3.77	12.16	0.66	3.02	13.25	24.04	3.17	12.58	4.14	13.53
30 to 40 acres	2.05	8.95	0.66	4.10	2.41	6.33	0.53	2.62	1.38	6.23
40 acres & above	1.03	8.18	0.66	5.73	4.82	26.63	2.12	18.22	1.73	14.11
Total	100.00	100.00	100.00	100.00	100.00	100.00	100.00	100.00	100.00	100.00

TABLE NO. 19

DISTRIBUTION OF ALL HOUSEHOLDS WITH LAND RIGHTS IN SAMPLE VILLAGES AND OF THE AREA HELD BY THEM AFTER ZAMINDARI ABOLITION BY TENURE AND BY SIZE OF HOLDING

Tenure	Bhumidhars			Sirdars			Asamis			Total		
Size Groups	No. of House-holds	Average Size	Area (in acres)	No. of House-holds	Average Size	Area (in acres)	No. of House-holds	Average Size	Area (in acres)	No. of House-holds	Average Size	Area (in acres)
Below 1 acre	84	0.53	44.52	389	0.61	237.29	25	0.41	10.21	498	0.59	292.02
1 to 3 acres	259	1.98	512.82	2,174	1.77	3,847.98	27	1.72	46.45	2,460	1.79	4,407.25
3 to 5 acres	385	3.64	1,401.40	1,626	3.66	5,951.16	12	3.76	45.10	2,023	3.66	7,397.66
5 to 10 acres	569	6.86	3,903.34	1,679	6.70	11,249.30	7	6.32	44.22	2,225	6.74	15,196.86
10 to 15 acres	318	11.49	3,653.82	708	11.58	8,198.64	—	—	—	1,026	11.55	11,852.46
15 to 20 acres	84	16.50	1,386.00	265	16.34	4,330.10	3	17.67	53.00	352	16.39	5,769.10
20 to 30 acres	151	23.52	3,551.52	194	23.73	4,603.62	—	—	—	345	23.64	8,155.14
30 to 40 acres	33	32.38	1,068.54	106	32.81	3,477.86	—	—	—	139	32.71	4,546.40
40 acres & above	84	61.48	5,164.32	35	44.27	1,549.45	—	—	—	119	56.42	6,713.77
Total	1,967	10.52	20,686.28	7,176	6.05	43,445.40	74	4.04	198.98	9,217	6.98	64,330.66

TABLE NO. 20

AVERAGE SIZE OF CULTIVATED HOLDINGS AND THE PERCENTAGE DISTRIBUTION OF ALL CULTIVATING HOUSEHOLDS IN THE SAMPLE VILLAGES AND OF ESTIMATED AREA CULTIVATED BY THEM AFTER ZAMINDARI ABOLITION

Variable				Percentage of Households to Total	Percentage of Cultivated Area to Total	Average size of Holding
A. TENURE						
(i) Bhumidhars	..	..	..	21.22	32.15	10.48
(ii) Sirdars	..	..	..	77.44	66.98	6.13
(iii) Asamis	..	..	..	0.80	0.61	5.39
(iv) Non-Tenure Holders	..	..	..	0.54	0.26	3.45
Total	..	..	..	100.00	100.00	7.04
B. REGION						
(i) Western	..	..	..	38.15	42.93	7.97
(ii) Central	..	..	..	23.04	16.89	5.19
(iii) Bundelkhand	..	..	..	13.11	20.24	10.93
(iv) Eastern	..	..	..	25.70	19.94	5.49
Total	..	..	..	100.00	100.00	7.08

TABLE NO. 20—*Contd.*

Variable			Percentage of Households to Total	Percentage of Cultivated Area to Total	Average size of Holding
C. OCCUPATION					
(*i*) Farmers	:	:	6.22	15.14	16.69
(*ii*) Peasants	:	:	84.15	80.76	6.59
(*iii*) Agricultural labourers	:		4.80	1.66	2.38
(*iv*) Miscellaneous	..		4.83	2.44	3.52
Total	:	:	100.00	100.00	6.87
D. CASTE					
(*i*) Upper Hindus	:	:	28.47	43.23	10.78
(*ii*) Scheduled	:	:	13.81	8.35	4.27
(*iii*) Others	:	:	57.72	48.42	5.97
Total	:	:	100.00	100.00	7.11

TABLE NO. 21

Estimates of Percentage Distribution of All Cultivating Households in the Sample Villages and of the Estimated Area of Cultivated Holdings after Zamindari Abolition by Size of Holding and Tenure

Present Principal Tenure Size Group	Bhumidhari		Sirdari		Asami		Non-Tenure Holder		All	
	Households	Area	Households	Area	Households	Area	Households	Area	Households	Area
Less than 1 acre	4.25	0.21	4.93	0.49	9.46	0.78	16.00	2.94	5.88	0.41
1 to 3 acres	13.19	2.49	29.56	8.82	22.97	7.74	52.00	25.58	25.36	6.85
3 to 5 acres	19.16	6.63	21.67	12.97	24.32	17.34	14.00	14.29	20.65	10.99
5 to 10 acres	30.21	19.76	25.37	27.63	32.43	41.70	12.00	20.50	26.67	25.21
10 to 15 acres	15.32	16.79	10.34	19.18	4.06	8.75	2.00	7.25	10.72	18.34
15 to 20 acres	4.25	6.69	3.45	9.30	4.06	13.29	—	—	3.53	8.48
20 to 30 acres	7.66	17.21	2.96	11.76	2.70	10.40	4.00	29.44	4.44	13.52
30 to 40 acres	1.71	5.20	1.48	8.15	—	—	—	—	1.31	7.15
40 acres & above	4.25	25.02	0.24	1.70	—	—	—	—	1.44	9.05
Total	100.00	100.00	100.00	100.00	100.00	100.00	100.00	100.00	100.00	100.00

TABLE NO. 22

Estimates of Cumulative Percentage Distribution of All Cultivating Households in the Sample Villages and of the Area of Cultivated Holdings after Zamindari Abolition by Size of Holding and Tenure

Present Principal Tenures / Size Group	Bhumidhars		Sirdars		Asamis		Non-Tenure Holders		All	
	Households	Area	Households	Area	Households	Area	Households	Area	Households	Area
Less than 1 acre	4.25	0.21	4.93	0.49	9.46	0.78	16.00	2.94	5.88	0.41
1 to 3 acres	17.44	2.70	34.49	9.31	32.43	8.52	68.00	28.52	31.24	7.26
3 to 5 acres	36.60	9.33	56.16	22.28	56.75	25.84	82.00	42.81	51.89	18.25
5 to 10 acres	66.81	29.09	81.53	49.91	89.18	67.56	94.00	63.31	78.56	43.46
10 to 15 acres	82.13	45.88	91.87	69.09	93.24	76.31	96.00	70.56	89.28	61.80
15 to 20 acres	86.38	52.57	95.32	78.39	97.30	89.60	—	—	92.81	70.28
20 to 30 acres	94.04	69.78	98.28	90.15	100.00	100.00	100.00	100.00	97.25	83.80
30 to 40 acres	95.75	74.98	99.76	98.30	—	—	—	—	98.56	90.95
40 acres & above	100.00	100.00	100.00	100.00	—	—	—	—	100.00	100.00

TABLE NO. 23

Estimates of Percentage Distribution of All Households in the Sample Villages and of the Estimated Area of their Cultivated Holdings before and after Zamindari Abolition by Size of Holding

Size Group	Households		Cultivated Area		Cumulative Percentages			
					Households		Cultivated Area	
	Before Zamindari Abolition	After Zamindari Abolition	Before Zamindari Abolition	After Zamindari Abolition	Before Zamindari Abolition	After Zamindari Abolition	Before Zamindari Abolition	After Zamindari Abolition
Less than 1 acre	3.80	5.88	0.29	0.41	3.80	5.88	0.29	0.41
1 to 3 acres	26.35	25.36	6.25	6.85	30.15	31.24	6.54	7.26
3 to 5 acres	21.38	20.65	10.41	10.99	51.53	51.89	16.95	18.25
5 to 10 acres	25.54	26.67	22.75	25.21	77.07	78.56	39.70	43.46
10 to 15 acres	11.73	10.72	17.42	18.34	88.80	89.28	57.12	61.80
15 to 20 acres	3.86	3.53	8.29	8.48	92.66	92.81	65.41	70.28
20 to 30 acres	3.79	4.44	11.68	13.52	96.45	97.25	77.09	83.80
30 to 40 acres	2.03	1.31	8.82	7.15	98.48	98.56	85.91	90.95
40 acres & above	1.52	1.44	14.09	9.05	100.00	100.00	100.00	100.00

TABLE NO. 24

PERCENTAGE DISTRIBUTION OF SAMPLE HOUSEHOLDS AND OF THE AREA OF THEIR CULTIVATED HOLDINGS BEFORE AND AFTER ZAMINDARI ABOLITION BY REGIONS

Size Group	Western Households Before Z.A.	After Z.A.	Western Area Before Z.A.	After Z.A.	Central Households Before Z.A.	After Z.A.	Central Area Before Z.A.	After Z.A.	Bundelkhand Households Before Z.A.	After Z.A.	Bundelkhand Area Before Z.A.	After Z.A.	Eastern Households Before Z.A.	After Z.A.	Eastern Area Before Z.A.	After Z.A.
Less than 1 acre	3.70	3.58	0.21	0.22	4.38	21.14	0.43	0.41	0.00	0.00	0.00	0.00	10.50	13.11	0.94	1.44
1 to 3 acres	15.83	15.63	3.31	3.42	36.25	37.28	13.51	14.05	9.09	8.43	1.17	1.26	36.50	36.89	8.72	11.98
3 to 5 acres	10.87	23.78	8.87	11.27	28.12	25.45	20.79	18.13	14.29	13.25	3.62	3.55	17.50	15.05	8.84	9.70
5 to 10 acres	33.33	32.57	27.09	27.92	16.25	19.53	21.24	25.21	36.36	37.35	17.65	19.79	17.50	19.42	16.31	23.08
10 to 15 acres	14.14	12.05	18.80	16.91	8.75	7.69	20.09	17.93	14.29	16.87	11.51	14.82	9.50	8.73	14.82	18.55
15 to 20 acres	3.70	3.91	7.39	8.48	4.37	4.14	13.97	13.62	5.19	3.62	5.80	4.20	2.08	2.43	4.63	6.94
20 to 30 acres	5.72	5.54	15.82	16.37	1.88	1.18	9.97	6.19	10.39	13.25	16.57	24.03	1.50	1.94	4.21	8.45
30 to 40 acres	2.36	1.96	9.89	8.06	0.00	0.59	0.00	4.46	3.90	2.41	9.90	6.35	2.50	0.49	10.76	2.60
40 acres and above	1.35	0.98	9.09	7.35	0.00	0.00	0.00	0.00	6.49	4.82	34.28	26.00	2.50	1.94	30.77	17.26
Total	100.00	100.00	100.00	100.00	100.00	100.00	100.00	100.00	100.00	100.00	100.00	100.00	100.00	100.00	100.00	100.00

Z.A. — Zamindari Abolition

TABLE NO. 25

PERCENTAGE DISTRIBUTION OF THE ESTIMATED AREA OF CULTIVATED HOLDINGS OF ALL HOUSEHOLDS IN THE SAMPLE VILLAGE AFTER ZAMINDARI ABOLITION BY FORM OF CULTIVATION AND BY THE PRINCIPAL TENURE OF THE CULTIVATORS

Present Principal Tenure / Size Group	Bhumidars				Sirdars			
	Personally Cultivated	Labour Cultivated	Share-Cropped	Total	Personally Cultivated	Labour Cultivated	Share-Cropped	Total
Less than 1 acre	90.48	0.00	9.52	100.00	100.00	0.00	0.00	100.00
1 to 3 acres	83.54	4.46	12.00	100.00	90.95	3.86	5.19	100.00
3 to 5 acres	93.80	4.06	2.14	100.00	87.61	1.39	11.00	100.00
5 to 10 acres	80.08	16.71	3.21	100.00	95.18	3.95	0.87	100.00
10 to 15 acres	75.78	17.55	6.67	100.00	83.21	15.81	0.98	100.00
15 to 20 acres	70.30	29.70	0.00	100.00	79.40	19.52	1.08	100.00
20 to 30 acres	68.00	26.51	5.49	100.00	81.41	10.06	8.53	100.00
30 to 40 acres	89.07	10.93	0.00	100.00	49.72	46.59	3.69	100.00
40 acres & above	0.00	100.00	0.00	100.00	0.00	100.00	0.00	100.00
Total	58.10	38.75	3.16	100.00	83.14	13.16	3.70	100.00

TABLE NO. 25—*Contd.*

Present Principal Tenure Size Group	Others				All			
	Personally Cultivated	Labour Cultivated	Share-Cropped	Total	Personally Cultivated	Labour Cultivated	Share-Cropped	Total
Less than 1 acre	100.00	0.00	0.00	100.00	98.42	0.00	1.58	100.00
1 to 3 acres	100.00	0.00	0.00	100.00	90.25	3.86	5.89	100.00
3 to 5 acres	100.00	0.00	0.00	100.00	88.95	1.88	9.17	100.00
5 to 10 acres	99.24	0.00	0.76	100.00	91.49	7.06	1.45	100.00
10 to 15 acres	100.00	0.00	0.00	100.00	81.12	16.25	2.63	100.00
15 to 20 acres	100.00	0.00	0.00	100.00	77.32	21.88	0.80	100.00
20 to 30 acres	100.00	0.00	0.00	100.00	76.21	16.58	7.21	100.00
30 to 40 acres	—	—	—	—	58.78	38.38	2.84	100.00
40 acres & above	—	—	—	—	—	100.00	0.00	100.00
Total	99.73	—	0.27	100.00	75.37	21.12	3.51	100.00

TABLE NO. 26

PERCENTAGE DISTRIBUTION OF THE AREA CULTIVATED BY SAMPLE HOUSEHOLDS AFTER ZAMINDARI ABOLITION BY SIZE GROUPS AND BY FORM OF CULTIVATION

Size Tenure & Region	Less than 3 acres	3-10 acres	10-20 acres	20-40 acres	40 acres & above	Total
TENURE						
A. Bhumidhar						
(i) Personally Cultivated	84.09	83.53	74.22	72.96	0.00	58.18
(ii) Labour Cultivated	4.10	13.53	21.01	22.84	100.00	38.66
(iii) Share-Cropped	11.81	2.94	4.77	4.20	0.00	3.16
Total	100.00	100.00	100.00	100.00	100.00	100.00
B. Sirdars						
(i) Personally Cultivated	91.43	92.76	81.96	68.43	0.00	83.08
(ii) Labour Cultivated	3.65	3.13	17.02	25.02	100.00	13.20
(iii) Share-Cropped	4.92	4.11	1.02	6.55	0.00	3.72
Total	100.00	100.00	100.00	100.00	100.00	100.00
C. Others						
(i) Personally Cultivated	100.00	99.24	100.00	100.00	—	99.73
(ii) Labour Cultivated	—	—	—	—	—	—
(iii) Share-Cropped	—	0.76	—	—	—	0.27
Total	100.00	100.00	100.00	100.00	—	100.00

TABLE NO. 26—*Contd.*

Size Tenure & Region		Less than 3 acres	3-10 acres	10-20 acres	20-40 acres	40 acres & above	Total
REGION							
A. *Western*							
(*i*) Personally Cultivated	..	82.53	94.81	87.29	84.92	0.00	83.07
(*ii*) Labour Cultivated	..	2.24	1.73	9.31	8.06	100.00	12.44
(*iii*) Share-Cropped	..	15.23	3.46	3.40	7.02	0.00	4.49
Total	..	100.00	100.00	100.00	100.00	100.00	100.00
B. *Central*							
(*i*) Personally Cultivated	..	96.96	88.09	91.94	32.30	0.00	84.64
(*ii*) Labour Cultivated	..	—	7.43	3.90	52.59	0.00	10.06
(*iii*) Share-Cropped	..	3.04	4.48	4.16	15.11	0.00	5.30
Total	..	100.00	100.00	100.00	100.00	00.00	100.00
C. *Bundelkhand*							
(*i*) Personally Cultivated	..	100.00	91.40	100.00	91.70	0.00	69.47
(*ii*) Labour Cultivated	..	—	6.80	—	8.30	100.00	30.11
(*iii*) Share-Cropped	..	—	1.80	—	—	0.00	0.42
Total	..	100.00	100.00	100.00	100.00	100.00	100.00
D. *Eastern*							
(*i*) Personally Cultivated	..	92.86	82.39	39.99	—	—	49.67
(*ii*) Labour Cultivated	..	5.93	15.50	59.16	100.00	100.00	49.26
(*iii*) Share-Cropped	..	1.21	2.11	0.85	—	—	1.07
Total	..	100.00	100.00	100.00	100.00	100.00	100.00

TABLE NO. 27

PERCENTAGE DISTRIBUTION OF AREA CULTIVATED BY ALL HOUSEHOLDS IN THE SAMPLE VILLAGES
AFTER ZAMINDARI ABOLITION BY BROAD SIZE GROUPS AND BY FORM OF CULTIVATION

Size Group			Personally Cultivated	Labour Cultivated	Share-Cropped	Total
1. Small—less than 5 acres	..	..	89.66	2.58	7.76	100.00
2. Medium—5 to 15 acres	..	..	87.12	10.94	1.94	100.00
3. Large—15 to 40 acres	..	..	72.26	23.46	4.28	100.00
4. Very Large—40 acres and above	..	..	0.00	100.00	0.00	100.00
All	..	..	75.37	21.12	3.51	100.00

TABLE NO. 28

AVERAGE SIZE OF CULTIVATED HOLDING BEFORE AND AFTER ZAMINDARI ABOLITION—
ESTIMATES FOR ALL CULTIVATING HOUSEHOLDS IN SAMPLE VILLAGES

				Before Zamindari Abolition	After Zamindari Abolition	Decrease in Average Size	Percentage Decrease in 'After' over 'Before'
				Acres	Acres	Acres	
A. PRINCIPAL PRESENT TENURE							
(i) Bhumidhari	:	:	:	12.37	10.48	1.89	15.28
(ii) Sirdari	:	:	:	6.49	6.13	0.36	5.54
(iii) Asami	:	:	:	5.80	5.39	0.41	7.07
(iv) Without tenure	:	:	:	3.53	3.45	0.08	2.27
All	:	:	:	7.73	7.04	0.69	8.93
B. REGION							
(i) Western	:	:	:	8.37	7.97	0.43	5.14
(ii) Central	:	:	:	5.25	5.19	0.06	1.14
(iii) Bundelkhand	:	:	:	11.42	10.93	0.49	4.29
(iv) Eastern	:	:	:	7.14	5.49	1.65	23.11
All	:	:	:	7.78	7.08.	0.70	9.00

TABLE NO. 28—Contd.

		Before Zamindari Abolition	After Zamindari Abolition	Decrease in Average Size	Percentage Decrease in 'After' over 'Before'
		Acres	Acres	Acres	
C. OCCUPATION					
(i) Farmers	..	21.83	16.69	5.15	23.59
(ii) Peasants	..	6.65	6.59	0.06	0.90
(iii) Agricultural Labourers	..	4.71	2.38	2.33	49.47
(iv) Miscellaneous	..	2.47	3.52	minus 1.05	minus 42.51
All	..	7.31	6.87	0.44	6.02
D. CASTE					
(i) Upper Hindus	..	11.93	10.78	1.15	9.63
(ii) Scheduled	..	4.36	4.27	0.09	2.06
(iii) Others	..	6.52	5.97	0.55	8.44
All	..	7.77	7.11	0.66	8.49
Total*	..	7.73	7.04	0.69	8.93

* Estimate on the basis of break-up into size-groups of holdings.

TABLE NO. 29

Distribution of All Cultivating Households and their Cultivated Holdings in Sample Villages before and after Zamindari Abolition by Size Groups

Size Group	Before Zamindari Abolition		After Zamindari Abolition		Variation in After Z.A. over Before Z.A.		Percentage Variation in After Z.A. over Before Z.A.	
	Households	Holdings Area (acres)	Households	Holdings Area (acres)	Households	Holdings Area (acres)	Households	Holdings Area (acres)
1. Small— Less than 5 acres	4,269	10,852.18	4,833	11,907.05	+564	+1,054.87	+13.21	+9.72
2. Medium— 5-15 acres	3,088	25,709.47	3,492	28,396.69	+404	+2,687.22	+13.08	+10.45
3. Large— 15-40 acres	802	18,431.23	841	19,015.96	+39	+584.73	+4.86	+3.17
4. Very Large 40 acres & above	126	9,019.34	101	5,902.24	−25	−3,117.10	−19.84	−34.56
Total	8,285	64,012.22	9,267	65,221.94	+982	+1,209.72	+11.85	+1.89

TABLE NO. 30

ESTIMATED PERCENTAGE DISTRIBUTION OF ALL CULTIVATING HOUSEHOLDS IN SAMPLE VILLAGES AND OF THEIR CULTIVATED HOLDINGS BEFORE AND AFTER ZAMINDARI ABOLITION BY SIZE OF CULTIVATED HOLDING

Size Group	Before Zamindari Abolition		After Zamindari Abolition		Variation in After Z.A. over Before Z.A.		Percentage Variation in After Z.A. over Before Z.A.	
	Households	Cultivated Holdings Area	Households	Cultivated Holdings Area	Households	Cultivated Holdings Area	Households	Cultivated Holdings Area
1. Small— Less than 5 acres	51.53	16.96	51.89	18.25	0.36	+1.29	+0.70	+7.61
2. Medium— 5 to 15 acres	37.27	40.16	37.39	43.55	+0.12	+3.39	+0.32	+0.79
3. Large— 15 to 40 acres	9.68	28.79	9.28	29.15	−0.40	+0.98	−4.31	+4.04
4. Very Large— 40 acres & above	1.52	14.09	1.44	9.05	−0.08	−5.04	−5.26	−37.33
Total	100.00	100.00	100.00	100.00	—	—	—	—

TABLE NO. 31

PERCENTAGE DISTRIBUTION OF AREA IN THE CULTIVATED HOLDINGS OF ALL HOUSEHOLDS IN THE SAMPLE VILLAGES BEFORE AND AFTER ZAMINDARI ABOLITION BY SIZE OF CULTIVATED HOLDING AND METHOD OF CULTIVATION

Size Groups	Before Zamindari Abolition				After Zamindari Abolition			
	Personally Cultivated	Labour Cultivated	Share-Cropped	Total	Personally Cultivated	Labour Cultivated	Share-Cropped	Total
1. Small— Less than 5 acres	10,270.47 (94.64)	213.41 (1.97)	368.30 (3.39)	100.00	10,675.19 (89.66)	307.57 (2.58)	924.29 (7.76)	100.00
2. Medium— 5 to 15 acres	21,878.79 (85.10)	3,166.50 (12.32)	664.18 (2.58)	100.00	24,740.29 (87.12)	3,104.40 (10.94)	552.00 (1.94)	100.00
3. Large 15 to 40 acres	13,646.62 (74.04)	4,379.39 (23.76)	405.22 (2.20)	100.00	13,740.10 (72.26)	4,462.61 (23.46)	813.25 (4.28)	100.00
4. Very large 40 acres & above	274.59 (3.05)	8,041.06 (89.15)	703.69 (7.80)	100.00	— (0.00)	5,902.24 (100.00)	— (0.00)	100.00
Total	46,070.47 (71.97)	15,800.36 (24.68)	2,141.39 (3.35)	100.00	49,155.58 (75.37)	13,776.82 (21.12)	2,289.54 (3.51)	100.00

TABLE NO. 31—*Contd.*

Size Groups	Change in After Zamindari Abolition over Before Zamindari Abolition			Percentage Change in After Zamindari Abolition over Before Zamindari Abolition		
	Personally Cultivated	Labour Cultivated	Share-Cropped	Personally Cultivated	Labour Cultivated	Share-Cropped
1. Small— Less than 5 acres ..	+404.72	+94.16	+555.99	+3.94	+44.12	+150.96
2. Medium— 5 to 15 acres ..	+2,861.50	−62.10	−112.18	+13.08	−1.96	−16.89
3. Large— 15 to 40 acres ..	+93.48	+83.22	+408.03	+6.85	+1.90	+100.69
4. Very large— 40 acres & above ..	−274.59	−2,138.82	−703.69	−100.00	−26.60	−100.00
Total ..	+3,085.11	−2,023.54	+148.15	+6.70	−12.81	+6.92

TABLE NO. 32

DISTRIBUTION OF SAMPLE HOUSEHOLDS EMPLOYING PERMANENT OUTSIDE LABOUR

Occupation	Sample Households		Households Employing Permanent Farm Servants		Number of Permanent Farm Servants		Average No. of Permanent* Farm Servants		Percentage of Col. 4 to 2	Percentage of Col. 5 to 3
	Before Zamindari Abolition	After Zamindari Abolition	Before Zamindari Abolition	After Zamindari Abolition	Before Zamindari Abolition	After Zamindari Abolition	Before Zamindari Abolition	After Zamindari Abolition		
1	2	3	4	5	6	7	8	9	10	11
1. Farming	75	78	51	45	124	80	2.43	1.77	68.00	57.70
2. Cultivation	485	487	7	8	10	9	1.43	1.13	1.44	1.64
3. Agr. Labourers	157	150	—	—	—	—	—	—	—	—
4. Non-Agricultural	48	50	4	5	5	5	1.25	1.00	8.33	10.00
Total	765	765	62	58	139	94	2.24	1.62	8.14	7.58

* Average number of Permanent Farm Servants per household employing Permanent Farm Servants.

TABLE NO. 33

DISTRIBUTION OF THE AREA HELD BY SUB-TENANTS (ASAMIS AND OTHERS ENTERED IN PART II OF KHATAUNI) AFTER ZAMINDARI ABOLITION IN SAMPLE VILLAGES GROUPED BY REGIONS

(Averages for 1957-58 to 1959-60)

Type of Sub-Tenancy	Western		Central		Bundelkhand		Eastern		Total	
	Area (acres)	Percent-age	Area (acres)	Percent-age	Area (acres)	Percent-age	Area (acres)	Percent-age	Area (acres)	Percent-age
1. *Asami* ..	37.66	8.26	73.83	34.53	43.24	21.52	78.27	30.53	232.99	20.61
2. *Adhivasis* of Class VIII	97.53	21.24	2.19	1.02	0.00	0.00	16.02	6.25	115.75	10.24
3. *Asami* without consent	323.99	70.56	137.82	64.45	157.66	78.48	162.11	63.22	781.58	69.15
Total ..	458.18	100.00	213.84	100.00	200.90	100.00	256.40	100.00	1,130.32	100.00

TABLE NO. 34

PERCENTAGE OF THE AREA FROM WHICH EJECTED TO THE TOTAL AREA OF HOLDINGS

Division	1940-41	1941-42	1942-43	1943-44	1944-45	1945-46	1946-47	1947-48	1988-49	1949-50
1. Meerut ..	0.45	0.58	0.53	0.46	0.56	0.15	0.04	0.14	0.13	0.05
2. Agra ..	0.57	0.57	0.56	0.48	0.71	0.11	0.04	0.10	0.08	0.07
3. Rohilkhand ..	0.32	0.40	0.44	0.37	0.46	0.11	0.06	0.14	0.34	0.04
4. Allahabad ..	0.21	0.25	0.32	0.33	0.58	0.05	—	0.11	0.09	0.03
5. Jhansi ..	0.25	0.17	0.22	0.21	0.64	0.04	0.01	0.11	0.06	—
6. Banaras ..	0.22	0.20	0.20	0.30	0.45	0.08	0.02	0.06	0.05	0.04
7. Gorakhpur ..	0.21	0.21	0.18	0.30	0.87	0.03	0.03	0.03	0.03	—
8. Lucknow ..	0.18	0.29	0.18	0.14	1.13	0.04	0.02	0.06	0.05	0.03
9. Faizabad ..	0.31	0.40	0.31	0.21	0.97	0.09	0.12	0.52	0.28	0.06
Total ..	0.29	0.34	0.32	0.30	0.70	0.77	0.03	0.15	0.13	0.04

Source: Revenue Administration Reports.

TABLE NO. 35

Transfer of Land in Sample Villages through Sale or Gift from 1951-52 to 1959-60

Region	Total Area* Under Holdings (in acres)	Area Transferred By			Total Sale Price Rs.	Price per acre Rs.	% of Area Sold to Total	% of Area given as gift to total
		Sale (in acres)	Gift (in acres)	Total (in acres)				
1. Western ..	22,237.76	1,679.11	28.80	1,707.91	4,13,994.00	246.55	7.55	0.13
2. Central ..	9,307.13	256.34	30.49	286.83	1,13,031.00	440.94	2.75	0.32
3. Bundelkhand ..	18,340.87	192.13	43.19	235.32	34,425.00	179.18	1.07	0.24
4. Eastern ..	11,458.91	245.58	70.70	316.28	2,09,500.00	853.08	2.14	0.67
Total ..	61,344.67	2,373.16	173.18	2,546.34	7,70,950.00	324.86	3.87	0.28

* Figures for the area of cultivated holdings in sample villages in 1959-60.

TABLE NO. 36

TRANSFER OF LAND THROUGH SALE BY SAMPLE HOUSEHOLDS ACCORDING TO TENURE, SIZE AND PURPOSE OF TRANSFER

Principal Tenure / Size Group	Bhumidhars					Sirdars				
	Social & Domestic Exp.	Repayment of Debt	Litigation	Unmanageable Holding	Total	Social & Domestic Exp.	Repayment of Debt	Litigation	Unmanageable Holding	Total
Less than 5 acres	9.56 (75.16)	0.91 (9.15)	2.25 (17.69)	— —	12.72 (100.00)	2.07 (22.00)	5.34 (56.75)	1.25 (13.28)	0.75 (7.97)	9.41 (100.00)
5 to 10 acres	9.97 (54.78)	— —	2.33 (12.80)	5.90 (32.42)	18.20 (100.00)	0.80 (26.06)	— —	2.27 (73.94)	— —	3.07 (100.00)
15 to 40 acres	22.73 (91.99)	1.65 (6.68)	— —	0.33 (1.33)	24.71 (100.00)	7.50 (92.36)	— —	0.72 (7.64)	— —	8.12 (100.00)
40 acres & more	—	—	—	1.88 (100.00)	1.88 (100.00)	—	—	—	—	—
Total	42.26 (73.48)	2.56 (4.45)	4.58 (7.97)	8.11 (14.10)	57.51 (100.00)	10.37 (50.34)	5.34 (25.92)	4.14 (20.10)	0.75 (3.64)	20.60 (100.00)

TABLE NO. 36—Contd.

Principal Tenure	Asamis					Total				
Size Group	Social & Domestic Exp.	Repayment of Debt	Litigation	Unmanagable Holding	Total	Social & Domestic Exp.	Repayment of Debt	Litigation	Unmanagable Holding	Total
Less than 5 acres	0.09 (5.03)	—	—	1.70 (94.97)	1.79 (100.00)	11.72 (49.00)	6.25 (26.13)	3.50 (14.63)	2.45 (10.24)	23.92 (100.00)
5 to 15 acres	—	—	—	—	—	10.77 (50.63)	—	4.60 (21.63)	5.90 (27.74)	21.27 (100.00)
15 to 40 acres	—	—	—	—	—	30.23 (92.08)	1.65 (5.03)	0.62 (1.89)	0.33 (1.00)	32.83 (100.00)
40 acres & above	—	—	—	—	—	—	—	—	1.88 (100.00)	1.88 (100.00)
Total	0.09 (5.03)	—	—	1.70 (94.97)	1.79 (100.00)	52.72 (65.98)	7.90 (9.89)	8.72 (10.91)	10.56 (13.22)	79.90 (100.00)

N.B. - Figures within bracket indicate percentages.

TABLE NO. 37

Transfer of Land through Sale by Sample Households according to Caste and Size

Caste & Size Groups		Upper	Other	Scheduled	Total
Less than 5 acres	..	14.00 (58.53)	7.51 (31.40)	2.41 (10.07)	23.92 (100.00)
5 to 15 acres	..	14.85 (69.82)	5.62 (26.42)	0.80 (3.76)	21.27 (100.00)
15 to 40 acres	..	19.36 (58.97)	13.47 (41.03)	—	32.83 (100.00)
40 acres and more	..	1.88 (100.00)	—	—	1.88 (100.00)
Total	..	50.09 (62.69)	26.60 (33.29)	3.21 (4.02)	79.90 (100.00)

TABLE NO. 38

TOTAL LAND PURCHASED BY SAMPLE HOUSEHOLDS ACCORDING TO TENURE, SIZE AND PURPOSE OF PURCHASE BETWEEN 1951-52 AND 1959-60

Principal Tenure and Purpose of Purchase — Size	Bhumidhars			Sirdars			Asamis			Total		
	Farming	Residential	Total	Farming	Residential	Total	Farming	Residential	Total	Farming	Residential	Total
Below 5 acres	23.97 (97.12)	0.71 (2.88)	24.68 (100.00)	6.77 (100.00)	—	6.77 (100.00)	6.40 (98.46)	0.10 (1.54)	6.50 (100.00)	37.14 (97.87)	0.81 (2.13)	37.95 (100.00)
5 to 15 acres	52.68 (100.00)	—	52.68 (100.00)	12.86 (100.00)	—	12.86 (100.00)	0.26 (100.00)	—	0.26 (100.00)	65.80 (100.00)	—	65.80 (100.00)
15 to 40 acres	15.99 (100.00)	—	15.99 (100.00)	3.12 (100.00)	—	3.12 (100.00)	—	—	—	19.11 (100.00)	—	19.11 (100.00)
40 acres and more	—	—	—	—	—	—	—	—	—	—	—	—
Total	92.64 (99.24)	0.71 (0.76)	93.35 (100.00)	22.75 (100.00)	—	22.75 (100.00)	6.66 (98.52)	0.10 (1.48)	6.76 (100.00)	122.05 (99.34)	0.81 (0.66)	122.86 (100.00)

TABLE NO. 39

TOTAL LAND PURCHASED BY SAMPLE HOUSEHOLDS BETWEEN 1951-52 AND 1959-60 ACCORDING TO CASTE AND SIZE GROUPS

Caste Size Group		Upper	Other	Scheduled	Total
Less than 5 acres	..	0.24 (0.63)	34.07 (89.78)	3.64 (9.59)	37.95 (100.00)
5 to 15 acres	..	41.59 (63.21)	21.41 (32.54)	2.80 (4.25)	65.80 (100.00)
15 to 40 acres	..	13.36 (69.91)	5.75 (30.09)	—	19.11 (100.00)
40 acres and more	..	—	—	—	—
Total	..	55.19 (44.92)	61.23 (49.84)	6.44 (5.24)	122.86 (100.00)

TABLE NO. 40

Percentage Distribution of Land by Different Uses

	Uttar Pradesh			Sample Villages		
	Before Zamindari Abolition[1]	After Zamindari Abolition[3]	Percentage Variation[4]	Before Zamindari Abolition[2]	After Zamindari Abolition[3]	Percentage Variation[4]
1. Cultivated area including current fallow ..	68.81	73.95	+ 8.23	64.44	69.89	+ 8.66
2. Old Fallow	1.21	0.68	—43.89	1.28	0.52	—59.66
3. Culturable Waste	13.57	10.72	—20.42	13.82	11.21	—18.74
4. Groves	2.25	1.96	—12.24	2.69	2.33	—13.08
5. Water	4.55	4.49	— 0.37	3.53	3.46	— 1.86
6. Land under non-agricultural uses ..	3.21	3.31	+ 3.90	2.58	3.08	+19.62
7. Graveyard and otherwise barren ..	6.40	4.89	—23.12	11.66	9.51	—18.26
Total	100.00	100.00		100.00	100.00	

[1] Based on the average of 1948-49—1950-51
[2] Based on the average of 1949-50—1951-52
[3] Based on the average of 1957-58—1959-60
[4] Percentage variations have been worked out from the actual area in acres for different uses.

TABLE NO. 41

EXPENDITURE ON NEW FARMS AND PERMANENT IMPROVEMENTS MADE BY THE SAMPLE HOUSEHOLDS

Region and Principal Tenure	Households		Percentage of 3 to 2	Total Expenditure	Expenditure per household	Expenditure per household incurring such expenditure
	Total	Incurring such expenditure				
1	2	3	4	5	6	7
				Rs.	Rs.	Rs.
REGION						
(i) Western ..	306	187	61.11	1,06,971.00	349.58	572.04
(ii) Central ..	169	63	37.28	30,845.00	182.51	489.60
(iii) Bundelkhand ..	83	43	51.28	36,690.00	442.05	853.26
(iv) Eastern ..	207	92	44.44	41,432.00	200.15	450.35
Total ..	765	385	50.33	2,15,938.00	282.27	560.88
TENURE						
(i) *Bhumidhars* ..	235	148	62.98	1,04,876.00	446.00	708.62
(ii) *Sirdars* ..	406	191	47.04	92,473.00	228.00	484.15
(iii) *Others* ..	124	46	44.44	18,589.00	150.00	257.80
Total ..	765	385	50.33	2,15,938.00	282.00	560.88

TABLE NO. 42

EXPENDITURE ON NEW FARM EQUIPMENT AND PERMANENT IMPROVEMENTS ON LAND INCURRED BY THE SAMPLE HOUSEHOLDS FROM 1952-53 TO 1959-60

Item	Total Expenditure Rs.	Percentage
1. Purchase of improved breeds of bullocks	1,64,863.00	76.35
2. Construction of *pucca* wells	24,290.00	11.25
3. Construction of *kuchcha* wells	3,165.00	1.46
4. Construction of irrigation channels	1,190.00	0.55
5. Persian wheels	5,227.00	2.42
6. Fencing	1,330.00	0.62
7. Iron ploughs	463.00	0.21
8. Cane crushers	3,154.00	1.46
9. Chaff-cutter	11,160.00	5.17
10. Miscellaneous	1,096.00	0.51
Total	2,15,938.00	100.00

INDEX